Eastern Europe 1740–1980

Eastern Europe 1740-1980

Feudalism to Communism

Robin Okey

Lecturer in History, University of Warwick

University of Minnesota Press
Minneapolis

Published by the University of Minnesota Press,
2037 University Avenue Southeast, Minneapolis, MN 55414
Printed in the United States of America.
Third Printing, 1985

Library of Congress Cataloging in Publication Data

Okey, Robin.
  Eastern Europe.

  Bibliography: p.
  Includes index.
  1. Europe, Eastern—History.   I. Title.
DJK38.O33   947   81–16436
ISBN 0–8166–1125–4   AACR2
ISBN 0–8166–1126–2 (pbk.)

Contents

Maps

To my father and the memory of my mother

Preface

This book surveys the history of the lands lying between Central Europe and Russia from the middle of the eighteenth century to the present. It is concerned, in other words, with what was once the Habsburg monarchy, partitioned Poland and Turkey in Europe, and is now the states of Poland, Czechoslovakia, Austria, Hungary, Romania, Yugoslavia, Bulgaria and Albania.

No general work can do justice to the eventful detail in which the history of each of these countries abounds. Its author must offer a perspective rather than tell a story, hoping to suggest enough of the region's fascination to persuade readers to pass on to lengthier studies on narrower fields. The perspective adopted here views Eastern Europe as a region which for two centuries has been striving after the 'modernity' seemingly embodied in certain of its western neighbours. From the time of the Enlightenment through the liberal and national movements of the last century on to the socialist experiments of our own day, East Europeans have struggled to emancipate themselves from a legacy of under-development and dependence. In the process they have experienced far-reaching changes: political change from a pattern of dynastic empires to one of republican nation-states; socio-economic change from a rurally based feudalism towards urbanism, industrialization and communism; cultural change from the folklore traditions of illiterate peasant communities to the norms of national cultures inculcated through schools and the modern media. The transformation has been marked by controversy and ambiguity. How much has instability owed to the implanting of alien ideas into unsuitable East European soil? Has the region's pervasive nationalism been curse or blessing? How far has the extension of independent statehood in the area really changed the balance of power between the interests of large nations and the aspirations of small ones? What verdict must one offer on the East European dream of national dignity and social well-being?

Of course, these themes are no longer peculiar to Eastern Europe. Much recent world history has been seen in terms of 'modernization' and its attendant stresses and strains. Eastern Europe, however, was the first area outside the advanced tip of Western Europe to set out on this road, and it still offers the most vivid illustrations of the twists and turns of the course. This is partly because of the length of time over which thoughtful East Europeans have been preoccupied with reform and partly because, as Europeans themselves, they felt an added pressure to emulate the achievements of their Western neighbours. Revivalist nationalism has never been as passionate as among Poles and Czechs, Serbs and Bulgarians, who had once possessed states playing a significant role in European affairs. The regaining of independence has nowhere proved so traumatic as in Eastern Europe after 1918. Nowhere has the fate of small nations become so caught up in the ideological and strategic confrontations of the great powers as in the nineteenth-century struggle of Teuton and Slav and the twentieth-century struggles of fascism, capitalism and communism. Hence the great crises with which the history of the area is studded: the revolutions of 1848, the Near Eastern imbroglio of 1875–8, the First World War, sparked off by the murder of the Habsburg heir by a Serb student, the Second World War precipitated by Hitler's desire for German 'living space' at the expense of the Slavs. In recent years, the focus of international conflict has begun to shift outside Europe, to South-East Asia, the Middle East, Africa and Latin America. But the events of 1956 in Hungary, 1968 in Czechoslovakia and 1980 in Poland are a reminder of the continued volatility of the old European storm centres.

Some more mundane comments are needed on the treatment of these themes. No attempt has been made to cover the history of Greece, even at the cursory level extended to Serbia and Bulgaria, because Greek development has always diverged markedly from that of her Balkan neighbours. Similarly, Austria after 1945 has been excluded from consideration since she alone of the successor states of the old Habsburg empire remained under non-communist rule in this period. Mention of Austria raises the question of the label used to describe the area covered in this book. 'East Central Europe' might appear a more suitable designation for a region including Vienna – or Prague – and this expression has been given currency by a number of recent writers. However, it seems no more logical to associate Bulgaria with Central Europe than to place Austria in the East, and I have plumped for the older and more euphonious term 'Eastern Europe'. Similarly, where place name changes have occurred, I have on the whole preferred the traditional forms, where these still predominate in the historical literature and maps which students will be consulting. Difficult cases are cited in the text or the index.

I have tried throughout the book to combine fact and interpretation, with just sufficient of the former to orientate the reader and to give substance to otherwise abstract arguments. Thus narrative passages tend to follow general ones, the better to illustrate them, and so that the full significance of the events mentioned may be appreciated. Chronological tables, maps and a glossary of unusual terms are added to supplement the factual element and to increase the usefulness of the book for the general reader. Unfortunately, it has not been possible to include accents or diacritic marks in the spelling of East European names, for which apologies are offered.

Eastern Europe is a complicated place. Its complexity may seem daunting at first. But a thorough study of the ethnic map and geography of the area will pay great dividends, for its largely stable ethnic and physical inheritance has shaped many regularities of attitude and assumption which underlie the confused flux of events. Thus the details of Balkan politics have always been tortuous but the basic objectives of the various Balkan peoples can be readily grasped. Those who attempt to learn some East European history are also amply rewarded should they visit the area. Street names (sometimes even town names) regularly commemorate famous people and events. People are aware of, and reflect, their past. Indeed, history dies hard in these parts. On a first visit to Budapest I was told by an archivist that I could not attend the archives the next day (20 August) as it was a public holiday. 'It is the day of the crowning of our King', she said, alluding to the coronation of St Stephen in 1000, a contemporary of Ethelred the Unready. Then she turned and added dryly, 'The Communists also have a name for it; they call it the day of the Proclamation of the Socialist Constitution.'

While such experiences have been the driving force behind the book, I am also much indebted to my colleagues, Professor Jack Scarisbrick and Dr David Washbrook, for their valuable comments on different sections of the manuscript, and to my publishers for all their patient forbearance while the same was in gestation.

1 The feudal inheritance

The history of Eastern Europe is grounded in geography. It is the funnel through which, over the centuries, successive migrations or invasions have passed from Central Asia, the cradle of so many races, to the European heartland. Huns, Avars, Slavs, Magyars, Tartars, Turks: all have come via the great plains to the north or round the Carpathians into the Danube basin or up the Balkan valleys from Asia Minor and the Hellespont, pushing back earlier peoples into the shelter of the mountains and settling themselves in the fertile plains and valleys until challenged in their turn. Thus has arisen that distinctive feature of Eastern Europe, the multiplicity of small and medium-sized nations lying athwart important strategic routes between two powerful and numerous peoples, the Germans to the west and the Russians to the east.

Of course, 'the lands between', as they have been called, differ markedly among themselves. Three distinct regions can be made out: in the north, the Great European Plain, corresponding roughly to the territory of modern Poland; in the centre, the Danubian basin flanked by the Alps, the elevated plateau of Bohemia–Moravia and the Carpathians, which shaped the old Habsburg monarchy, and to the south, beyond the Danube, the mountainous reaches of the Balkans. But greatly as the experience of these separate regions has varied, history has time and again underlined the ultimate interdependence set by geography; as in 1683, when a Polish army marching south through the Moravian Gap relieved Vienna, the Danubian capital, from Turkish besiegers striking through the Balkans; as in 1943–4, when many anticipated a Balkan landing by Western forces and advance through to the plains of Central and Northern Europe to forestall the communization of the whole area by the Soviet Red Army. At a deeper level, it is the struggle of a large number of relatively minor peoples to achieve full independent national development in difficult strategic circumstances which imparts a related rhythm to East European history as a whole.

The medieval background

The initial impulse of this rhythm stems from the so-called Volkerwanderung or migration of peoples which followed the collapse of the Roman empire. In the sixth and seventh centuries Slav peoples, already installed in Poland, moved into Bohemia and the Balkans. But they did not entirely disperse the earlier inhabitants, particularly the fore-fathers of the modern Albanians in their west Balkan mountain fortress and the Latin-speaking Romanians north of the Danube, and they failed to withstand totally the pressure of later arrivals, like the Asiatic Magyars (or Hungarians), who settled in the Danube basin in 896, or the Germans, who pushed downwards from Bavaria through the Austrian Alps, inwards into the mountainous girdle of Slav Bohemia and eastwards from the Elbe into nascent Poland. This settlement pattern by which Slavs came to form the majority of the population of Eastern Europe, but had to share it with a large minority of assorted non-Slavs, was to have fateful consequences for the area. Gradually splitting up into separate groups – the east Slav Russians and Ukrainians, the west Slav Poles, Czechs and Slovaks and the south Slav Serbs, Croats, Slovenes and Bulgars (of which the last family was isolated from the others by non-Slav settlement) – the Slavic peoples lost the initiative which numbers might have given them.

But this is to anticipate. The Middle Ages were not concerned with such overall racial considerations. This was a period in which the various individual ethnic groups, Slav and non-Slav, gradually organized themselves politically into states, with royal dynasties, a measure of centralized administration and clearly defined territories. Thus from the tenth century Magyar Hungary arose under the Arpads, Czech Bohemia under the Premyslids, and Poland under the Piasts. To the west, the German speakers of the Austrian Alps were grouped in the duchy of Austria, already under Habsburg rule in the thirteenth century. In the Balkans, the medieval Serbs, Croats and Bulgars all boasted national kingdoms, albeit with sharply fluctuating fortunes. But not all the identifiable peoples of Eastern Europe achieved statehood in this way. The Albanians continued to live a decentralized tribal existence in their mountain eyrie. The Slovenes in the north-west of modern Yugoslavia, the Slovaks and the Ukrainians all submitted to the rule of more powerful neighbours. The Romanians occupied an intermediary position, their western branch in Transylvania falling under Magyar rule, but the eastern establishing not one national kingdom, but the self-governing principalities of Wallachia and Moldavia from the fourteenth century. It was to this division, between those who had formed a state and those who had not, that the socialist Friedrich Engels alluded in his famous distinction between the historic and the non-historic nations of Europe. The Middle Ages already saw the pattern of subjection of one people to another which was so decisively to influence the course of Eastern European history in the era of national awakening.

Although the political organization of medieval Eastern Europe was ethnic in origin, it was hardly national in operation in the modern sense. Most states, even if they had a dominant nationality, were multi-national in population and, in accordance with feudal principle, allotted power to the privileged noble order rather than the members of a particular ethnic group. Feudal society showed closer ties between the privileged elites of separate states than between these elites and the peasant masses of their own country. Culture, too, apart from folk culture, was cosmopolitan in style, bound up with the values of a universal Christendom and transmitted through the language of the Church. Indeed, throughout medieval Eastern Europe the spoken languages were hardly used in administration or in literature before the sixteenth century, with the exception of German and in some instances Polish and Czech. Hence the decisive break in cultural traditions was not between racial groups, but between Catholic and Orthodox (consummated after the final split between Rome and the Ecumenical Patriarch in 1054), which introduced a further complexity into the East European mosaic. Since the formation of a kingdom required recognition from the international community it generally coincided with acceptance of Christianity and reception of the Crown through papal or patriarchal grant. Logically enough, it was the peoples nearer the East, the Bulgars, Serbs and Romanians who joined the Russians and Ukrainians in adopting Orthodoxy, while the more western Croats, Slovenes, Slovaks, Czechs, Magyars and Poles adopted Roman Catholicism. The unorganized Albanians divided, characteristically, down the middle. Once made, the choice determined also the alphabet used, whether Latin or Cyrillic, and the literary and administrative language, Latin for Catholics, Greek or Church Slavonic for Orthodox peoples.

Physical features of Eastern Europe

This said, it remains true that the medieval kingdoms of Eastern Europe had national traditions of a kind. States had been founded around a dominant ethnic group, and nobles, if not originally belonging to this group, tended to gravitate towards it in their spoken language and customs. Of course, the patriotism of such states, recorded in many a medieval chronicle, was a feudal patriotism, confined to a privileged noble elite which, in Poland and Hungary, actually arrogated to itself alone the title 'natio' or nation. It was not the determining force in society, merely one of many strands – ethnic, social, political and religious – which interwove in the intricate pattern of medieval society. Eastern Europe was already a complicated place. But it was not yet more complicated than the West. Ethnic and political alignments in the medieval British Isles were no less 'Balkanized' than those of the contemporary Balkans. Although the density of population was substantially less in the East, and the steady demand for German skilled labour suggests the existence there of an economic and cultural lag over against the West, the very energy with which native rulers encouraged German colonization shows that the desire to catch up was high. Certainly the spate of town-building in late medieval Poland confirms a picture of vigorous growth. A fifteenth-century traveller could compare the Serbian city of Pec to Paris, and Charles IV of Bohemia (1346–78) and Matthias Corvinus of Hungary (1458–90) were among the most powerful and cultivated sovereigns of their age. At the end of the Middle Ages, Eastern Europe, if not yet quite in the same league, was by no means far behind the civilization of the West.

The sixteenth-century turning point

It was in the sixteenth and seventeenth centuries, the period beginning with the Renaissance and the Reformation, that the crucial change occurred that made Eastern Europe thereafter a land apart, so remote from West European experience that the nineteenth-century Austrian statesman, Metternich, could speak of Asia as beginning at the gates of Vienna and successive generations of East Europeans could see hope only in the heady language of 'awakening', 'rebirth', 'resurrection', ultimately, 'revolution'. Already in the late Middle Ages, Western Europe was witnessing a slackening of the ties of the old feudal order. The shrinking of the labour supply after the Black Death tilted the balance of forces between landlords and serfs somewhat in the latters' favour. Unpaid or forced serf labour on the lord's demesne, the hallmark of feudalism, finally yielded to cash rents, and peasants came to enjoy greater personal rights of movement and inheritance and to acquire a surplus which brought them into a money economy. Demesne lands were either rented out to peasants or cultivated by hired as much as by servile labour. Meanwhile, the growth of towns and commerce, spurred on by rising population and geographical discoveries, promoted the enrichment of the urban classes and the diffusion of their influence among a peasantry with cash to spare. With the invention of printing and the increase in literacy, horizons widened, and in some societies, particularly those won for the Protestant Reformation, signs emerged that a modern national consciousness was replacing the narrower, more personal or regional allegiances of medieval times. Finally, under what historians used to call misleadingly the 'New Monarchy', the power of the central administration increased and the rudiments of the modern bureaucratic machine were fashioned, operated, as often as not, by men of non-noble birth. Thus, in place of a purely feudal order based on the land came (in Italy and the Low Countries at least) a more open, urban-orientated society where wealth and earning rivalled, if they did not yet eclipse, birth as the criterion of status. Modernity was at hand.

For a while, it seemed that Eastern Europe might follow a parallel course. Cash dues prevailed over labour service in late medieval Hungary; wealthy peasant sons studied in sixteenth-century Polish universities; in Bohemia, where the proto-Protestant martyr John Huss was a national hero, Protestantism was enthusiastically embraced, as it was throughout the region in the towns. But there was to be no flowering. Feudal forces were strong enough to reverse the trend. For one thing, the urban bourgeoisie, still weaker in Eastern Europe than the West, suffered from the dynamic development elsewhere which tended to reduce Eastern Europe to the level of provider of raw materials, chiefly grain, to an expanding West. Taking advantage of the grain trade's rural origins to wrest control of it from the urban merchants, the East European nobility decisively asserted its dominance over the towns and pressed ahead to consolidate the weakened demesne economy so as to maximize the profits of grain export. But this required the revival of forced serf labour to man the demesnes. Secure in their feudal diets, the nobles in province after province from the late fifteenth century began to pour out edicts restricting free peasant movement and tightening up half-forgotten labour regulations.

So stood matters in the mid sixteenth century when the Ottoman conquest, last of the great Asian invasions, reached its climax. Having crushed the Bulgar and Serb medieval empires in 1362–71 and 1389 respectively, the Turks completed their subjugation of the Balkans in the fifteenth century, and by 1550 had overrun two-thirds of Hungary, asserted their suzerainty over the Romanian principalities, and laid seige to Vienna itself. In the almost constant warfare which followed until their final expulsion from Hungary in 1699, in which we must include the intra-European Thirty Years War, the fabric of urban life took a further hammering; the only victors were the feudal-military aristocracy and the Habsburg dynasty. The death of the Hungarian king in battle with the Turks in 1526, by a quirk of dynastic marriage politics, brought under a single sceptre the hereditary Habsburg Austrian lands and the prestigious medieval kingdoms of Bohemia and Hungary. Already *de facto* Holy Roman Emperors in Germany, the Habsburgs now became rulers of a Christian super-state inhabited by German-speaking Austrians, Czechs, Magyars, Italians, Romanians and half a dozen smaller Slav nationalities. Thereafter, like the Bourbons of France, they energetically asserted their power over dissident nobles, whether the Czech Protestants, whose autonomist pretensions they crushed in the Battle of the White Mountain in 1620 or the part-Calvinist gentry of Hungary. Unlike the Bourbons, they did not enlist the services of talented bourgeois in this task but imposed on Bohemia and Hungary a nobility of their own, in the former country totally replacing, in the latter merely overlaying, the native elite. The effect of the Turkish onslaught and the Habsburg response was thus to strengthen the nobility in its bid for economic dominance. The peasants, in the language of feudalism, became 'bound to the soil', their tenure no longer secure. Cut off from the market by heavy dues in kind and the nobles' resumption of their profitable wine sale monopoly, toiling for up to six days a week on noble demesnes which had grown to account for 15–50 per cent of the region's arable land, the peasants had been reduced by the seventeenth century to what historians have called the 'second serfdom'. Meanwhile, the nobles made good their victory over the towns. By exempting themselves from tolls and municipal administration, usurping the regulation of market prices and whittling away bourgeois representation in the diets, they reversed the process occurring in much of the West, so that, far from rising towns influencing the values of the nobility, it was the towns themselves that were feudalized. Deprived of trade with the West and a peasant market, the East European town withered – in one Polish town only 28 per cent of the houses that had existed in the mid sixteenth century remained in 1811 – and noble dominion triumphed over a stagnant society.

It was a society growing apart from the West, nationally as well as socially. The conquests of the Ottomans over the Balkan Slavs and of the Habsburgs over the Czechs destroyed these peoples' native ruling class and reduced them to purely peasant status. Military and religious turmoil, bringing in its wake flocks of refugees, shifting colonists and mass conversions, wrought havoc with the region's ethnic map. Christian Slavs fled northwards before the Turks or followed in their baggage-train; Turkish and Tartar settlements dotted the Balkans; the Habsburg resettlement of Hungary after the Turkish retreat helped make Magyars a minority in their own land amidst a mosaic of Germans, Slovaks, Serbs, Romanians and Ruthenians. The numerous Slavs and Albanians who accepted Islam formed distinct groupings alongside their old Christian compatriots whose languages they still spoke. In the Christian world, the Habsburg-led Counter Reformation failed to eliminate Protestantism from Hungary and actually added to the religious confusion by creating the new Uniate Church among Habsburg Romanians and Polish Ukrainians as a kind of half-way house for these formerly Orthodox people on the road to Rome. When Western Europe was seeing a consolidation of national consciousness, in much of the East, what awareness there had been sank beneath the rising tide of feudal and religious loyalties. Outside Poland, ethnic and, as often as not, religious subjection complemented social subordination for the Slav peoples. Illiterate and leaderless, the peasant masses, in the Balkans especially, often ceased to identify in terms of the medieval national kingdoms at all and became, in their self-image, just 'Christians' or 'Orthodox' or 'Latins' (Catholics). The very names of East European peoples were replaced in the consciousness of learned Europe by provincial or racial tags, often with derogatory force. Czechs were Bohemians, Serbs Rascians, Slovenes Wends, Romanians Wallachs, Ukrainians Ruthenians and so on. Where there had been a recognizable pattern in 1400, the late seventeenth century disclosed an astonishing tangle of linguistic and religious allegiances mutely subsisting behind the facade of dynastic-feudal might.

The eighteenth century: state and society

So Eastern Europe entered the eighteenth century. To Western observers it was a society of decline. 'Nothing can be more melancholy', wrote Lady Mary Wortley Montagu in 1717, 'than to travel through Hungary, reflecting on the former flourishing state of that kingdom, and to see such a noble spot of earth almost uninhabited.' Half a century later, on the road from Cracow to Warsaw, Archdeacon Coxe felt driven to comment: 'Without having actually travelled it, I could hardly have conceived so comfortless a region . . . a forlorn stillness and solitude prevailed almost throughout the whole extent with very few symptoms of an inhabited, and still less of a civilised, country.' Nor was European Turkey any better. Journeying through its 'wastes', another English traveller concluded, 'the whole of this fine country is in a very backward state of cultivation and is not very likely to improve so long as it shall remain under the ignorant and oppressive government of the Turks.'

This last comment underlines the nature of the East European problem as viewed from other parts. Its difficulties were not just the great stretches of mountain and marshy plain barely tamed by a scanty population – and at a likely 22 million in 1700, compared to 140 million today, the entire region held few more people than contemporary France – but were aggravated by a harsh and retrograde social order. Formally the three states into which the region was now divided differed sharply. Poland was still a nation state, the Habsburg monarchy a loose congery of peoples presided over by a dynasty, Turkey a 'centralized' Oriental despotism with an Islamic culture and a Byzantine allure. But backwardness and feudalism were common to them all; men's lack of mastery over nature went hand in hand with their all too crude mastery over each other.

This was no accident. Feudalism in historical perspective is a regime of under-development. It appears where governments lack the resources to organize administration over far-flung territories and maintain themselves by bartering their responsibilities to local leaders in return for grants of land and honours. The principle underlying this initial arrangement, centred originally around military service, is then replicated between the local leaders and their tenants in turn, and in the organization of parallel religious and economic elites, so that feudal society becomes a honeycomb of interlocking hierarchies, their mutual relations governed by a bewildering maze of privileges, charters, grants, jurisdictions, exemptions, statutes, constitutions and the like. Where in the West increased urbanization, mobility and literacy provided the potential for a different pattern of society, moving towards a sense of common citizenship, to the east, as we have seen, social and political organization continued to reflect the older form, based on the co-operation of elites at the expense of the unprivileged masses. Flexible in structure, for the feudal principle of interlocking allegiances can be extended almost indefinitely, Austria, Poland and Turkey were correspondingly cumbersome in operation and narrowly based in popular support.

At the start of the eighteenth century, no strong consciousness of having slipped behind existed in these three states, particularly not in Austria as she emerged victorious from long wars with the Turks. The Habsburgs, presiding over the very parody of a feudal state, made up of the kingdoms of Bohemia, Hungary and Croatia, a grand principality, six duchies, four counties, a principality, a grand duchy and a margravate, were so enamoured of the dynastic principle that the ornate baroque buildings with which they beautified Vienna in the aftermath of triumph were decorated with the two headed eagle, symbol of their wider claims to their family's lands in Spain and overseas. Only the great general, Prince Eugen, fully appreciated the inherent weakness of a realm every one of whose constituent parts retained its own traditional constitution, and where the only pan-imperial agencies were the war ministry and the treasury. Hungary, whose diet claimed legislative equality with the sovereign and whose autonomous county administrations reserved the right to register or reject royal edicts, preserved a particular independence *vis-à-vis* Vienna. For this lack of common government the so-called Pragmatic Sanction of 1713, by which the emperor, Charles VI (1711–40), had bound his separate possessions to accept in perpetuity the heirs of the Habsburg line, could only be a partial substitute.

Poland appeared deceptively more straightforward. In fact, it was the product of a sixteenth-century fusion between the medieval Polish state and the multi-national and still separately administered grand duchy of Lithuania. With Germans in the west, Lithuanians, White Russians, and Ukrainians in the east, and about a million Jews, eighteenth-century Poland was no more than half Polish in population. Real power in the Republic, as it was officially called, lay not with the monarch, whose position had been elective since 1572, but with the Polish diet or Sejm and even more so with the sixty or so provincial dietines dominated by the magnate class. Seventeenth-century Poland had seen the withering away both of the state's power to levy taxes and customs, and of the political influence of the numerous gentry who had once lent republicans' professions some genuine popular content. Nothing better illustrated this than the growing abuse of the ostensibly democratic liberum veto, by which a single delegate could bring the entire proceedings of a session of the diet to an end. Applied six times between 1650 and 1700, eight times in the reign of August I (1703–35) and thirteen times under August II (1735–64), the veto in fact allowed overmighty magnates or foreign powers, manipulating client gentry deputies in the diet, to plunge the state into anarchy.

Central power was not reduced to such desperate straits in the Turkish empire, but its position there was hardly enviable either. The shrinking of Ottoman boundaries demoralized a political system founded on the rewards of conquest. In the principalities of Wallachia–Moldavia the sultan formally delegated his powers to Christian hospodars or governors chosen from the wealthy Greek community of Constantinople. Elsewhere such powers were often seized illegally by provincial governors. Without the wide authority granted non-Muslim hierarchs in the cultural affairs of their flock, or the extensive autonomies allowed to certain regions (not to speak of the virtual independence of groups like the Suliotes of Epirus or the mountaineers of Montenegro), the inadequacy of the corruption-ridden administration would have been still further exposed. But the Porte made up in terror for what it lacked in efficiency. Six hospodars met violent deaths at its hands between 1769 and 1821; and unsuccessful grand viziers and generals had to expect garrotting.

Regimes so constituted could hardly fulfil the functions of government in a modern sense. They fell short even in feudal terms. Although the feudal state was founded on military power, eighteenth-century Turkey could put into the field only 25,000 of its feudal spahis, as against 200,000 in the sixteenth century, and its professional janissaries, by a characteristic quirk, had largely degenerated into artisans who acquired the coveted status by purchase. In Poland, the anti-monarchical diet would not finance a standing army of more than 12,000 men, while the Austrian army's efficiency was gravely inhibited by the fact that recruiting and equipment still fell to the individual provinces.

Military weakness was in part a function of fiscal failure. Taxation was old-fashioned, clumsy and discriminatory rather than heavy in absolute terms. A great deal of it still came from rulers' imposts on mines and customs and the income of royal estates, which encouraged the sultan to seize land in Turkey and impoverished the Polish treasury as royal lands were alienated. Direct taxes fell mostly on those least able to pay, the Turkish Christians in the Balkans or the peasants everywhere. Nobles in Hungary and Poland were tax-free by law, so that Poland's late eighteenth-century revenues were one-fourtieth those of France, and Hungary contributed a mere seventh of the direct taxes of the Habsburg treasury. So complex were the expedients that could be adopted to fend off bankruptcy that more than half seventeenth-century Turkey's revenues came from payments compounding for various kinds of communal state service, which had themselves for the most part previously been substituted for taxes. Much of the money so laboriously obtained went on sustaining the lavish routine of court, for the medieval association of the royal household with the state lived on. As against 4.5 million gulden for the civil administration and 8 million for the peacetime army, the Austria of Charles VI continued to spend 2 million on the court to maintain the emperor and his 2000 paid courtiers on their round of hunting and ceremonial.

Traditionally, economic prosperity has been seen as a way out of state insolvency. The late seventeenth-century Austrian cameralist economists advanced quite a sophisticated programme for protective tariffs, dismantling the restrictive controls of the gilds and encouraging native industry. But East European states operated too sluggishly to respond to such calls. Ottoman economic energies were exhausted by the provisioning of the vast city of Constantinople, in itself no mean task. Separate Austrian provinces and in Poland even the greater estates had their own system of tolls. The production of goods was left to the gilds, a typical feudal institution based on hierarchy and privileged monopoly.

Just as it delegated economic production to the gilds, the feudal state entrusted education and welfare to the Church. Primary education was dispensed by parish priests; secondary education by the religious orders; in Turkey both levels by grades of Koranic schools. The universities, whether the medieval foundations of Vienna, Prague and Cracow or the handful of later claimants to the title had low academic reputations and, like the censorship of publishable material, were in Jesuit hands. Hospitals and orphanages were nearly always religious foundations and in Turkey fountains, libraries, hospices, even bridges also. The quality of the service provided was low. If as many as 10,000 students were receiving a secondary education from the Jesuits in Poland in 1700, only one in ten late seventeenth-century Moravian communes had a school of any kind, and this was probably typical. Doctors had to be driven by the army to attend to plague victims in Bohemia in 1713, and further afield, there were no doctors at all. Only one had professional training in all Bosnia as late as 1878. Nevertheless, with a parochial system extending to every village in the land, with 2163 religious houses in the Habsburg monarchy (1770) and 693 in Poland (1750), paralleled by 1000 mosques and 700 Koranic schools in Ottoman Bosnia alone, religion had an omnipresence and prestige scarcely imaginable today. The result was hardly one that a later generation would approve.

Travellers found Balkan mountaineers who lived in fear of hell for every breach of their creed's exacting fasts quite without compunction in the taking of human life. Everywhere among the common people religious fervour took the form of hatred of rival beliefs rather than real knowledge of their own. The princes of the Church lived in pomp and riches equalled only by the very greatest nobles; more than half Carniola belonged to the Church, three-eighths of Moravia and Silesia. In a single feast in the Serb Orthodox monastery of Hopov in Hungary in 1757, the monks consumed two pigs, eight brace of turkey, four of geese, ten of chicken, five of mallard and 220 kilogrammes of fish, which they washed down with three barrels of brandy and thirty-one of wine. But then, the Church was a vital arm of the state, fulfilling ideological and welfare functions for which no bureaucracy existed. In return it exacted power, wealth and a spiritual monopoly. The Turks punished conversion from Islam by death and attached multitudinous restrictions to the building and repair of Christian churches. Protestantism was proscribed in Austria and Bohemia and afforded the barest of tolerance in Hungary and Poland, which did not prevent the Mayor of Thorn in Poland and eight leading

Protestant burghers from being led to the gallows in 1723 for giving offence to the religion of the state.

Relying on the Church in all cultural matters, the government turned to the nobles to help it out in secular administration. Excepting the kadis or Islamic judges of Turkey, landowners were the sole administrative and judicial authorities on their estates; many of them inherited powers of life and death over their serfs. But the term 'noble' covered a wide range of different conditions. Most powerful of all were the magnates, distinguishable not by any legal status (except in Hungary), but by the sheer size of their estates. In Poland, families like the Radziwills, the Czartoryskis and the Potockis, each with armed retinues numbering thousands and a semi-royal state and style, wielded immense power. Hungarian families like the Esterhazys, with 100 villages, forty marketplaces and thirty castles or palaces, matched their wealth if not their influence, as did the fifty-one princely families of Bohemia whose estates dominated a province where, after the expulsion of the Protestant elite, nobles totalled only a few hundred all told. Opulence and crudity often competed in the homes of these great feudalites for we should beware of attributing to them, at this time, the sophistication of a Versailles. Polish mansions might have enormous ornate beds but no chairs, majestic tapestries and flaking ceilings. If this was true of many magnates, how much more primitive was the life-style of the mass of what we may call the gentry, the middle landowners owning at most a village or two, who numbered perhaps 25,000 families in Hungary, 40,000 in Poland, 5,000 in the Romanian principalities? Here, equipped with the sabre, belted kontusz or cloak and saffron-coloured boots of the Polish national costume, were the mustachioed, shaven-headed upholders of Polish 'Sarmatianism' (the cult of Poland's distinctive origins and the 'golden liberty' of the nobles); alternatively, ensconced in their unpretentious thatched and whitewashed timber homes, the proud, parochial patriots who shouted 'extra Hungariam non est vita' ('there is no life outside Hungary') and ran the Hungarian county administrations. But below the gentry again, and peculiar to Poland and Hungary, were the swarming petty nobility, often products of communal ennoblements in the past, who cultivated their plots like peasants and were distinguishable from them only by their greater literacy and political rights. For in Poland and Hungary, with some 10 per cent and 5 per cent of the population respectively of noble rank, only nobles could own land, hold public office or claim citizenship and voting rights in the 'nation'.

If these were the noble societies *par excellence* they had, however, their equivalent elsewhere, in the caste spirit of the Romanian boyars and the fierce particularism of the begs and agas of Bosnia, whose Slavic ancestors had accepted Islam to preserve their land. Nothing better illustrates the power of feudalism in Eastern Europe than the emergence of the Bosnian Muslim aristocracy, since formally Ottoman statecraft knew nothing either of hereditary tenure of fiefs or provincial autonomies on European lines. Indeed, the development of the second serfdom north of the Danube was paralleled by the rise in the Turkish empire alongside the relatively paternalistic spahis or fief-holders of a new category of landlord, the chiftluk sahibije, who introduced forced labour to the Balkan peasantry. The economic initiative that the East European nobility had shown in the late sixteenth century and early seventeenth century when they succeeded in wresting the corn and wine trade from bourgeois hands was relapsing into a willingness to rely on *force majeure* and a determination to maintain the privileged position won, rather than use it for economic development. Independent research in Poland, Hungary and Romania has shown that the most important item of noble income came from the monopoly of the sale of wine, not the growing and sale of corn which would have entailed more effort. Observing the nobles' role it is hard not to echo the judgement of a poet of the later awakening, the Hungarian Sandor Petofi (1823–49):

Nothing but idleness is life,
I'm idle, therefore I'm alive,
Peasants may work until they die,
A Magyar nobleman am I.

It was indeed peasants who bore the brunt of noble policies; but again, the term, 'peasant', is deceptively general. There was a world of difference between the life-style of the fisher-folk of Dalmatia, the Danube delta or the Pripet marshes; the stock-rearers of the Balkans and the steppe-like Hungarian plains; the tillers of central Bohemia and Poland; the charcoal burners and metal workers of the forested upland of the Carpathians, Bohemia and the Austrian Alps. It was the Czech and Polish agriculturalist, behind his plough, 'bound to the soil' and subject to onerous labour service for his lord, who came closest to the conventional image of the East European serf. Here and in Hungary was the classic region of the second serfdom, with its division of land into 'rustical', where the peasant, his dues once paid, had a tenuous hold on his plot and the use of its produce, and 'dominical', worked as the lord's demesne or let out on bad terms to small cotters. Here the beginnings of a permanent crop rotation could be seen, land (except in parts of Hungary) was scarce and settlement stable. Elsewhere, in Romania and the Balkans, land was still plentiful and stock-rearing more common. Even the three-field system was unknown; Romanian peasants either shifted their plots as they chose, or repartitioned them annually using primitive fallow techniques. Few Serbian rural settlements appear to be more than 300 years old. The eighteenth-century south Slavs still lived a communal existence in their zadrugas or joint-households under the discipline of male and female elders. On their barren heights, Montenegrins and Albanians retained tribal organization, the blood-feud and the immemorial pursuit of cattle-raiding. Balkan peasants, though subject to harsh and arbitrary taxation, were not serfs in the technical sense; they were not bound to the soil and had tenure of their land, provided they met their obligations. Perhaps their relative freedom owed something to the rugged terrain, for the Tyrolean peasants were free and labour duties in the other Austrian Alpine provinces were comparatively light. Labour service, after all, was essentially the product of the arable regime of the plains.

Nevertheless, the gradual worsening of the rural population's position was clear everywhere. In the servile areas, labour demands had been pushed up to several days a week for a peasant household with a full plot; households owning less than a full plot owed proportionately less. The Romanian boyars and the Balkan chiftluk sahibije were forcing up labour service and the tithe on produce, while the Ottoman practice of farming out taxes to rapacious collectors increased peasant burdens. Difficult as it is to quantify for earlier periods, it seems that over 40 per cent of eighteenth-century Galician peasants' gross production went to the lords alone and that 75 per cent of a Polish peasant's time was spent working to acquit his various obligations. At a later date, it appears that Austrian peasants were giving up 17 per cent of their income to the state and 24 per cent to the lord in the 1840s, and that a mid nineteenth-century Bosnian peasant retained little more than a third of his harvest.

Population pressure was already beginning to worsen these

burdens, as war-devastated areas recouped inhabitants. In the eighteenth century the population of Hungary rose from 4 million to 8.5 million; of Bohemia from 1.5 million to over 3 million; of Poland from 6 million to 12 million. In one area of Poland the proportion of peasants holding at least half a full plot fell from 58 per cent in 1565 to 11 per cent two centuries later. Cracow University had a fifth of its students of peasant origin in the sixteenth century; in the eighteenth century such a phenomenon was unknown. Although a quarter plot was generally the minimum on which a family could be sustained, those holding less than this – smallholders, cotters and landless, – outnumbered the rest by four to one in Bohemia, two to one in German Austria, and three to two in Hungary in the later eighteenth century. They scraped an existance together from domestic industry, petty trading or by hiring out their labour. Hungary had 200,000 vintners. Peasants shared their homes with their animals, sometimes in the same one room, in wooden cabins in northern parts, which Coxe called 'receptacles of filth and poverty', simple stone or baked mud structures in the Balkans, and often in the treeless Romanian and Hungarian plains dug-outs wholly or partially underground – 31,000 were still recorded in the Romanian census of 1911. Throughout the area, soup and porridge dominated the diet, for which cereal grains and cabbage adapted to a form of *sauerkraut* were used. Bread was reported to be a luxury in Silesia in 1755; meat was reserved for feast days; potatoes did not become common till the nineteenth century. Famine and epidemics, commonly linked with war, wreaked periodic devastation, reducing the population of Bohemia by virtually a half in the Thirty Years' War, and that of Hungary by a sixth in the War of Hungarian Independence (1705–11).

What was the mental world of these rural communities which made up the vast majority of the population? Peasant life was not all bleakness. Human nature with its instinct for hierarchy provided, even at this lowly level, distinctive roles with corresponding opportunities for pride and ambition; whether among the cowherds and shepherds of the Hungarian plains, the estate clerks and millers of Bohemia or the village herdsmen or zadruga elders of the Balkans. The numerous festivals of the religious calendar, with its intricate interweaving of Christian and pagan ritual with the rhythm of the seasons, offered a focus for communal relaxation. Among the Serb Orthodox, young girls danced in the open air on the eve of Palm Sunday to celebrate the triumph of spring and the awakening of Lazarus; on Palm Sunday they bathed before sunrise and danced with the fairies; it was the boys' turn for a pre-dawn dip on St George's Day. On Whitsun, games and processions took place, condemned by the clergy, in honour of Leljo, the old Serbian god of love. That at least must have been fun. Creative energies found expression too, in the astonishingly prolific products of folk art, costume, music and poetry. Among the humble Slovaks alone, a late nineteenth-century lawyer collected 30,000 songs; a twentieth-century musicologist, 50,000 more.

Communities with this creative vigour in them were not simply the passive recipients of their fate. If the savagely punished risings marking the sixteenth century were not repeated on such a scale – the Hungarian peasant chief, Dozsa, of 1514 had, after all, been seated on a red-hot iron throne with a molten crown on his head while his famished supporters were encouraged by thongs to dance around him and appease their hunger by plunging their teeth into his roasting flesh – eighteenth-century peasants readily availed themselves of the few opportunities for legal redress like the appeals system on royal estates in Poland and that established in Hungary after 1764. A more common way out of oppression was simply migration: from central Poland to the freer Cossack lands of the Ukraine, from the populous north and west of Hungary to the empty plains won back from the Turks, whose lords initially encouraged settlement by relaxing feudal ties from the boyar regime of the Principalities to neighbouring Transylvania or Bulgaria; from the Balkans to south Hungary in the great Serb exoduses of 1690 and 1737. But militant defiance was not excluded either. Thousands participated in movements in Bohemia in 1775, Hungary in 1755 and 1764–5, Transylvania in 1784, the Polish Ukraine in 1769, Macedonia in the 1720s, and (free Muslim peasants) Bosnia in the 1750s. For the unmarried young Balkan Christian, as for the peasant migrant of the Ukraine, the lairs of the Haiduk outlaws and the free Cossack communities offered institutionalized outlets for the freedom-loving instinct.

How far were peasants sustained over the centuries by a consciousness of nationality setting them apart from alien lords? It is hard to say. In northern Moravia, Czech-speaking communities referred to themselves as 'us' and their speech as 'our language'. On the other hand must be set the famous poetic sagas of the Serbs, centred around the disastrous Serbian defeat by the Turks at

Kosovo in 1389, to which has been attributed the survival of Serbian national consciousness under Turkish rule. A study of the sagas arouses some scepticism about the clarity of this folk vision, for the principal hero, Kraljevic Marko, is a somewhat ambiguous figure, on easy terms and occasionally even in alliance with Turkish pashas and chiefs. Perhaps religious differences from their masters rather than specific national awareness contributed to the preservation of separate identity among the mass of the Serbs, as it separated the Orthodox Cossacks (only later 'Ukrainians') from the Poles, and the Serbs from the Catholic Croats. But the hierarchy of the Orthodox Church gave some Serbs and Bulgars, and more Greeks, the opportunity for some education, and among this elite are clear signs of a distinctive ethnic consciousness. For was not the Serb Orthodox Church, in the words of one of its early eighteenth-century metropolitans, 'the only visible symbol and name by which we give witness among other peoples and creeds to what was once the dignity and glory of our race which had its Tsar and Patriarch'? Where a distinctive religion was absent, national feeling can still be found among isolated intellectuals of nations which had a history; for example, in the unpublished 'Apologia for the Bohemian language' of the late seventeenth-century Czech Jesuit, Balbin, or his Croat contemporary Krizanic's *Panslav Theories*. There is nothing similar in more anonymous groups like the Slovaks of Hungary or Slovenes of the south-eastern Alps, whose folk poetry glorifies a foreigner, the fifteenth-century Magyar king Matthias. Yet too much can be made of this. Probably the significant fact is that peasant societies remained keenly, often aggressively, alive to ethnic differences. 'A German will as soon do a good turn to a Slav as a snake will warm itself upon ice', ran a Czech saying. An eighteenth-century German traveller showed the readiness of the age for ethnic generalization when he wrote of the Romanian peasants of Transylvania, not yet dignified with a national name:

The Wallach is still a peculiar type of humanity, extraordinarily neglected by niggardly nature in the mountains which are his favourite habitat. One finds many of them who have hardly anything human about them except the human form and even that is distorted and disfigured by goiters and other defects. They remain rude and savage .... They seldom figure in history and, when they do, the pen of the historian shrinks from recording their acts.

'There is nothing', he added 'more dangerous than an offended Wallach.'

Slumbering ethnic hostilities go far to explain the peasants' aversion to the towns. It was a symptom of East European backwardness that these had failed to develop into genuine centres for the surrounding countryside, but for the most part remained alien to their hinterland in language and creed. In Poland townsmen were often Germans and Jews amid a Polish, Lithuanian, White Russian or Ukrainian peasantry; in the Habsburg monarchy, they were Germans among Slavs and Magyars; in the Balkans, they were Turks or non-Slavic Christians in a Slav sea. By contrast, 'there are no members of the Serb nation but peasants', wrote the founder of the Serbian cultural revival. Towns were small: few exceeded a population of 10,000, with Constantinople (400,000), Vienna (120,000), Prague (50,000), Warsaw (30,000) and Bucharest leading the field in the mid eighteenth century. Hungary's forty-eight royal towns contained only 5 per cent of the country's total population. 'Royal' status meant a town had a charter of municipal government unlike many smaller marketplaces which were totally subject to the feudal lord on whose ground they stood. In either case, though, towns reflected the character of feudalism, with only a minority of privileged 'burghers', oligarchic corporations and a penchant for caste-conscious legislation. Thus we hear that in 1714 the Hungarian town of Kosice ordered low-class women wearing over-colourful dresses to have them ripped off by the public executioner. No further details of this thought-provoking measure are available.

Commerce was the fortune of larger towns, particularly along the Balkan routes to the Danube, then Vienna or Trieste, for Turkey was increasing her export of raw materials – grain and cotton – after a brief experiment with manufacturing self-sufficiency. There were 2000 Ottoman merchants in Hungary by the mid eighteenth century, and large merchants from south Germany had their own organization in Vienna. But smaller towns were commonly quite agricultural in life-style with the burghers in Hungary at least, giving themselves up to viticulture and not more than a quarter of the population actually pursuing a craft. Here was no rising bourgeoisie. The Hungarian and Polish royal towns alike held a single vote between them in their country's respective diets, nor was burgher representation much more meaningful in the diets of Austria and Bohemia. Although domestic industry was widespread, engaging some 400,000 textile workers in Bohemia and Moravia for example, industry in the sense of large-scale manufacture existed only on a handful of noble estates. In a more traditional sense, as mining and metal work, it was carried on in remote, mountainous areas in Upper Austria, north Hungary and the Carpathians that had been its preserve for centuries, utterly removed from the connotations which 'industry' evokes today.

Conclusion

It is not difficult to see why to the aspiring nineteenth century the era described in this chapter should have seemed, in the phrase of the Czech revivalists, 'a time of darkness'. Feudal society erected into principles of government the very things which most men since 1789 have seen as their moral duty to oppose – social and religious inequality. It set the value of one infant – the future Joseph II – so high that a papal nuncio and sixteen bishops presided at his christening, and the value of the common people so cheap that in a single year 200 witches could be burnt in the mountains of Bohemia (1651) and 115 gipsies hanged in one Hungarian county alone (1782). It made the testimony of one Balkan Muslim equal in weight to that of twenty Christians, and disbursed 9 million florins (£1 million) of confiscated Jesuit property to pay off noble debts just two years after famine and disease had killed off 250,000 Bohemians, with much less governmental relief. It was harsh, unjust and inefficient, and it made the poor pay for its inefficiency. But this alone is an incomplete picture. The society which raised caste distinctions to a height unknown today could also reveal a paternalism and a homeliness we have lost. 'My dear children,' the dowager empress told irate peasants who sought her out in Vienna in 1712 about hunting abuses, 'I know that you are poor, if the emperor were at home he would surely help you'. A British traveller in Epirus in 1805 was entertained by a rendition of Christian rebel songs after which the Ottoman governor led the dancing in bare feet. Classes, peoples, cultures lived cheek by jowl, at once infinitely apart and inextricably entwined. The Habsburgs spoke Viennese dialect and corresponded in French; numerous Ottoman sultans were descended from Christian slaves; Islamicized Bosnian begs celebrated the Christian festivals of their forefathers; Hungarian professors wrote patriotic Latin histories and spoke Slovak at home; the elegant polonaise was in origin a peasant dance, while folk poetry often described, in garbled form, episodes in the lives of the mighty some centuries before. We are dealing here with a world which cannot be glibly labelled with a term reflecting later values and experience.

This insight has given rise to the concept of a traditional or pre-modern society, from which modern society had to grow, through the transformation of social and political values and the transition to a new form of economic organization. These processes of transformation and transition will be at the heart of this book. However the concept of traditional society is not without its dangers. Abstracted to suggest some timeless realm, where the common people live out their lives beyond the reach of government or ideas, responding only to the wishes of local lord or priest and the rhythm of the seasons, it can imply too one-sided a view of developments in the modern period, in which everything is explained in terms of new forces and theories breaking through the crust of custom. In reality, no society is ever wholly static or uninfluenced by political vicissitudes. The Thirty Years' War which halved the population of Bohemia and the Ottoman conquest which changed the status of every Balkan Christian are only the most obvious examples. Well-nigh impossible though it is to form a clear picture of the mind of the masses, we should not assume that this was a *tabula rasa* or mere repository of exotic 'lore'. Undoubtedly collective consciousnesses were shaping, slowly and obscurely compared with later times, to be sure, in which ethnic religious and social circumstances played their part.

Herein lies the drama of 'modernization'. Too often those who undertook it – enlightened rulers and 'national awakeners' alike – exaggerated the power of new ideas to remould their complex inheritance. Modernization proved a Pandora's box which, once opened, released forces hard to control. The imperatives of the future – economic, technological, administrative – encountered the imperatives of the past – ethnic, social, geographic. The encounter is still continuing. Only powerful motives could impel a process which has proved so turbulent. To these we must now turn.

2 Enlightenment

The second half of the eighteenth century is the turning point in East European history. It was the age when the states of the region reaped the legacy of earlier backwardness; the age of the dismemberment of Poland, the humiliation of Austria and Turkey, the germination of the anti-feudal and pro-nationalist sentiments of later generations; and it was the age of enlightened despotism.

Enlightenment and its associated images are the constant refrain of the eighteenth century. 'We, nurtured on our sweet dreams of enlightenment, will scarce credit that in the purportedly so enlightened eighteenth century all this priestcraft really still exists', cried the Prussian traveller Nicolai in Vienna in 1780. 'At last', exulted the Austrian ambassador to Berlin in 1774 on news that general primary education was to be introduced in Austria, 'the time has come when the truth is emerging in new splendour from the dark clouds which have enveloped it, and is entering upon its rights.' What underlay the rhetoric? The light of Enlightenment was the light of human reason, exalted as the tool of intellectual inquiry by Descartes, employed to reveal the secrets of the physical universe by Newton and applied to problems of human society by Locke. The achievement of the eighteenth-century *philosophes* was chiefly to popularize the insights of these great predecessors and, by applying them to fresh fields, to build up a systematic body of knowledge. Political thinkers gave ideas of the sovereign's responsibility, even accountability, for the good of his subjects a new meaning. The physiocrat economists advocated tax reforms and an improvement in the position of the peasants. Voltaire and others stressed freedom of conscience and intellectual inquiry as a condition of progress. Greater humanity was urged in education, in the treatment of the sick and infirm and in prison reform. The *philosophes*' attack on the traditions of the *ancien régime* in the name of rationally conceived 'Laws of Nature' reflected Western Europe's long evolution away from exclusively feudal norms.

The penetration of the Enlightenment into Eastern Europe in the eighteenth century therefore represented the first signs of *rapprochement* between two areas which for generations had been drifting apart. Why was this so? Could a philosophy born of one milieu sink sound roots in another? This was the crucial question of eighteenth-century Eastern Europe as, in a sense, it is of modern East European history as a whole. Liberals and nationalists of the nineteenth century gave it an enthusiastically affirmative answer. To them, the East European Enlightenment was an upsurge of the human spirit, preluding the popular 'awakenings' of their own day and the return of the region to the fold of European progress. The storms of the twentieth century have inclined modern historians to a greater scepticism. In a common view, the East European reform movements owed more to the ambitions of rulers and the imperatives of political survival than to a genuine enthusiasm for 'philosophy' which, as subsequent events were to show, was only superficial. If the young Empress Maria Theresa succeeded to the Habsburg throne in 1740 to find Frederick of Prussia encamped in her wealthiest province, Silesia, and just £7,000 in the treasury to finance her unsuccessful campaign to drive him out; if, in the first Partition of Poland in 1772, the Poles, having no good map of their country, had to use their enemies' which unsurprisingly decided all points against them; if, during their disastrous war with Russia of 1768–74, the Turks refused to credit reports that a Russian fleet was approaching the Mediterranean because they did not believe it geographically possible to reach that sea from the Baltic, the lesson in each case was the same: knowledge and organization are power. The age of Enlightenment was a time of increased competitiveness between states, in which the weakest went to the wall. Faced with the threat of a rising Prussia and Russia, which were ruled by energetic westernizers with philosophic pretensions, little wonder that the states of our region turned to the new creed for salvation. Enlightened despotism, then, was more despotic than it was enlightened, and its failure foreshadowed further tribulations along the bumpy road to modernity.

This interpretation is more plausible than the ultra-idealistic one which preceded it, but nonetheless it seems rather over-dismissive of the fascination which new ways of thinking exercised in the East European milieu. Consider only two guide books to Bohemia, each typical of its time, from 1712 and 1794. The first explains the origins of the Czech people in terms of the biblical story of the

Eastern Europe in the mid eighteenth century

Tower of Babel, then lapses, after five pages of desultory information (language, dress, etc.) into a gazetteer of Bohemian kings and place names. The second, dismissing 'mythological' versions of Czech origins with reference to the work of the first scholarly Czech philologist on the word 'Czech', launches into a sophisticated analysis of the roles of heredity, environment and experience in the formation of national character and an exhaustive statistical account of Bohemian demography, society and culture. Between the two works has intervened that urge for rational inquiry and systematized knowledge which is the motive-force of Enlightenment. The access of intellectual energy which this comparison implies was indispensable to the eighteenth-century reforms, for the mere fact that reform was necessary in no way guaranteed that, ir the absence of generalized intellectual stimulus, it would be carried out. Crisis does not always, of itself, bring cure, as the case of eighteenth-century Turkey shows only too well.

Besides, the movement for political renewal transcended the ambitions of enlightened despots. The 'condition of Poland' question became the subject of vast pamphlet literature. Even in the remote Romanian principalities, 208 petitions and memoranda for reform have been traced to the period 1769–1828. The upheavals in Hungary between 1790 and 1791 produced about 500 pamphlets on socio-political themes, the freeing of the press in Vienna in the 1780s, some 2000. Though by no means all these writings were 'enlightened', their very number testifies to a widespread awareness of alternatives to the *status quo*. The impact of the West on eighteenth-century Eastern Europe should neither be romanticized nor minimized. Before we consider the political upheavals which resulted, we must first establish the contours of cultural influence that took form in the transmission of ideas from one setting to another, marking out what was retained, what lost and what distorted in the process.

The ideas: the concept of an East European Enlightenment

At first, reform ideas were largely the possession of fringe groups in East European society with special ties in the West, like the Hungarian Protestants (often educated abroad), German-speaking Lutherans in western Poland, freemasons or Catholics influenced by the officially disfavoured Jansenist tendency. But from the

1730s, a breaking down of psychological barriers against the West can be seen in the wider community also. Once the religious hostilities of the seventeenth century began to recede, German Austria was open to influence by the syntheses of Enlightenment propounded by the north German Protestants, Leibnitz and Wolff. Absorption into a common German literary culture steadily pushed out the Italian theatre and homely *Hanswurst* drama of the Catholic baroque. The Jesuits too, lost their grip on intellectual life as, after the 1750s, rival orders, Jansenists and 'reform Catholics', captured the majority of influential teaching posts in the monarchy's seminaries and theology faculties. 'Must one shout one's head off that a saint may hear?' commented the reforming abbot Rautenstrauch on traditional liturgical practices. The same rationalistic streak revealed itself in Gerhard van Swieten, Maria Theresa's Jansenist-influenced personal doctor, whose memorandum against the persecution of witches advanced medical reasons against the traditional proofs of guilt. It was van Swieten, as head of a censorship freed from Jesuit control, who fought to get Montesquieu's *Spirit of the Laws* allowed into Austria. In the freer climate the printer Trattner, who established his press in Vienna in 1748, could make a fortune from reprinting foreign material. By the 1760s Vienna had an intelligentsia for the first time.

In Poland, too, the growing vogue of foreign dress, previously considered an indecency, signalled a decline in 'Sarmatian' exclusiveness. Bavarians, Viennese, Saxons, Italians and Frenchmen made Warsaw from the middle of the century a centre of foreign bookshops, soon complemented by an expanding Polish newspaper press. The number of books appearing in Polish rose from 280 in 1740 to 650 in 1760. Polish Jesuits cannily followed the trend, publishing five French grammars in the 1750s alone, and increasing the number of their French-speaking members from 40 in 1740 to 283 in the 1770s. By the end of the century Montesquieu, Rousseau and Voltaire, d'Alembert, Diderot, Condillac and Condorcet, Holbach, Mably, de Mettrie and Morelly, Hume, Bentham, Locke and Burke, Leibnitz and Herder, Vico, Beccaria and the physiocrats had all appeared in Polish translation. Hungary followed suit a little later, for a well-known poetic lament of 1782 for the Magyar national costume showed the influence of foreign fashion, via Hungarians at the Viennese court. More than 100 translations of French seventeenth-century works, as well as Locke, had already appeared by mid century and by the 1790s Rousseau's *Social*

Contract was also available, in Latin. The first Magyar newspaper appeared in 1780, to be followed within a dozen years by the first Magyar literary journals, cultural societies and permanent theatre. Further afield, the famous Wallachian boyar family Cantacuzino possessed the *Encyclopédie* in 1777, and the Bucharest Metropolitan Church Library was subscribing to the *Journal Général de la Litterature*, the *Journal des Savants* and the *Journal Encyclopédique* in 1800. Condillac's *Logic* had appeared in Romanian, and Locke, Voltaire, Wolff, Beccaria and Montesquieu were also known. In the few Greek academies of the Balkans, a number of German and Italian-educated monks taught their pupils the philosophy of Natural Law. Some Serbs, too, gained ideas of 'Europe' via the Nakaz or enlightened governmental programme of Catherine the Great (1767), or even from Russian translations of Protestant and Jesuit histories which had been commissioned for the benefit of backward Russians by the grandfather of westernization, Peter the Great. For those brought up on an exclusive fare of medieval saints' lives, the factual objectivity of these works came as a revelation.

This brief survey suggests different levels of penetration of the new ideas. In the German-speaking areas around Vienna, in Bohemia and in north-west Poland, the cultural pattern came to resemble that of Central rather than Eastern Europe. Enlightenment numbered many doctors, engineers, civil servants, soldiers and other professional men of bourgeois origin in its ranks, and took on a scientific and technological as well as a literary and educational dimension. In the minerologists Faerber and Born, the plant and animal expert Peithner, the veterinologist Knobloch and the mathematician and economist Gerstner, first director of the technical high school in Prague, Bohemia had a team of scientists of which any European country could have been proud, men who helped lay the intellectual foundation for Bohemia's economic maturity in the nineteenth century. Joseph von Sonnenfels, (1732–1817) is perhaps the representative figure of this German Austrian Enlightenment. The son of a Jewish middle-class convert to Christianity, later ennobled, he demonstrated in his personal career the freer social climate that was dawning, while his interests as journalist, economist, founding professor of political science at Vienna, arbiter of German literary taste and law reformer reflected the new emphases of the age. Frequently called on by the government as a skilful committee-man, it was he who persuaded

Maria Theresa to abolish torture in Austria. Sonnenfels held no brief for serfdom, 'that stain on the constitution where it is tolerated . . .'. Yet, as the pillar of a rising enlightened 'establishment' he was no revolutionary or radical either. His acceptance of absolute monarchy, provided it was based on Natural Law not feudal custom reflected Wolff's adaptation of French thought to Central Europe's conservative political traditions.

In Poland and Hungary, a second zone, noble-dominated societies offered infertile soil for a Sonnenfels. There was a place, though, for the enterprising burgher of Danzig or Warsaw – such a man as Nax, economist and mathematician, member of the Polish Physical Society and head of the state hydraulics department – or for plebeian priests, like the Polish polymath natural scientists, Kluk and S. Staszic, or the Slovak-Hungarian Lutheran pastor and agricultural pioneer, Tessedik. But it is the career of the Piarist monk Stanislav Konarski (1700–73), which best illustrates the preponderantly literary and noble-orientated reform movement in these two countries. Konarski was liberated from a youthful traditionalism by foreign education and researches in Polish legal history, which exposed him to the oligarchic fraud of the gentry republic of his own day (p. 23). In 1740 he founded his noble college to offer the country's future elite a more progressive education. A Polish patriot priest rather than radical philosopher, he nonetheless recommended Protestant books to his students and, through his eloquent attacks on the liberum veto and empty libertarian rhetoric, helped spread an awareness of the need for reform, 'I did not write to expose the nation to shame', he claimed, in terms often used hereafter by East European reformers to reconcile national pride with foreign precept, 'for the French write things a thousand times worse about France and the English about England, not for the sake of insult but of improvement.'

Konarski kept his doubts about the social side of the Polish constitution – serfdom – to himself and his friends, but after his death, coincidentally with the spread of physiocratic economic doctrines in Poland and the expansion of the bourgeoisie and intelligentsia of Warsaw, this question, too, came to be voiced. Should the emancipation of the peasantry take place gradually as even the westerners Mably and Rousseau advised, or at once? Should it cover all or only 'deserving' peasants? Was it enough to grant peasants personal liberty and legal protection, or should they also be freed from labour service and become, effectively, tenants on the English model? Should a system of national education precede social reform to prepare the ground? How could the development of industry and urban life be dovetailed in with the regeneration of agriculture? All these questions were debated, without consensus, in the Poland of the 1780s.

Beyond Poland and central Hungary, on the Habsburg periphery and in the Balkans, stretched a third zone where reform ideas were more a matter of individual conviction than public debate. These individuals, too, came from limited groups, leading boyar families and higher clergy in the principalities, the Romanian Uniate clergy of Transylvania and the Greek and Serbian merchants of the larger towns. By and large, the Romanian Enlightenment was unsubstantial until after 1800. 'We have French books and novels; all other books are melancholy! We are enlightened; all the older writers are hypocrites', boasted some young eighteenth-century Wallachians unconvincingly. Only two Romanians travelled to Western Europe and six to Central Europe in the second half of the eighteenth century. Yet, where there was contact with a wider world, there could be a meaningful Orthodox Enlightenment, lacking the scientific and technological enthusiasm and the social radicalism of more advanced milieux, but sincere in its intellectual curiosity, devotion to reason and abhorrence of superstition. We have a good idea of its nature from the life and work of a remarkable Serb monk, Dositej Obradovic, who lived from about 1742 to 1811. Born in the Serb community of south Hungary, Obradovic derived a lifelong anti-clericalism from his youthful monastic experiences – 'a good book is worth a dozen bell-towers', he once said – and, by reaction, an incipient humanitarian Deism, which was strengthened by his travels in the Near East, England, France and Germany. His message was simple: to bring up children to 'love of man and good nature' would free even lowly nations from the 'eternal night of despair and ignorance'. So simple was it that Obradovic drew on himself the ridicule of a traditionalist who told him people had been quite capable of thinking before he came along to tell them how. To this, the sage replied with a delightful self-depreciating anecdote which tells us much of the climate in which he worked. It seems the bishop of Montenegro once set up the unsuspecting Dositej to put the following highly enlightened questions to an irascible and old-fashioned abbot: 'What is a rainbow and why is it multi-coloured?' Glaring at Dositej, the abbot promptly replied, 'Do you see that ass of mine?' 'Yes,' said the puzzled sage, 'but that's not what I asked you'. 'I know very well what you asked me', retorted the abbot scornfully, 'but let me tell you that my ass is far more intelligent than you are. That ass knows husks when he sees them in front of him, and if you don't believe me see how he bites them, and you don't even know what a rainbow is! A rainbow is a rainbow, it isn't some kind of ring is it? And you ask me why it's multi-coloured, O wretched one, could it be a rainbow if it weren't multi-coloured? Or have you ever seen a black one?' The repartee was devastating, admitted Obradovic, but it was not what he meant by rational thinking.

Some would question whether Sonnenfels, Konarski and Obradovic can be fitted into a common framework of 'East European Enlightenment'. Yet, though attenuated in scope, Obradovic's philosophy retained the rationalist core of the enlightened creed. To find Enlightenment falsely so-called, it would be necessary to go on to Bulgaria and the famous 'Slav-Bulgarian History' of Paisi, dubbed the 'father of the Bulgarian Enlightenment', although his vague enthusiasm for learning and emotional calls for national awakening do not redeem his totally uncritical acceptance of myths in his sources in a way Obradovic would have scorned.

Except for such as Paisi, it is possible to generalize about the Enlightenment in our region, while remembering that its range and influence shaded off as it moved east and south. Everywhere its adherents were drawn preponderantly from the upper reaches of society, few in number, but influential: high officials, magnates, senior clergy, sometimes bourgeois, less commonly gentry. 140 subscribed to the first Magyar literary journal, as against 150,000 who bought a Magyar almanack in 1809. Its spokesmen, too, were social propagandists rather than original thinkers, stirred by a strong, often anguished, desire to see their wayward lands conform to the standards of a rationally organized society. 'Poland sleeps to the scorn of learned Europe,' cried Kluk, 'She groans at her poverty, but will not change her inveterate ways.' 'Unfortunately it is true', wrote the reforming Austrian jurist Martini, 'that with regard to the Protestants we are well behind but . . . a few years ago the gap was still greater. With patience and steadfastness we will catch them up yet; indeed, with God's help, overtake them.'

Not labouring on the frontiers of knowledge, East European reformers tended to regard Enlightenment rather simplistically as a set of unquestioned truisms, to ascribe all their ills to feudalism or foreign oppressors and envisage the rational society in Utopian terms. After all, as the Hungarian Jacobin Martinovics wrote, the truths of the Social Contract were 'so simple'. No doubt it was this lack of philosophic depth which enabled so many priests to participate in a movement whose ultimate implications raised awkward questions of materialism and atheism. Let reason guide man to the rational exploitation of available resources, natural and human, for the benefit of mankind. To this end, let minerological, hydrological and agronomic research advance, and canal, drainage and river regulation projects be taken in hand. Let human talents be nurtured concomitantly through the expansion of education at primary and secondary levels, and through health and welfare services worthy of a human society. Let a purified Church, free from superstition, bigotry and the corrupting taint of temporal power and wealth, subserve these ends in the pristine spirit of the gospels.

Plainly this programme clashed with the practice of feudalism. Yet, if the Viennese press came to specialize in stereotypes of sterling peasants and wicked lords, were these more than sentimental effusions in face of the fact that enlightened ideas were largely confined to the privileged classes themselves? Was not an Enlightenment which produced the 'radical' Hungarian count Fekete, who sent Voltaire a hundred bottles of Tokay with every batch of his indifferent French verses, more superficial fashion than powerful creed? This is the ground on which critics of the concept of East European Enlightenment prefer to stand.

Far more dynamic movements than East Europe Enlightenment are open to ridicule if their purest theory is contrasted with their practice. But the whole argument can be turned on its head. If a measure of 'philosophy' had become a desirable social accomplishment for the upper classes by the late eighteenth century, this was no triviality but a significant sociological fact, as any but our own functional age would recognize. Since the traditional political and economic structure of the region largely revolved around sustaining the life-style of privilege, changes in leisure patterns reflected much broader changes in society at large. The transition from drunken and gluttonous revelry to the sophistication of the salon (or the gambling table) paralleled the abandonment of native dress, the decline of permanent residence of magnates on their estates, the increasing vogue for expensive noble building – some 211 new mansions were built in Hungary under Maria Theresa alone. Ultimately, the life-style of Enlightenment was part of a wider evolution, at least for the upper classes, from the close-knit patriarchal norms of feudal society to new perspectives, cultural, economic and political. It portended the more general reorganization of society. This is the theme of transition favoured by the Marxist historiography now dominant in the region, which seeks not to minimize the concept of an East European Enlightenment but to root it in the context of socio-economic change.

This transition cannot simply be aligned with the passage from feudalism to capitalism, whose culmination still lay well in the future. Yet, as Western Europe advanced, growing market opportunities were inclining larger landowners to a more systematic, even on occasion, more capitalist exploitation of their estates. They might simply, like the Romanian boyars or the Muslim chiftluk sahibije of north-west Bulgaria, press up peasants' labour service to benefit from expanding grain demand, in this case from Constantinople. They might set up factories on their land, like many great nobles in Bohemia and Moravia. Under the explicit influence of the Enlightenment, they might experiment with peasant reform, either by converting feudal forced labour into capitalist money rent (the Polish Count Andrzej Zamoyski doubled his revenues in this way) or extending personal liberty or founding model farms, like the Hungarian counts Festetics and Szechenyi. Such advanced reforms were few, but in general, agricultural handbooks multiplied after 1750, and estate records were better kept. From the 1780s, Hungarian figures show the first sharp upturn for centuries in grain yields. Nor were advances confined to agriculture. Warsaw made a spectacular leap forward from a town of 30,000 to 120,000 in the second half of the century. According to recent studies, the Cracow region of southern Poland had a far better integrated economy at this time than had been thought, with peasants participating in the market to an unsuspected extent. It was an age of some achievement in canal-building (in Poland), port construction (in Trieste) and government-sponsored industry (in Bohemia and Lower Austria), helped by the migration of skilled workers from the West and the reservoir of labour provided by a rapidly rising population.

It would be as hazardous, though, to give priority to these economic changes as to the political and intellectual pressures that have been discussed. What we may call East European Enlightenment was a complex interaction of all these. Threatened politically, aware of the cultural roots of the challenge, moving away from a traditional life-style to one sustainable only by new methods, the East European elite (north of the Danube, at least) was open to change. This interaction had not yet reached a high level of integration. In other words, because Romanian boyars were growingly interested in export opportunities in corn, they were not necessarily the more enlightened. Indeed, they were more likely to be tightening up their feudal obligations rather than reforming them. In the very long term, social evolution would impel political, intellectual and economic tendencies to converge towards .the liberal bourgeois capitalist society of the later nineteenth century and Marxist theory. But in the medium term, unevenness of development makes any such generalization difficult. The Marxist concept of transition is a convenient, if, for specific situations, rather vacuous catch-all for these complexities.

East European Enlightenment was as much a matter of mood as of social theory or practice. The Polish journal *Monitor* put its finger on this in an article of the 1780s:

the coarse habits of our forefathers have almost vanished from our midst, the passions so usual in other days as a result of ignorance and idleness have no longer a place among us. Manners have been moderated by knowledge, serving in part the ends of science, in part those of entertainment.

What would be the impact of a movement both pervasive and vague? Politically, it seemed to presuppose more active, hence more centralized government, yet it appealed to nobles and small nation intellectuals, both groups with anti-centralist traditions. Socially, its distaste for feudalism entailed no consensus as to the scope or manner of reform.

Uncertainty was natural. Precedents for the social renewal some people encouraged hardly existed, and diffuse ideas had not yet hardened into political programmes. Pressure for change did not come, as later, from below (for 'Jacobin' revolutionism appeared only at the tail-end of the period), but from a section of the privileged class itself, facing traditional perils – suspicious peasants, reactionary priests, regional separatists, foreign jealousies and the continued conservatism of most of the lesser nobles. In the absence of a tradition for the politics of Enlightenment, personality took over, the cautious erred on the side of caution, the impatient on that of change. Bitter experience would show how difficult it was to strike a balance.

The practice: enlightened despotism

This background to eighteenth-century politics has been discussed in detail because its importance can hardly be overestimated. To be sure, this was still a time when the personal qualities of the sovereigns mattered enormously. Traditions of fealty, long-standing claims of the state to supervise the Church, time-honoured practices of economic management were to hand for the energetic ruler to grasp for the overhaul of the state. So, over thousands of corpses Mehmet IV and the Koprulu brothers had restored Ottoman fortunes in the seventeenth century. What was now required, however, was something more. Not terror and authority, which fell with the man who imposed them, but new institutions and a new spirit of ongoing vitality, implying adjustment in the relations between the sovereign and his traditional feudal props – magnates, lesser nobles and Church – which could be eased only by some common commitment to a new order such as has been described.

Eighteenth-century Turkey provides a perfect illustration of this. Ottoman patriotism was not dead, nor did Turkey lack statesmen who realized the need for change. As early as 1721 the grand vizier Ibrahim sent an envoy to Paris 'to make a thorough study of the means of civilisation and education, and report on those capable of application in Turkey'. Nine years later his 'Frankish manners' helped lose him his life in a popular insurrection. After the loss of Muslim Crimea to the Russians in 1783, Sultan Selim III (1789–1807), who corresponded with Louis XVI, abolished tax-farming and feudal fiefs and established a regular army with European-style uniforms and a military college using French instructors; he too perished at the hands of united janissaries and ulema (priests). The solitary printing press established in 1729 was closed in 1742 to reopen only in 1784, and no less a man than the energetic grand vizier Raghib Pasha (who may even have planned to have Voltaire translated into Turkish), dared, it seems, to reopen the geometric school, closed by janissary pressure, only secretly in his private house. Hence the disarray of the central power in the 1790s before mutinous janissaries in Belgrade, Bosnian begs, virtually independent pashas in Bulgaria and Albania, and bellicose Suliote and Montenegrin Christian highlanders.

An important consequence of Turkey's decline was the emergence of the Eastern question into European diplomacy, and the dawning of fresh hopes among Balkan Christians. The Russo-Turkish treaty of Kutchuk Kainardji in 1774, in which Russia extracted her famous right of protection over the Orthodox subjects of the Porte, would, wrote the Austrian diplomat Thugut, not only menace the existence of the Ottoman empire but cast its shadow over all the European powers, 'giving birth to endless ills and troubles'. Its immediate effect was to stimulate the Romanian principalities to begin the long tradition of overtures by Balkan Orthodox peoples to Europe and progress against the 'Oriental barbarism' of the Ottomans. Where the Turks had, relatively speaking, power without Enlightenment, the Romanians had a modicum of Enlightenment but no power. Their continual appeals against the arbitrary hospodar regime for qualified, accountable officials, free trade in corn, a free press and inviolability of property sometimes made explicit the ultimate desire for autonomy or independence. But such aspirations stumbled against the fact that client buffers between powerful states were useful in time of war (when promises might be made), but were apt to be ignored at the peace conference.

Political Enlightenment in practice was on the cards only in the two Christian states of the region, the Habsburg monarchy and Poland. It is associated with three reigns, those of Maria Theresa (1740–80) and Joseph II (1780–90) of Austria and Stanislas Augustus Poniatowski of Poland (1764–95).

A successful ruler of great common sense, a pious Catholic and devoted wife and mother (she had sixteen children), Maria Theresa figures in Austrian historiography as a cross between Good Queen Bess and Queen Victoria. Much has been made of the fact that she herself was untouched by 'philosophy'. Her early experiences on the throne when she found her Bohemian ministers virtually conducting their own policy in the war against Prussia had made plain enough to her the need for more centralized government. These views were shared by her able and equally non-doctrinaire minister, Haugwitz. Immediately on conclusion of the War of the Austrian Succession, into which the Austro-Prussian conflict had grown, the two carried through the reforms of 1748–9 which demonstrated Maria Theresa's determination not to permit noble privilege to interfere with the efficiency of the state. She established the strength of the standing army at 108,000 men, to be financed partly by a novel tax on noble land, though assessed at only half the peasant rate. Then, having coerced the diets into acquiescence and deprived them of their control over the recruitment and provisioning of troops, she merged the Bohemian chancellery in a directorium for all the Austro-Bohemian lands, and extended the control of central government over local adminstration at the district level.

Although these initial reforms required no philosophical explanation, as Maria Theresa's reign advanced she became increasingly surrounded by people for whom the Enlightenment mattered. Mention has been made of her personal physician Gerhard van Swieten. Her confessor Müller was also inclined towards Jansenism. In Prince Kaunitz, her chancellor and leading statesman, she had a typical aristocrat of the enlightened school, an urbane and witty rationalist who combined the mannerisms of the courtier with those of the man of letters. The empress (whose prejudices were so strong that she consulted Jewish financiers from behind a screen) gave great credence to Sonnenfels, a baptized Jew, and ennobled a Calvinist industrialist. Maria's reforms could be conceived no doubt, for the most part, by traditional wisdom, but their implementation against the forces of inertia and vested interest required an alliance with Enlightenment.

After the Seven Years War had exposed continuing inadequacies, a second reform period began in the 1760s which went well beyond the first. The reorganization of the central administration of 1760–2, unlike that of 1748, was inspired by Montesquieu's principle of the division of powers; its main feature was the creation of a state council with an advisory brief for the monarchy as a whole. It was becoming clearer that determined action was necessary to improve the condition of the peasants, the chief source of recruits and taxes. Although Maria Theresa's benevolence may have been motivated by *raison d'état* and Christian piety, significantly the official she appointed to investigate the problem – Franz Anton Blanc, a former pupil of Wolff's – formulated a solution in terms of Natural Law: the peasant had a natural right to satisfy his own needs and those of his family before the state and landowner could exact their share of his income. Famine in 1771 and disturbances in 1775 speeded the Bohemian patent which forbade lords to claim labour service from their serfs in excess of three days a week. Unlike earlier patents (1680 and 1738), this one was enforced. It was paralleled in other provinces.

Naturally, enlightened elements in government circles wished to turn the centralizing drive against the Hungarian nobility too who, in the words of an exasperated state councillor in 1762, 'misjudging [their] freedom and preferring momentary desires to the good of the Empire and [their] own true needs, lack all conception of the obligations of a part of the state to the whole'. Here, however, the empress showed her native caution. Despite counsels to dismantle the Hungarian county autonomy, she contented herself with imposing an unenforceable urbarium – or patent – on lord–serf relations (1767) and leaving unsummoned the Hungarian diet, which on the three occasions it had met had refused her greatest wish – the taxing of noble land.

Change was easier where the instinct for improvement encountered less powerful vested interests. The gilds, even the Jesuits, could not match Magyar nobles. 'Care for the general state economy is undoubtedly to be seen as the most important task of the political authorities' ran an imperial edict of 1768. The systematic mercantilism advocated by the seventeenth-century cameralists could at length be put into practice, aided by the common protective tariff for all the Austrian–Bohemian lands introduced in 1775. Trieste trebled in size in Maria Theresa's reign, helping to compensate for the failure of Charles VI's attempt to break into the Oriental trade through Ostend in his Belgian lands. Not until the plethora of financial incentives, bounties, premiums and monopolies was scaled down after 1770 however did native industry really acquire the competitive thrust to forge ahead. Industrial workers in Lower Austria doubled in the 1780s under Maria's successor. Austria now had 280 factories, about 100 of them in and around Vienna. 65 per cent of her exports and only a sixth of her imports were finished products. Bourgeois manufacturers were making their appearance.

Since eighteenth-century progressive thought bound up economic progress with the diffusion of knowledge, we should not be surprised at the bold decision in 1774 (1777 in Hungary) to introduce a system of universal primary education into Austria. Again, the real breakthrough came in Joseph's reign. In 1781 only 208,000 out of 776,000 children of school-age attended school in the monarchy's non-Magyar lands; in 1790 the figure was 174,000 in Bohemia alone, over two-thirds of those eligible. The inspirer of the scheme, Felbiger, like the reorganizer of secondary education, was a clergyman, for the empress bypassed her enlightened officials for this sensitive role; but both men were 'reform Catholics'. This was a period of steady retreat by the conservative wing of the Church. The anti-clerical Kaunitz exploited an increasingly rationalistic climate to ascribe the original acceptance of Christianity by rulers to 'moderation of its principles and the excellence of its moral teachings'. It was not just the state's interests, therefore, but 'the essence of Christianity' which was contravened when unlettered boys of 14 took monastic vows, constant feast days interfered with commerce and benefit of clergy allowed criminals to go unpunished. As the pope seemed slow to agree, these customs were abolished without him, but pressure from the powers did force him, by disbanding the Jesuit order (in 1773), to remove the chief symbol of the former pretensions of the Church.

Such wide reforms cannot be traced to a single cause. Maria Theresa's energetic personality was an important factor. Land patents, mercantilist programmes, the concept of a 'God-pleasing equality' all pre-dated her reign. What was new was the number of people with a commitment to carry them out and on the other side a certain intellectual lassitude of feudal and clerical forces whose resistance, always passive, was undermined by the fact that so many of their members had gone over to the new ways. It was as a great landowner that Kaunitz commented on pleas for the restoration of the Bohemian chancellery that he 'could not understand how the very servants of Your Majesty can so far forget themselves to oppose a well-established system in order to substitute it for one which is clearly in contradiction with all the rules of a reasonable form of government.' The essence of Maria Theresa's achievement was to draw this intellectually alert section of the feudal elite into the service of the rising state bureaucracy; like Frederick in Prussia and Catherine in Russia, she had updated the old alliance of sovereign and nobility, not abolished it.

Maria Theresa died in 1780. Unlike her, her son and successor Joseph was as acquainted with the philosophers as any of his ministers and resolved indeed to 'make Philosophy the legislator of my Empire'. The fact that Joseph was also a martinet, inordinately ambitious for personal glory, does not disqualify him as an 'enlightened' ruler, as some have claimed. No ideology has yet succeeded in banishing ambition, nor did the philosophers (unlike nineteenth-century liberals) unanimously repudiate absolute monarchy as an instrument of their ideals. Actually Joseph's ten-year reign was to test to the limit, and beyond, the capacity of the Habsburg lands to admit reforms, throwing into relief the achievements and limitations of Enlightenment in East European society. It was a reign destined to a tragic end.

Joseph was certainly a man in a hurry; 6000 edicts testify to the reforming zeal of this repressed and passionate widower. A significant early measure was his Toleration Edict of 1781, always unacceptable to his mother, which removed disincentives for skilled Protestants to settle in Austria and, more important, brought the numerous Hungarian Protestants into Hungarian official life. But Joseph undoubtedly believed, too, that it was wrong 'to save people's souls in spite of them, to coerce their conscience'. Attempts to ascribe all his measures to '*raison d'état*' not 'philosophy' are beside the point because they assume naively that the state interest is always plain to see, irrespective of intellectual assumptions. Many of Joseph's acts, like his freeing of the press, though no doubt intended by him ultimately to conduce to the strengthening of the state, would have seemed calculated to have the opposite effect to more old-fashioned statesmen. The unhindered circulation of anti-Joseph pamphlets, the criminal code of 1787 which abolished the death penalty and established equality before the law, the concern for popular welfare symbolized by the founding of the vast Vienna general hospital with its 2000 beds all reflected a despotism nothing if not enlightened.

Of course, Joseph's methods were likely to grate on some, like the convicted nobles he set to sweeping the street, or conservative clerics appalled at civil marriage and divorce, the closure of 700 monasteries, and the restrictions on links with Rome. There were even somewhat utopian enlightened intellectuals who regretted that the Toleration Edict did not go far enough (it went further than the famous 1689 Toleration Act of liberal England) or that the criminal code still contained harsh penalties. But the measure of popular indignation, particularly to his religious measures, has probably been exaggerated by writers of the nineteenth-century Catholic revival. What is interesting about the hectic early years of Joseph's reign is not that his innovations should have been opposed, but that they had so many supporters, like the able clerics who came forward to staff his new provincial general seminaries and helped to inculcate 'Josephinism', or the view of the Church as a kind of moral arm of the enlightened state. Nor was Joseph embarrassed by his grant of personal freedom to the serfs and reduction of landlords' judicial powers (1781) or even, initially, by his centralizing measures in Hungary, which included the abolition of the county system, the removal of the Hungarian royal Crown to Vienna and replacement of Latin by German as the offical language. Indeed, future leaders of the Hungarian national revival like Kazinczy and Berzevicky, both, significantly, Protestants, described themselves as Josephinists and worked in the German administration.

But Joseph's restlessness led him further. Avid for martial fare he allowed Russia to inveigle him into a disastrous war with Turkey in the Balkans which forced him into unpopular fiscal and requisitioning measures. To make matters worse, in the middle of the war he decided to upgrade the tax survey he had commissioned in 1785 into a scheme for the transformation of feudalism in his domain. The resulting tax law of 1789 ordered that henceforth all labour service by peasants was to cease, to be replaced by an annual rent to the lord amounting to 17.8 per cent of the peasant's income, with a further 12.2 per cent going to the state. This was nothing less than the physiocratic programme of the single state land-based tax and reliance on a prosperous peasant class.

In pressing ahead with the tax law despite the repeated warnings of the Chancellery and the head of the Tax Commission, Count Zinzendorff, Joseph had finally stepped outside that wide area where his reforms could find an echo in the sentiments of the cultured notables around him. Count Zinzendorff, a progressive iron industrialist on his estates and a supporter of equal noble–peasant taxation, bitterly attacked the enforced commutation of feudal labour service in the language of Enlightenment. 'Is the right of property to be protected or not, are contracts to be held or not?' he challenged the emperor, adding that Joseph's attack on noble property exceeded the bounds of a 'moderate form of government'. Zinzendorff's defection symbolized the collapse of a reform consensus. Joseph was left alone to face the perils of a deteriorating military situation, revolt in the Austrian Netherlands, recalcitrant Catholic peasants in the Tyrol and a mutinous Hungarian noble opposition, withholding war supplies and intriguing with Prussia. Suddenly, in the midst of these troubles, he sickened and on his death-bed, as news reached him, by every post, of disturbances throughout his domains, revoked much of what he had done, restoring to the Hungarians their constitution and their Crown.

Joseph II is one of the most intriguing and controversial monarchs in European history. What light does his rise and fall throw on the dilemma of East European Enlightenment? Wangermann, in his thought-provoking *From Joseph II to the Jacobin Trials*, argues that Joseph's last years, marked by war, reintroduction of censorship and political police and harassment of freemasons and dissidents, reveal his true character as a despot, contemptuous of the genuine free thought that was beginning to emerge in the Viennese press and in the ranks of intelligent artisans. This is to exaggerate the extent and importance of Paris-style Jacobinism in the still somewhat immature Habsburg milieu and to overplay the rather mild repressions of a hard-pressed regime. A. J. P. Taylor sums up the Josephine Enlightenment from the other extreme. Joseph was too radical for his times. His was 'a revolutionary policy for a revolutionary class', he was 'the Convention in a single man'. But the implied comparison with the French Revolution overlooks the fact that Joseph neither installed a 'cult of reason' in place of orthodox Christianity – he actually appropriated monastic funds only so as to found 1700 new parishes – nor opposed the order of nobility as such, though, in accordance with a long standing moral tradition, he expressed repugnance at noble arrogance. The commutation of labour services ordered by the tax law had been implemented on certain Polish estates, as we have seen (p. 45), and had been gradually introduced on Austrian Crown estates since the last years of Maria Theresa's reign. It offered landowners a status not dissimilar to that which they held in Hungary and Poland after the definitive abolition of feudalism in the mid nineteenth century, and both these societies remained of predominantly noble stamp.

Yet if Joseph's policies were hardly revolutionary taken singly, they were undoubtedly felt to be so in their cumulative effect. By the tax law, the noble percentage of peasant income (17.8 per cent) was pitched too low for lesser nobles, lacking ready cash, to be able to finance their demesne farms on the capitalist wage labour system that the law presupposed, while in Hungary they were prevented from moving off the land into the civil service, as happened in the next century, by the fact that German was to be the language of administration. But over and above this, Joseph's chief error was to associate Enlightenment with the absolute monarchy alone; all criticism of his rule he denounced as obscurantist reaction.

It was a pardonable exaggeration as far as the noble and clerical opposition was concerned. The dispute with the Magyars can be seen fairly as the clash of a modernizing regime with a feudal economic order, whose exponents, like the contemporary French *parlementaires*, had acquired sufficient of the language of liberty and natural rights to deck out their own interests in the guise of enlightened patriotism. But it was not just a question of 'feudal reaction'. The novel calls made between 1788 and 1792 for a Magyar-speaking administration and army corps, together with the influential multi-volume inquiry into Hungarian circumstances commissioned by the 1791 diet, point the influence of a nascent cultural revival tracing its own distinctive descent from Enlightenment ideals. Of this, Joseph had no inkling. He viewed a complex social issue in black and white moral terms, a common failing of the eighteenth century. The Magyar question exposed the limits of his kind of centralized enlightened despotism. Its natural supporters were a thin band of high officials and great magnates of advanced education and pan-imperial loyalties but limited radicalism. Yet any attempt to develop a more far-reaching policy would have meant trying to win over the gentry or other groups, who were both less well educated and more regional in their outlook.

All this the new emperor, Leopold II, saw much more clearly than his famous brother. By suspending the tax reform and calling the Hungarian diet, while also encouraging non-Magyars and non-nobles in Hungary to stake their claims, Leopold cut the ground from under the Magyar opposition's feet. The conclusion of peace with Turkey and Prussia deprived it of its last possible source of support. Having reasserted the Monarchy's power, it seems Leopold envisaged some kind of constitution for his subjects which would have combined elements of noble, royal and bourgeois Enlightenment somewhat on the lines of Montesquieu. But in 1792 the wise Leopold died unexpectedly. This was the end of the Austrian Enlightenment. By now the French Revolution was throwing its shadow over monarchical and aristocratic reformer alike. Leopold's son Francis II exhibited a lethargic and conservative temperament. In 1795 the execution of a handful of maladroit 'Jacobin' conspirators in Vienna and Hungary signalled the start of a long period of reaction.

The previous year, the Polish Enlightenment, and with it the Polish state, had also come to a bloody end. Poland's experience parallels and in places extends that of the monarchy. Its problem, too, was how to extend the reform spirit which prevailed in cultural and economic matters into more controversial spheres of government and social privilege. At least the common nationality of sovereign, magnates and lesser nobles in Poland appeared to boost the chances of accommodation. Moreover, in King Stanislas Augustus Poniatowski, bibliophile, patron of the arts, amateur physicist and a devotee of English civic virtues, the Poles had the very model of Enlightenment, dedicated 'to the restoration of the political fortunes of my country and the development of my nation's genius'. Against this had to be set Poland's greater exposure to foreign pressures (partly because her large non-Polish minorities gave ample pretexts for intervention) and the weak, elective basis of the monarchy, which sapped its powers of leadership.

The Polish reform movement is commonly dated to the year of Stanislas Augustus's election in 1764 as the first native monarch for sixty years. The outset of his reign saw agreement on the removal of internal tolls, currency reform, standardization of weights and measures and a national tariff and postal service; later followed by two important canals linking the Baltic to the Black Sea, state geological surveys and the founding of a complex of state industries on the royal estates at Grodno. In the Commission of National Education set up in 1773 the Poles acquired, too, what was effectively Europe's first ministry of education. Its charter – 'the good of every individual is the goal of the government, the true interest of the supreme power is to protect, defend and assure the rights of the citizens' – reads like a paraphrase of the *philosophes*. Half the children in the commission's secondary schools were non-noble, though it could do little at the primary level.

What Poland lacked was the powerful state bureaucracy of Theresan Austria, but she was soon to have the strongest of incentives to create one. The militant opposition of a section of the nobility to Russian influence precipitated an international crisis, a Russo-Turkish war and the entry of Austria and Prussia into Polish affairs, in order to prevent Russian influence from growing still further. The upshot was the division of one-third of the helpless commonwealth among her three neighbours in 1773 (known to history as the First Partition of Poland) with Austria receiving Galicia, Russia the eastern borderlands and Prussia the Baltic coast. In the aftermath, the diet consented to strengthen the executive power, electing five members from its ranks to form a Permanent Council under the king's presidency whose members headed departments which were in effect ministries. Feudalism, however, and an only slightly modified liberum veto remained inviolate, for the 1780 diet threw out the enlightened legal code on which the reforming party had set its heart. But the 1780s proved to be a decade of cumulative pressure for change, impelled partly by traditionalist magnates who resented the comparatively stable and monarchical regime of the Permanent Council, but in greater measure by the prospering middle gentry and the emerging bourgeoisie of Warsaw. Irked by the Russian tutelage over the Permanent Council, these varied elements overthrew it in 1788, turned to Prussia and inaugurated the reform era known in Polish history as the Four Year Diet (1788–92).

The crowning achievement of these years was the new constitution of May 1791. For the first time a leading section of Polish society broke with its feudal past. The qualification for political rights was made property, not noble birth; nobility became the automatic reward for meritorious state service, fifty seats in the diet were allotted to the towns and a standing army of 80,000 proclaimed. Of course, the extension rather than abolition of nobility and the vague reference to putting peasantry 'under the protection of the law' bespoke the moderation of the Polish reformers. They were a coalition of progressive gentry and wealthy burghers with the former still well on top. But the advance on the diet of 1780, or the Hungarian diet of 1791, was great. Too great, in the event, for conservative magnates appealed to Russia to intervene, thereby unwittingly precipitating the Second Partition of Poland. The stricken state moved to the left, gave General Kosciuszko, a Polish veteran of the American Revolution, dictatorial powers and called a *levée en masse*.

As events moved inexorably to a Third Partition and the erasure of Poland from the map of Europe (1795) plans were brought forward to accord the bourgeoisie an equal share in government, labour service was suspended and the prospect of permanent changes dangled before the peasant's eyes. In the republic's last days Polish Jacobins, led mainly by landless nobles in Warsaw, came to the fore urging revolutionary justice and forced requisitioning from the rich.

The collapse of the policies of Joseph and the Polish progressives meant the defeat of the first great reform movement in Eastern Europe. What difficulties this movement faced may be seen from the engaging cynicism of a Polish noble's letter to Joseph II criticizing his pro-peasant plans:

Assuredly one can only admire the views of Your Majesty, filled as they are with goodness and humanity. Certain it is that our nature revolts at the very idea of belting with blows him who is our own kind and the support and provider of our existence. Nevertheless I testify that the subordination which is in some measure even more necessary in economic than in military affairs can only be maintained in Galicia through corporal punishment.

Whether the historian chooses to emphasize the considerable reform endeavours made in Eastern Europe in this period or the continuing prevalence of feudal norms is, since both sides of the coin are undeniable, largely a reflection of his judgement of Eastern European history as a whole, indeed, of the entire question of the relationship of under-developed areas to more advanced ones. The East European Enlightenment faced the difficulty that, during the slow transition from a fully fledged feudalism, the social premises for an alternative order would long be incomplete. The co-operation of monarch and bureaucratic nobles as under Maria Theresa and, in different form, Poland's Permanent Council, could not be a permanent solution in an age of steady change, but the coalescence of landowners and bourgeois, which was to provide the basis of nineteenth-century Eastern Europe's distinctive liberalism and which appeared to be foreshadowed in Poland's last years, was still premature.

This situation was not as different from that of eighteenth-century Western Europe as is sometimes supposed. Enlightenment there too, as Venturi has argued, had markedly aristocratic origins and pointed only obscurely to a new political order. It took the French years of bloody strife before their reform movement crystallized into a successful bourgeois revolution. Nevertheless, the French movement did succeed while those of Eastern Europe faltered. Henceforth the Eastern European state was to be more extreme in its conservatism and the advocates of change correspondingly more revolutionary than in the West. This is not to say that nothing had been achieved. The memories of the Polish Enlightenment, somewhat over-coloured, lived on to inspire the national movement of the nineteenth century. Joseph's ideals of non-sectarianism, civic equality, and honest, paternalist administration set the tone of a powerful Austrian state patriotism till well into the next century and heavily influenced the awakening nationalities of the Balkans. The legacy of Enlightenment, much stronger in our region than in eighteenth-century Russia, can still be detected in the more liberal spirit which informs East European communism in comparison with its Soviet counterpart.

3 Liberalism and nationalism

The *ancien régime* under threat

With the deaths of Joseph and Leopold and the exile of Stanislas August, the first phase of modernization had come to an end. But events originating in revolutionary France were soon to show that the check was only temporary. In 1792 the French declared war on Austria and Prussia; where Enlightenment had penetrated fitfully through books, liberty, equality and fraternity were to be spread by force of arms. Even if it wished, Eastern Europe could no longer remain aloof from the ideological tussles of the West.

The years of almost continuous war from 1792 to 1815 mark a watershed in modern European history, despite the fact that the Vienna Congress of 1815 very much restored the pre-revolutionary *status quo* after France's final defeat. The princes of Italy and to a lesser extent Germany (only thirty-nine, instead of 300, loosely linked in a German confederation) were returned to their thrones; Austria gave up Belgium and received compensation in the form of Lombardy–Venetia in north Italy, including the Venetian province of Dalmatia; Poland was again partioned between Austria, Prussia and Russia, on somewhat different terms from 1795, with Russia now taking the lion's share, including Warsaw, and Austria the province of Galicia. Nonetheless, this defiant rejection of the principles of 1789 could not erase the memory of the hopes it had extinguished, or the victor's fears of doctrines which had helped France to humiliating dominance for so long. In 1805 and 1809 French armies had entered Vienna in triumph, in 1806 Berlin and in 1812 Moscow. Whether summoning into existence the Polish duchy of Warsaw (1806–13), conjuring up the kingdom of Italy (1805–14) and the Yugoslav Illyrian provinces (1809–13), dangling before the tsar visions of a Turkish partition, or appealing dramatically to the Hungarians to regain their national independence in his cause, Napoleon had brilliantly set the national question

before the minds of his contemporaries. His lieutenants had
similarly brought the social question to life again. 'There is nothing
feudal any more', cried the Polish reformer Staszicz in 1807 after
the abolition of serfdom by the French-sponsored duchy of Warsaw.
'Four years, I wish they had been here four centuries', observed
Emperor Francis on surveying the roads the French had built
during their brief occupation of Dalmatia.

Nonetheless, historians have sometimes exaggerated the role of
the Napoleonic interlude in inspiring the liberal and national
movements of nineteenth-century Eastern Europe. Societies often
but slightly touched by half a century of Enlightenment were not
suddenly shaken to their foundations by the passage of a French
army or the declaration of the rights of man. The Hungarian
gentry ignored Napoleon's appeal to rise. Bohemian peasants,
disturbingly interested in the French Revolution according to
Habsburg officials in 1792, were apparently permanently alienated
by the execution of Louis XVI the next year. In the Illyrian
provinces, French attempts to standardize the local Slav dialects
into an official language foundered on regional discord.

The French message took deepest root in areas where reform
sentiment had already made significant headway before 1789, as in
Poland. 20,000 Polish legionaries served under the French flag
between 1798 and 1802, hoping for the resurrection of an
independent Poland as their reward. The duchy of Warsaw, an
area of some 40,000 square miles, which Napoleon created in 1806,
was not quite what they had expected, but at least it was a Polish
state which successfully instituted the strong central government
and noble–burgher partnership that the reformers of the Four
Year Diet had striven unavailingly to achieve. But not all Poles in
these stressful times sided with France. As foreign minister of Tsar
Alexander in 1804–6, the great magnate Adam Czartoryski worked
for the reform of Europe along more moderate lines and an anti-
French European federation in which Poland would regain her
1772 borders under Russian aegis. It was in partial response to
such promptings that in 1815 Alexander carved out a kingdom of
Poland from his territories and endowed it with a constitution and
a diet; partial because the so-called Congress Kingdom covered
only a fifth of pre-partition Poland and excluded large Ukrainian,
Lithuanian and White Russian speaking territories which had
belonged to the former commonwealth.

Thus, in one way or another, the Poles gave notice of that

'Polish Question' which was to preoccupy Europe for a century. These years, too, saw the emergence of the Balkan question in its modern form. The revolt of the Serbs of the Belgrade Pashalik against Ottoman rule in 1804 was supported by numbers of educated Romanians, Greeks and Habsburg Serbs, who lent a localized peasant revolt something of the allure of a struggle for self-determination of Balkan Christians against Muslim misrule. The enlightened Dositej Obradovic became responsible for education in the Serbs' embryo administration, and the Serb leader Karageorge commissioned a copy of the Napoleonic code; even if the illiterate Karageorge's actual criminal code reflected primitive Serbian circumstances more accurately by recognizing only crimes against the state – murder, theft of livestock and abduction of women. Eventually, after the failure of Karageorge's bid for outright independence, his successor Milos settled for a limited autonomy under Constantinople, despatching the murdered Karageorge's head to the Sultan to seal the bargain.

However dubious the Serb movement may be as an example of French revolutionary influences in the Balkans, both the Serbian and the Polish question suggest three conclusions of the highest importance. First, in ethnically diverse Eastern Europe the call to justice and liberty would be seen pre-eminently as a call to national independence. Second, the suppressed peoples of Europe could pursue this independence by revolutionary or gradualist means, for the tactics of the legionaries and Czartoryski in Poland were paralleled by those of Karageorge and Milos in Serbia. Third, whatever the effect of the revolutionary era in radicalizing the people of Eastern Europe, it is hard to overrate its impact in making their rulers more conservative.

Indeed, the post–1815 years were to show that the most striking legacy of the revolutionary interregnum was the complete cessation of reform from above. Already in the first decade of his reign the Austrian Emperor Francis had dismantled the liberal features of the Josephinist experiment, restoring a reinvigorated censorship to the police, restricting the commutation of feudal labour service and clamping down on all forms of association. Soon after 1815 the once liberal-minded Tsar Alexander succumbed to reactionary influences and took steps against the Polish constitution he himself had granted; press censorship was tightened up in 1819; the following year an obscurantist minister of education replaced a Voltairian reformer. In 1819, too, the Karlsbad decrees clamped down on liberal and national agitation in the German confederation.

The Karlsbad decrees were sponsored by a man who brought to the conservative cause greater stability of character than the tsar and more intellectual sophistication than his own emperor: Francis II's chancellor from 1809 to 1848, the celebrated Prince Clemenz von Metternich. Elegantly aristocratic and outrageously conceited – 'error never had access to my mind', as he once remarked – Metternich (1773–1859) believed his diplomatic skill had won the war against Napoleon and now alone could secure the peace. Agitation after 1815 by Spanish liberals, German students, Italian *carbonari* and Greek patriots convinced him that Europe, 'visited by a plague', was 'an object of pity to a man of intellect, of horror to a man of virtue'. For – man's nature and society's needs being immutable – what but pathological folly, or ambition, could see in revolution anything but a pointless treadmill of social upheaval and internecine strife before society sank back exhausted into a 'repose'? Sadly, though, progress had turned the mind of presumptuous man, infecting him with a fatuous belief in his own powers and an equally fatuous contempt for the social order inherited from his forbears. Naive idealists on the one hand, predatory self-seekers on the other: these composed the revolutionary foe. 'It is principally the middle orders of society that this moral gangrene has infected,' wrote Metternich, for 'the masses are and always will be conservative.'

It is not difficult to see in Metternich the rationalist aristocrat of the eighteenth-century Enlightenment, shocked into intransigent conservatism by the revolutionary excesses he had observed as a youth in France. A man of wide scientific interests, a Josephinian in religion, and a successful innovator on his own estates, Metternich held fast to the enlightened preference for a mechanistic rather than a transcendental world view. His historic role, however, was to apply rationalism to question, not the illogic of the *ancien régime*, but that of the revolutionary Utopia and to conclude from mechanistic philosophy, not man's duty to adjust benevolently the workings of society, but the great dangers of upsetting the balance that underlay the whole. Balance was at the heart of Metternich's political credo. Internally, he wished to restore an equilibrium between the component territories and nationalities of the Habsburg monarchy. Externally, he sought to conserve the congress system of the powers and the Holy Alliance of Austria, Prussia and Russia into instruments for the suppression of disorder anywhere in Europe. The years 1815–48 have been called the Age of Metternich.

Metternich quite justly denied that he was a reactionary. The advances made in the preceding half century were too far-reaching to be reversed. Much of enlightened despotism had, anyway, aimed at strengthening the state and was accordingly retained: centralized administration, subordination of Church to state; general primary education as a training in civic patriotism; economic development. But even the Enlightenment's concern for intellectual freedom and social reform, at which the post-1815 regimes did demur, was extremely hard to jettison.

Neither efficient bureaucrats, nor the doctors, lawyers, engineers, vets, surveyors or estate managers increasingly demanded by developing societies could be obtained without greatly extended facilities for higher education. New universities opened in Lemberg (1817) and Warsaw (1816); technical high schools, the first of their kind in Europe, in Prague (1806) and Vienna (1815). Despite repression and mass emigration the intelligentsia of the Congress Kingdom still grew from some 7500 to 11,700 members between 1830 and 1863. Where only a handful of papers existed in major centres in 1790, literally hundreds were being published by 1848.

Even more significant, attempts to shore up the social order were being undermined by economic change. The eighteenth-century population upsurge continued. In the Habsburg monarchy, numbers went up by 50 per cent in the first half of the new century; in Poland and the Principalities, still more. Towns grew faster than the surrounding countryside: Vienna from 240,000 to 408,000 between 1818 and 1846; Budapest from 60,000 to 140,000; Prague from 79,000 to 115,000. In the first three decades of the century both Warsaw and Bucharest passed from 80,000 to 130,000 inhabitants. This unprecedentedly sustained rise of population was made possible only by a steadily improving economic performance. High grain prices in the Napoleonic wars had stimulated capitalist farming methods, and after 1815 the ability of enterprising landowners to turn to sheep-farming, sugar-beet, sugar refining and distilling partly circumvented the subsequent price fall. Increased cultivation of the potato, with its high nutritional value, naturally helped. In more advanced areas, industry offered increasing scope for employment of surplus rural labour.

In keeping with the *étatiste* traditions of the eighteenth century, governments played a substantial role in this developmental process.

Not only were the great road and canal-building projects of the Enlightenment brought to completion, in 1841 Austria planned the most ambitious state railway system up to that time, linking the capital to Saxony, Bavaria, Lombardy and Trieste, and rounding off privately financed routes begun years earlier; the Congress Kingdom government also completed the Warsaw–Vienna line (begun in 1845) under state control. An Austrian state bank was founded in 1816, a state bank in Warsaw in 1828. Austrian gilds lost their privileges in 1811; foreign entrepreneurs were as welcome as in the eighteenth century. Eastern Europe was to be safeguarded against Western ideas, not Western technology. The English gave Poland and Bohemia their machine goods industries, and the Viennese their mechanized cotton spinning; Englishmen built the first Austrian locomotive, inaugurated the steamship services of Trieste and the Danube, and took charge of Viennese gas-lighting. German or Swiss Protestants and Jews virtually monopolized the breed of Viennese financiers, and Jewish bankers were important in Warsaw. The role of Salomon Rothschild, Metternich's personal friend, who was an Austrian baron but needed exceptional permission to acquire an estate, because Jews lacked civil equality, exemplifies the curious modern–conservative compromise of the Metternichian era.

For all that, something was happening. Mechanization of cotton spinning, introduced into Bohemia in the 1790s, dominated cotton production by the 1820s, and was soon applied to wool and linen. A Bohemian factory proletariat came into existence, only some 50,000 strong in the 1830s, true (about a seventh of the domestic workers), but still the spearhead of a process which saw coal production and raw cotton imports quadruple and iron production double between the 1820s and the 1840s, while trade between Austria and Hungary rose from £1.7 million to £4 million a year. Meanwhile the Congress Kingdom finance minister, Drucki-Lubecki (1821–9), was presiding over a state-orchestrated economic expansion which created a state metallurgical complex in the Dabrowa basin and stimulated a Lodz-based cotton manufacture that had multiplied thirtyfold by the 1840s. Not for nothing have recent economic historians emphasized the importance of the first half of the nineteenth century as the culminating stage in 'proto-industrialization', preparing the way for the achievement of industrial society later in the century.

In absolute terms and relative to Western countries, production

The partitions of Poland

was still low. The monarchy produced 1,182,600 tons of coal in 1851 against nearly 4.5 million in France; it had some 550 steam engines in the mid 1840s against France's 4114. Moreover, there were wide regional variations – Hungary had only eighty of the steam engines, Croatia four – while outside the monarchy and Poland industrialization could not be spoken of. Yet in these regions, too, there was an economic quickening. The area of cultivated land almost doubled and the price of rural property trebled in the Romanian principalities in the second quarter of the nineteenth century. A comprehensive road-building programme facilitated a 275 per cent increase in Moldavia's grain exports in a decade. Galatz and Braila began to develop as significant ports as Odessa and Trieste had in the previous century. Nor was European Turkey entirely passive: her exports to Austria doubled in the years 1814–38, enabling something of a Serbian and Bulgarian commercial bourgeoisie to grow up alongside the traditional Greek, Tsintsar and Jewish merchant class; indeed Bulgarian historians have calculated an eight fold increase in trade between Bulgarian lands and England and France in the period 1820–50.

Set against this background of development, the ideological issues of the Napoleonic years could have seemed a mere distraction. Was this not, after all, the age of Austrian Biedermeier, when comfortable Viennese burghers gave themselves up to the pleasure of domesticity, the music of Beethoven, Schubert and Schumann, and the theatre of Nestroy and Grillparzer? Metternich for one took this positive view. 'Austria is sometimes assured of standing still,' he wrote once. 'Nothing of the sort. We move with the times but we are not in any danger of moving away from our principles.'

Such complacency was ill-judged. Metternich's period of office spanned the years of fastest development Eastern Europe had known, but also a period of unprecedented disaffection. The paradox is superficial. It was precisely the gradually changing economic environment which set in motion forces with which traditional absolutist regimes were unequipped to cope.

Basically, two cankers rotted the restoration handiwork. One was the institutional backwardness of the absolute state itself, which put it at the mercy of its ruler's vagaries. The achievement of the enlightened despots had been to establish bureaucratic control over their territories, but they had not rationalized powers at the top which remained in their hands and those of a handful of trusted advisers. As government grew more complex such a system required further formalization; Western liberal constitutionalism developed a distinction between a legislative power, lodged in a popularly elected assembly, and an executive power, wielded by ministers responsible individually for particular departments and collectively in cabinet for binding advice to the sovereign. The suspicious Emperor Francis, however, rejected all attempts, by Metternich and others, to get him to accept an adaptation of these principles to the conditions of absolute monarchy, which would have distinguished between a legislative state council (nominated by Francis, of course) and a committee of executive ministers meeting regularly to formulate collective, non-binding advice. In fact, during Francis' reign the state council ceased to exercise any general function and become embroiled in pointless demarcation disputes with organs of day to day administration; modern executive ministries failed to emerge, and cabinet discussion was displaced by one to one contact between the sovereign and whoever he chose to consult on particular problems. The result was lack of cohesion and endless delays. After Francis's death in 1835, a quarrelsome trio composed of Metternich, the Archduke Ludwig and Count Kolowrat carried on a lame-duck, unofficial regency in the name of his son Ferdinand, who was a half-wit. Absolutism had struck again!

This vacuum at the centre helps explain why the Habsburg state failed in its appointed task as guardian of social cohesion after 1815. In an age when an emerging public opinion was particularly sensitive to economic issues, it trebled the national debt between 1825 and 1847, because it preferred loans to direct taxation which would hit nobles; it kept credit facilities at a derisory level, because it preferred to deal with a few big bankers; and it published no budget, because it despised public opinion and the figures would have been sobering anyway. As a result, probably no single factor so radicalized educated Austrian opinion as rumours of impending state bankruptcy. In an age of mounting social problems, when house-building totally failed to keep pace with the flow of people into the large towns; when machine production and international market cycles began to swell the ranks of the un-employed; and when an expanding low-paid, fixed income bureauc-racy proved peculiarly vulnerable to sharp food price changes, it was doubly unfortunate that Austria had a government caught between traditions of fussy and increasingly ineffectual paternalism and the modern ethos of *laissez-faire*. The boasted 'welfare state' had done next to nothing to anticipate the problems of industrial-ization which assailed it with growing force in the 1840s, bringing in turn the Bohemian Erzgebirge miners' famine in 1843, the Prague cotton printers' rising in 1844 and the mass destitution in Vienna and Prague in the following years. Nor did the welfare state have any policy but 'leave alone' in the face of the steady decline of the feudal system on the land, where population pressure increased the number of dwarf-holders and landless, and inefficient serf labour revealed its unsuitability for market-orientated farming. Ominously, peasants grew steadily more reluctant to meet their feudal obligations. From the mid 1830s the noble diets of Lower

Austria and Hungary themselves unavailingly requested change.

This malaise of government was not confined to Austria. In the Congress Kingdom the army chief, Grand Duke Constantine, the viceroy, Zajaczek, and the tsar's representative Novosiltsov were constantly at odds; similar confusion prevailed in the Principalities between boyar-dominated assembles, the princes and the Russian consuls; a quarrel between Milos and his council precipitated the ex-pig merchant's deposition and flight in 1839. In an age steadily growing away from absolutism the ruling factors were turning unsuccessfully to half-baked makeshift, whose only rationale was the absence of liberal or democratic principle. The traditional pretensions of autocracy contrasted hollowly with its inability to maintain control, particularly in the economic sphere. Hence not just patriotism but the doubled price of rye and the increased cost of beer and vodka swept the Russians temporarily out of Warsaw in the Polish rising of 1830–1.

If governmental inadequacy was the first canker of absolutism, the second was the failure to maintain Eastern Europe free from ideological contamination. Metternich's external balance was destroyed by successive lurches to the left in European politics. Britain's withdrawal from the congress system in 1822, Tsar Nicholas's endorsement of the Greek revolt against the Turks in 1827, and the July 1830 revolution in France preluded ever more confident movements nearer at hand for liberal and national goals in Germany and Italy. From their Parisian headquarters, 9000 Polish *émigrés* kept up vigorous propaganda in all three sections of partitioned Poland; in Austria itself the notorious censorship could not stop the Leipzig *émigré* publication *Grenzboten* from being widely read; the room of the radical Magyar poet Petofi was hung with lithographs of Danton, Robespierre, Marat and St Just; and even lowly Serbia in 1839 began to send youths for study abroad. On the eve of 1848 Metternich's 'system' was a dirty word and liberalism and nationalism concepts to conjure with in Eastern Europe.

Liberalism

Naturally, such terms as 'liberalism' and 'nationalism' could not have exactly the same connotations here as in the lands of their origin. Indeed, important differences existed between the liberalisms of industrial England, ex-republican France and politically divided

Germany, where professional and administrative groups played a larger role. Yet in all these countries, liberalism was the creed of the middle classes, however composed, whose numerical and economic strength led them to demand political power and the reorganization of society according to individual rather than inherited distinctions. Liberalism was Enlightenment from below.

Liberalism in Eastern Europe could hardly be as decisively a movement of the middle class because, for all the tendencies just described, this was still small and weak. Even in comparatively developed areas around Vienna and in the Czech lands the role of capitalists was significantly less than in Germany, which these areas most closely resembled. The captains of industry and finance trod cautiously in Austria because they were commonly of alien origin, and besides, the former, at least, were still mainly laying the foundations of later success. A mere month before he was overthrown, Metternich joked to Salomon Rothschild not to rock the boat, 'for if the devil comes for me he will take you too'.

Hence early nineteenth-century Eastern Europe presents a remarkable phenomenon: a liberalism originating with and for some time dominated by the noble class, strongest in the three noble communities *par excellence* of the Austro-Germans, the Magyars and the Poles. What lay behind this noble liberalism? Was it a contradiction in terms, a case of mistaken identity? Not altogether, for in two ways the situation of East European nobles was more analogous to that of the West European middle classes than might at first appear. For one thing, politically they frequently occupied the middle ground between the masses and the governing elite. Cut off from the latter because of alien rule in the case of the Poles and Magyars or by bureaucratic absolutism in the case of the Austrians, the nobles could easily find themselves alienated by official censorship or ineptitude, and provoked, like Western liberals, to press for a political role commensurate with their social and economic status. Government intransigence risked the destruction of feudalism from below and without compensation, as in France. Would it not be better to dismantle it peacefully from above, especially when researches like those of Szechenyi (see p. 72) showed that free agricultural labour was up to three times more productive than serf labour? The second explanation for noble liberalism relates to the social structure of the East European nobility, particularly in Poland and Hungary. There was simply a very large number of nobles in those countries, who could not all be held comparable with the restricted elites of England and France. The Polish urban intelligentsia which was taking shape at this time had a bourgeois life-style but was built up largely from impoverished noble migrants. Hungarian nobles, some 544,000 strong in 1840, were almost as numerous as the urban population of 575,000, and since all nobles had the vote they had the semblance of a claim to be living in a more democratic society than England had been before the 1832 Reform Act. In particular, the 30,000 or so families of the middle gentry, which by the 1830s and 1840s had acquired a fairly homogenous political outlook, voiced in journals and newspapers, have often been equated with the middle class of the West. The case can be made still more forcibly for the many Hungarian liberal noble leaders who were landless, or almost so, and made their way in life as members of the free professions: a lawyer like Kossuth, a writer and civil servant like Eötvös, a historian like Szalay, a journalist like Szemere. Here were people for whom the liberal message of equality of opportunity undoubtedly held more appeal than the closed society of feudalism.

Examples will make the process plainer. One alienated noble, to whom the first manifestation of Austrian liberalism may be traced, was the independent minded young Count Anton von Auersperg, whose *Wanderings of a Vienna Poet* (published in 1831 under the pseudonym Anastasius Grün) made an impassioned plea for free speech. Another was Baron Andrian-Werburg, author of *Austria and Her Future* (1842) and apparently frustrated by failure to advance rapidly enough through the ponderous Austrian civil service. As yet the protest of these talented but somewhat lordly individuals was an ambiguous one, muffled by family ties, dynastic loyalty, and disdain for the more whole-hearted radicals encouraged by their influential testimony. Its concrete proposals in Andrian-Werburg's work were for reinvigorated provincial diets, representative of bourgeois and peasants as well as nobles, and offering a counterweight to a federal assembly and government. In the 1840s the diets of Lower Austria and Bohemia did begin to press for the extension of their powers. By this time other potential foci of opposition were appearing where, alongside liberal nobles, representatives of the business world, academics, professional people and even civil servants assembled to express views on what should be done; such were the Lower Austrian Manufacturers Association (1839), the Literary and Artistic Concordia (1840), the Juridical–Political Reading Union or Leseverein (1842) and the student societies. Their toleration points to the authorities' increasing uncertainty, although these may also have felt that there was not so much to fear from the haphazard mix of bourgeois liberalism, Josephinist nostalgia and noble liberal conservatism that characterized the societies' discussions. Only two points united all the reformers; abolition of serfdom and of censorship. Outside Austria the exiles and their vigorous journal *Grenzboten* took a more consistently bourgeois line: a strong central parliament rather than a decentralized federation; representation by property franchise, or even universal suffrage, rather than by orders. This was the influential programme of the Bohemian-born Franz Schuselka, a prolific political pamphleteer in his German exile.

In Poland and Hungary the noble element in liberalism was much stronger. In Hungary only nobles had political rights; although non-nobles had civil equality in partitioned Poland and even played a leading role under Marcinkowski in the smaller Prussian zone, politics in Galicia and the Congress Kingdom remained very much a noble affair. In 1819 the Niemojowski brothers launched an attack on censorship in the Warsaw diet. Despite their immediate disciplining, the campaign for an extension of constitutional and national rights continued both openly, in the Patriotic Society founded in 1821, and covertly in secret student societies, notably at Wilno University. Meanwhile, Francis had finally been forced to convene the Hungarian diet after an unconstitutional interregnum of fourteen years (1825). The deputy Nagy in the language of liberalism called for guarantees for press freedom and against Habsburg absolutism. A generation of struggle between the Hungarian diet and Vienna had begun.

At this stage neither of the movements could really be described as liberal. 'No radical in England can inveigh more violently against taxation than do the liberals of Hungary', wrote the Englishman Paget of his observations of the Hungarian diet of 1835, 'but they mix up their invective so strongly with the privileges of nobility, that it would be difficult to recognise anything like the same principle in their opposition to it.' But change was on the way. In Poland's case it was speeded by the experience of the 1830–1 insurrection in Russian Poland when the revolutionaries subordinated peasant claims for land ownership to constitutional and military priorities. 'Cold reason for the moment silenced the cry of humanity', explained a revolutionary in elegant French. This kind of rationality did not impress the peasants, whose consequent apathy in large contributed to the revolt's humiliating collapse. Left-wing patriots drew their conclusions. In 1836 the manifesto of the largely *émigré* noble Polish Democratic Society proclaimed peasant ownership of their land without compensation the cornerstone of the society's policy. At least the radical wing of the Polish nobility was committed to a fundamental restructuring of Polish society.

The Hungarian nobility in its turn was awoken to reality by the north Hungarian peasant revolt of 1831, the most serious in the country since 1514. In this case, however, the effect was to reinforce the impact of a remarkable book published the previous year – the *Credit* of Count Stephen Szechenyi, with which Hungarian liberalism may be said to have taken form. For Szechenyi argued that it was the feudal system, not Hungary's subordination to Vienna, that caused the nation's backwardness. What society could obtain credit for modernization when a battery of laws protected feudal property from the creditor? How could that credit which, in its primal sense of mutual trust, had blessed mighty England with her spirit of association and public zeal be brought to Hungary other than by lowering the barriers between noble and non-noble and sharing the burdens of taxation and power? If Szechenyi's concrete constitutional proposals were modest and gradualist, as befitted the second largest landowner in Hungary, his land drainage and river regulation schemes, his sponsorship of Danube steamship services and textile manufacturers, not least his advocacy of casinos (social clubs) and scientific horse-breeding (for Szechenyi knew the Magyar gentry, and he was a great admirer of the English aristocracy!) were brilliant practical propaganda for a change of attitudes. Unlike the Poles, the Magyars proceeded crab-wise towards reform, dogged by conservative Vienna and her magnate supporters in Hungary and by the hesitations of the reformers themselves. The diet of 1832–6 voted for peasants' rights to perpetual redemption of servile obligations, that of 1840 for full equality between Catholics and Protestants, that of 1843–4 for non-noble right to land ownership and office and, in principle, a compulsory end to the lord–serf relationship. When the diet reassembled in 1847 the united opposition under Kossuth was pledged to the final stage in the liberal programme; the establishment of a modern responsible government free of Vienna's tutelage in a wholly defeudalized Hungary, where serfs were no more, nobles paid taxes and burghers sat in parliament.

Austria, Poland and Hungary were the focal points of East European liberalism in the first half of the nineteenth century. Beyond them liberals might be found, mainly in the Principalities, but hardly a liberal movement. Tudor Vladimirescu's revolt in Moldavia in 1821 had a liberal inspiration but failed to rouse an apathetic population. It served, though, as a prologue to the Greek War of Independence against the Turks, and Russian intervention on the Christian side in the Russo-Turkish war of 1827–9. The Treaty of Adrianople, which followed Russian victory, not only established a Greek state but entitled Russia to supervise a change of administration in the Principalities, where the replacement of the Phanariot hospodars by native princes was confirmed. Under the so-called Organic Regulation (1832) both provinces acquired institutions combining enlightened despotism and boyar oligarchy, and a land settlement weighted in the boyars' favour. An intelligentsia did begin to emerge, when in 1835 Wallachia and in 1842 Moldavia restricted public office to diploma holders, and the officially noble colleges opened their doors to non-nobles also. Foreign study also began to be an option. Nevertheless, Kogalniceanu, Ghica and the *Progress* journal group in Moldavia, Radulescu, Balcescu and the Bratiano brothers from the secret revolutionary society 'Fraternity' were as yet only on the fringes of politics. The Principalities truly displayed that noble pseudo-liberalism which historians more often attribute, rather unfairly, to Poland and Hungary. As for the Balkans, their turn must await Chapter 4. Suffice it to say here that, although expulsion of the autocratic old tyrant Milos was followed by a wider trading right, a civil code based on individual private property (1844) and the institution of a regular bureaucracy and legal process, this represented not so much contemporary liberalism as the belated penetration to the Balkans of enlightened paternalism.

Eastern European liberalism was an elusive, complex creed, as any ideology must be which is grafted from one milieu on to another. At one level it displayed the emotionalism and idealism of the student youth of developing lands, drunk on ideas from afar: English constitutional monarchy, French democracy, American republicanism, even Utopian socialism. At another level, it was only partly emancipated from preceding native traditions, enlightened, Josephinist or noble libertarian. It had no united view of the future order. The division between a Werburg and a Schuselka in Austria was duplicated, approximately, in the split in Poland between the Polish Democratic Society, and Prince Adam Czartoryski's moderate conservativism, in Hungary in the split between Kossuth's support for traditional county autonomy and Eötvös's preference for centralism (though Eötvös was no democrat). As to peasant emancipation, much dispute continued as to whether this should be with land or without, how it should be compensated, and through what financial mechanism.

However a certain common ethos can be made out. East European liberals were not a revolutionary class pushing aggressively into the unknown, but the spokesmen of a fairly small, educated stratum, usually members of the privileged order they condemned and often linked to it still by ties of sentiment and interest. Of course, there were also plebeian elements coming to the fore. The 'Polish People', an *émigré* group of peasant participants in the 1831 campaign, with its own programme of peasant communism would have been unthinkable half a century earlier. Tancsics, a proponent of emancipation without compensation, himself of peasant stock, and Petofi, a butcher's son, brilliant poet and libertarian radical, introduced new strands into Hungarian public life in the 1840s. The spokesmen of the reviving Czech nation, Palacky, Rieger, Havlicek, Brauner and others, were the talented offspring of a peasantry that had begun to spill out of the countryside into Bohemia's German-dominated towns. Despite all this, the key theme of political discourse before the revolutionary cataclysm of 1848 was not overturn and class conflict, but the call for a timely piece of social engineering. The conviction of being caught up in a world historical process of transcendent power helped ease for many an otherwise painful accommodation to new ideas. 'In face of the unrelenting onward march of time', as Kossuth said, 'to hold fast to the old would be as impossible and absurd as to demand that the Danube should cease to flow or flow upstream.' Whether such convictions aroused enthusiasm or resignation depended partly on status and partly on temperament; either way, liberalism, was embraced because it offered a new framework and new principles. 'Believe me, noble states', the reformer Kölcsey told the Hungarian diet in 1834, 'that this spirit [of peasant rebellion] can neither be vanquished nor curbed, but must be tamed down by community of interests, and reconciled to society by the words *Freedom* and *Property*'.

Alongside 'freedom' and 'property', which need no commentary, 'community of interests' is the key phrase here. How to restore the cohesion in society which ideological breakdown and socio-economic change had shattered? Here was the core of the liberal problem. Hence the appeal for East European liberals as for the *juste milieu* school in contemporary France and the German *Rechtstaat* theorists of the concept of law, as the linchpin of a new civil society, which in treating all equally would ensure their mutual respect, facilitating necessary reforms without social revolution. Law, rather than the people, would be sovereign. Hence also the East European liberals' preoccupation with another aspect of classical liberalism which above all seemed calculated to guarantee that 'community of interests' they craved – the idea of nationality.

Nationalism

Throughout Eastern Europe countless monuments attest to the immense emotional force that the idea of nationality has had, and still holds, in these parts. Let only one, secluded in a minor square of Budapest, be mentioned here. Around the four sides of a rectangular block are carved idealized figures representing different aspects of the national life – a milkmaid holding a pitcher, a young student, a peasant rake in hand, a dignified frock-coated old gentleman, a middle-aged lady seated sideways clasping an open bible.... All of them gaze out at the bystander with an ernest intensity, as if caught in external meditation on the opening line from the famous Vörösmarty poem (1837) that runs along the top frieze: 'Remain, O Magyar, forever faithful to thy fatherland.' On top of the plinth Vörösmarty himself sits brooding over the scene in pensive pose. The theme is hackneyed but its execution is genuinely moving, even to the outsider.

This attraction of the nation for the East European reformer has already been partly explained. We may go further. Liberalism lauded the value of association for common purpose, condemned feudal inequalities and stressed the fitness of all for progress. Was not a nation the highest form of association, and the subjection of entire peoples to servile status the most iniquitous act of feudalism, as their rebirth would be the clearest sign that the feudal order had had its day? This much is plain. Yet it must be stressed that the appeal of nationalism in nineteenth-century Eastern Europe had deeper roots even than these and touched upon essentially psychological motivations that cannot be strait jacketed into a liberal creed. The East European reformer, as we have seen, sustained an intellectual life drawn very largely from Western models. In this relationship with a more advanced world there was necessarily a fund of tension – the contrast between the model and the reality of the motherland could energize and inspire; it could also jolt and deflate. 'Poor little fatherland, how filthy you are', sighed the much travelled Szechenyi. Moments of euphoric hope alternated with spasms of deepest despair. Szechenyi described his life as that of a madman, consumed equally by grief and by joy, as he alternated between pessimism and optimism on his country's fate. The young Jevrem Grujic, a Serb scholarship holder, having left Heidelberg University where the history professor had called Serbs barbarians, found his ardent patriotism severely shaken by his overwhelming first impressions of mighty Paris; within two years, however, he had jointly published a French pamphlet on the south Slavs so ecstatically nationalistic that it claimed Sir Thomas More could never have written his *Utopia* if he had seen Serb peasant society. 'There, before my eyes moist with tears, stretches that land, once the cradle, now the grave-yard of my people', lamented the Slovak poet, Kollar, in his 'Daughter of the Slavs' written at the University of Jena in Eastern Germany, an area wrested by the Germans from the Slavs centuries before; but the poem went on to prophesy a messianic resurrection of the Slavs to world leadership and glory.

The nascent East European intelligentsia was inspired by two of the most powerful instincts of humankind; pride and emulation. But in the end only the fool is sustained by pride alone. Generally small, often despised, always backward, how could the nationalities of Eastern Europe have indulged their patriotic visions unless uplifted by a powerful, dynamizing creed, going beyond the rational tenets of liberalism? The romantic movement supplies the answer.

Romanticism was a reaction of sensitive spirits against the stress of the Enlightenment on the universality of human reason and scientific law. By contrast, the Romantics claimed that Nature was diverse, the individual soul unique and true wisdom the fruit, not of abstract ratiocination, but of an intuitive empathy with the mystery of life. Wordsworth wrote 'Tis murder to dissect', and found inspiration in the humble and lowly: a highland reaper, a forsaken Indian woman, a shepherd. So the romantic spirit, adapted to the political sphere, could have a striking relevance for the insignificant national group or for any people which felt itself deficient in the rationalistically conceived means of civilization and progress. Rousseau had urged the Poles to cherish their national customs. Johann Gottfried Herder (1744–1803) adjured the Slavs, 'now sunk so low', to rise from 'their long, enervating sleep' and reinstate their forgotten history and folklore 'in the portrait of mankind'. For in Herder's philosophy man was no abstracted intellect, but a social being who could grow to fulfilment only as a member of a people, nurtured by its heritage and values. Since this heritage was transmitted through language, language acquired a fundamental importance for Herder as a people's distinctive mark. But the process of maturation did not end with the ethnic group. Just as the individual grew to maturity through his people, so all peoples were part of a broader humanity, to which all brought their distinctive gifts. The essence of nature was diversity; humanity would be the poorer for the loss of the humblest people's contribution, for what was humanity other than the sum total of the potential of mankind! Hence the importance of the lowly Slavs.

The Herderian concept of national character and its role in the destinies of mankind was to have an incalculable effect on the small nation intellectuals of Europe, particularly for the fillip it gave to Pan-Slavism, the doctrine of the essential unity and greatness of the Slavs. To the Czech historian Palacky, Herder was 'the apostle of humanity'; the great Polish poet, Mickiewicz, echoed him when he called folksong the memory of the peoples. With his scorn for serfdom, nobility and arbitrary power, Herder appeared to have pointed the way to an intoxicating synthesis of national feeling and liberal ideology. But the deepest level of his appeal was its legitimation of national pride:

My heart beats when I hear the names of Alexander the Good, of Stephen the Great, of Michael the Brave, and I am not ashamed to tell you that these men are for me more important than Alexander the Great, Hannibal and Caesar.... Their battles have a greater interest, because they were won by Rumanians.... I regard as my fatherland all that territory where Rumanian is spoken.

Thus ran the opening lecture of Kogalniceaunu's course on national history at the Michael Academy in Jassy in 1843; if space permitted it would be instructive to parallel it with similar sentiments from the Magyar Kolcsey, the Slovak Stur, or the Pole Lelewel.

Lest the ethnocentrism repel, let it be remembered that they were preached against a background of cosmopolitan culture shared by Eastern Europe's educated classes. Kogalniceanu had been trained in France and Germany; Stur spoke Slovak, Czech, Polish, Russian, Serbo-Croat, Latin, German, Magyar and French; Lelewel almost as many. Nationalism was an international movement arising from a common grounding in classical and European culture. Kollar had acquired his Pan-Slav philosophy through German Romanticism, Palacky his patriotism in Hungarian Pressburg. German was the mother-tongue of the founder of the Croat literary language Gaj, and the language in which Szechenyi kept his private diary. It was Goethe who urged Vuk Karadzic to publish the epic poems of the Serb peasantry, in which process modern Serbian took shape, and the patriotic Magyar novelist, Jokai, who said of his associates in 1848, 'We were all Frenchmen. We read only Lamartine, Michelet, Louis Blanc, Sue, Victor Hugo and Béranger.

The seed-bed of nationalism lay, then, in places of education; in the universities of Germany and Poland, the Protestant lyceums of Hungary (much frequented by Slavs, regardless of religion, for the charismatic Stur taught here) the academies of Jassy and Bucharest, the Serb high schools of Belgrade and the Vojvodina, the Catholic seminaries of Croatia and the Romanian Uniate seminary of Blaj in Transylvania. Its bearers were the young, its instruments books. It followed that nationalism reached further than liberalism, for as a social and political, rather than a cultural philosophy, the latter required more than ideas and a nucleus of enthusiastic acolytes to take root. We can speak of a Slovak, Serb, even a Bulgar nationalism in this period more confidently than of a Slovak, Serb or Bulgar liberalism. But it also followed that nationalism, common in concept, diverged in form. How, by the Herderian perspective, which made culture and language the heart of the nation, could it be otherwise when some nations, like the Germans of Austria and the Poles, disposed of literary traditions of richness and antiquity, while many minor peoples lacked even an established system of writing their languages?

Among culturally mature nations literature was under less pressure than elsewhere to serve merely imitative or propagandist functions, but could freely and forcefully give expression to the well-springs of national feeling. Seen in this light the preoccupation of Grillparzer, Austria's leading dramatist, with Habsburg themes, as compared to the wider Pan-German patriotism of Austria's leading poet Anastasius Grün, pointed to a fateful uncertainty in the allegiance of Austrian Germans; they alone among the peoples of Eastern Europe had, in the Habsburg monarchy they dominated, a powerful alternative object of loyalty to the area where their language was spoken. There was no such uncertainty among the Poles. In the years following the defeated insurrection of 1831 Polish exiles created a literature of romantic messianism of astonishing intensity. The works of Mickiewicz, Slowacki and Krasinski, transformed Poland into the symbol of suffering humanity, a divine voice unjustly silenced, endowed by her wrongs with a moral primacy which would guide the world upon her resurrection. At the climax of the pious Mickiewicz's *Godfather's eve* the hero Konrad, an idealized symbol of Polish student youth, faints as he begins to curse God himself for Poland's fate. The exiles died far from their motherland but their imagery and sentiments lived on in the Polish consciousness.

Before other nations could receive similar inspiration in their own tongue the instrument thereto had to be cast into shape; grammar, vocabulary, prosody, often the very alphabet itself had to be painstakingly agreed. Sometimes the inception of this work preceded the Romantic age. The Josephinist Kazinczy (1759–1831) had done much to modernize Magyar vocabulary before the creation of a national library at Szechenyi's instigation (1827) set formal seal to the process of linguistic renewal. By the 1840s one of the main aims of the reform movement, the replacement of Latin by Magyar as the language of Hungarian public life, had been achieved. In Bohemia the Josephinist abbot, Dobrovsky (1755–1829), had similarly reconstructed the Czech literary language, which received further support from the foundation of the Czech Museum (1818) with its Czech journals and the Czech Matice, a patriotic Czech book club (1831). Opposition to Viennese centralism by the German-speaking Bohemian nobility aided this movement which lacked the advantage Magyar had, in the shape of a socially prestigious Magyar-speaking gentry class. Not till the 1840s did the Slovaks of Hungary, on Stur's urgings, finally resolve to abandon Czech as their literary language in favour of a speech based on living Slovak dialects.

Some dilemmas were especially painful. Should the Catholic Croats base their literary language on the Kajkavski dialect of their capital Zagreb or the Stokavski dialect some Croats shared with the Orthodox Serbs? Should the tiny Slovene people desert its separate speech and throw in its lot with the rest of the south Slavs? Should the Serbs reject the sentimental heritage of a Russian-influenced literary medium and orthography for forms closer to popular usage, or the Romanians exchange the Cyrillic alphabet of their religion for the Latin script of their cousins by race? No masterpiece *à la* Mickiewicz could adorn the patriotic name while such basics remained unresolved. In the event, the first famous original work of the East European revival, Kollar's 'Daughter of the Slavs' (1824), a paean to Pan-Slavism in more than 600 Czech sonnets, has been pronounced by modern critics more remarkable for its politics than its literary merits. But this is beside the point. To contemporaries the main thing was that so ambitious a poem should have been attempted in Czech at all. Intoxicated by their beautiful dreams of national redemption the revivalists clambered laboriously up a ladder which, as in the fable of *Jack and the Beanstalk*, led up into the clouds they knew not where. Alphabet, grammar, collections of folk literature, translations, popular dramas, original belles-lettres, historiography, cultural institutions, native opera; these, in approximate order, were but rungs to be conquered, one by one, in a labour of love and pride.

Of course, this is not to say that the cultural movements possessed no political *arrière-pensées*. Where political traditions existed, as in Hungary and Poland, the cultural revival naturally reinforced them, as we have seen. It was in these years, too, that the Serbian government formulated its secret goal of restoring the great realm of the medieval Serbian Tsar Dusan, that Romanian patriots conceived the idea of the union of all Romanians in one state, that Croat intellectuals broached the concept, only ostensibly non-political, of a South Slav Illyria of Serbs, Croats and Slovenes. Yet a readily explicable vagueness attaches to all their schemes, as even more to those conversations behind closed doors where, so a contemporary tells us, Czech patriots privately raised the question of the revival of the old Bohemian kingdom's historic right. For articulate nationalism remained very much a minority phenomenon, restricted both in its social appeal and its geographic range around the provincial capital. In 1847 the Czech Matice still had only 2329 members in a population of 4 million; Gaj's newspaper *Danica Horvatska, Slavonska i Dalmatinska* which settled the question of literary Croat, had 300 subscribers; of the 1000 copies of Presern's poems printed in 1847, which in the longer term did more than anything to preserve Slovene as a medium of culture, a mere thirty-three had been sold by 1849. As the great nineteenth-century Austrian historian, Springer, shrewdly observed, Czech patriots before 1848 (and *ipso facto* those of smaller nations) were incapable of an active political role, because they did not yet represent the Czech nation as a whole, but only one party in the nation. They *were* beginning to voice demands for the greater use of Czech in public life, in the courts, in secondary and higher education and in administration, which could not but ultimately impinge on the political functioning of the state. But as yet, in the authorities' eyes, Slav nationalism did not appear to be a menace of the order of German or Magyar constitutionalism. Metternich was sarcastic on Czech nationalism; for him it was an 'urge' which gave rise to 'unimportant aberrations' when people had nothing better to do, but at times of general excitement it had 'as much influence on man as salad beans in an outbreak of cholera'.

Metternich was obviously wrong in his assessment of the importance of cultural nationalism, but was he also wrong in his evident contempt for it as sentiment and cause? The classical Marxist critique of nationalism as the product of the emerging bourgeoisie's struggle to dominate the national market cannot be sustained, at least for this first phase of nationalist activity. So much is recognized by the most thorough recent East European historians of early nationalism, the Czech Hroch, and the Hungarian Niederhauser. Even Kossuth's famous campaign to boycott Austrian goods was a case of nationalism exploiting economic issues for its own ends rather than vice versa. From quite a different, right-wing perspective, Elie Kedourie has presented a subtler critique in his brilliant polemic *Nationalism*. Kedourie draws attention to the prominence of small groups of intellectuals in nationalist movements, and the difficulties they experienced in demarcating literary languages to argue that linguistic nationalism of the Herderian kind is inherently an artificial phenomenon, in which bogus cultural roots are manufactured to bolster the interests of clerical elites, jostling for power over the corpse of the old order. Less aggressively put, the claim that nineteenth-century nationalism marked a clear break with the past, spearheaded by intellectuals, has been widely accepted.

Even in this milder form such a view needs qualification. For one thing, the 'intellectuals' of the minor East European peoples were usually men of humble origin who cannot be so lightly separated from the communities from which they sprang. More precisely, their fathers were very often members of the slightly better off, more independently situated stratum of the rural population – millers, brewers, estate officials in Bohemia; parish priests or village headmen in Orthodox or Uniate populations; alternatively, as Hroch has shown, they had considerable support from urban artisans even before aspiring peasants began migrating to the towns. Scanty though the evidence is, it seems likely that national consciousness was not absent in these milieux. The diaries of Josef Dlask and F. J. Vavak, two late eighteenth-century prosperous Czech peasants, reveal a surprising grasp of Czech history and the old Czech chronicles. The Austrian Count Hartig, writing in 1850, observes that 'a feeling of jealousy of the Czechs against Austrians and a wish to resurrect the nation and the language of that people had never been extinguished'. True, Hartig also ascribes the new linguistic rivalries of Bohemia to the ambitions of the educated, not to the ordinary peasants. But it would be wrong to assume, as is often done, that because traditional peasant communities live peacefully side by side with others of alien origin, they lack generalized notions of identity (beyond religion) and own allegiance only to their own locality. Hartig's testimony suggests the more plausible view that, while European pre-industrial societies generally had a reasonably clear abstract grasp of nationality (for peasants can conceptualize, and the idea is not a difficult one), for common sense reasons they did not translate it into concrete hatred for their alien neighbours, until a modern state infrastructure made coexistence too complicated. If this is so, two conclusions follow. First, the national movements of the nineteenth century did not 'artificially' create nations and national feeling; whenever this actually was attempted, as in the propaganda for united Illyrian or Czechoslovak nations and languages, it failed. Second, though the national revivalists did not succeed in engaging the active interests of the masses for their patriotic activities, they were not wrong to claim that these activities articulated an underlying popular consciousness. The 'national awakening' was a reality. The self-conscious nationalists, unlike the ambitious of yore who had accepted denationalization for fame and fortune, chose to link their achievement to the advancement of their peoples. It was a choice which the democratizing spirit of the age made possible, and in the longer term eminently practical; but for the pioneers it still had more of idealism and of pathos than of opportunism.

There is another side of the coin. If the Herderian claims of cultural tradition were not as baseless as modern historians have sometimes assumed, by the same token cultural nationalism could hardly be the innocent babe which nationalist apologetics depicted, seeking only its right to live with malice towards none. In so far as nations built on the past, they absorbed the memories of past iniquities; in so far as they claimed rights, they presupposed wrongs which history did not fail to reveal. In short, the Herderian vision of a contented community of nations moving towards a better humanity was vitiated from the start. Already by the 1840s Magyars were at loggerheads with Croats, Serbs, Romanians and Slovaks about the use of Magyar as the official language throughout Hungary. Earlier still (in 1836) a Bohemian German, Professor Exner, caustically parodied the roots of Czech anti-Germanism:

True more than a quarter of the population |of Bohemia| is German, but they are intruders; true, they have had property and estate here for centuries, but once they did not have them; true, Czech monarchs summoned them, only to the disadvantage of the Czechs; true, the present predominance of the Germans is ordained by Bohemia's rulers, but these are foreign rulers, conquerors, . . true, they cannot attain their goal as long as a powerful Austrian Monarchy survives, so long as they cannot attach themselves to the great Slav Mother, but . . . .

Exner spoke even truer than he knew. Right up to 1848 hardly anyone outside our region and few enough inside anticipated the tragic convulsions that were to end an era as stimulating as any Eastern Europe had known. But a Viennese observer early in 1848 did speculate:

I am curious to see if our love of freedom can reconcile itself with Hungarian, Polish, Bohemian and Illyrian patriotism. If these other people place their nationalism as high as we do our constitutionalism then I do not see how we can agree with them.

He was about to find out.

4 Storm and settlement, 1848–70

1848: the events

Throughout Europe successive crop failures from 1845, and severe industrial depression in the towns in 1847 increased the likelihood that the common people would stand behind the mutinous educated classes. On 22 February 1848, revolution broke out in Paris: by 25 February Louis Philippe was heading for exile in England.

This event provided the stimulus for protest all over Central and Eastern Europe. On 3 March Kossuth, who had been seeking for a means to break the party stalemate in the Hungarian diet, now carried the Lower House for his programme of constitutional reform. On 9 March the Viennese Leseverein petitioned the emperor for the abolition of censorship, judicial reform and more representative provincial diets. On 11 March leaders of Czech and German life in Prague formulated similar requests, with an additional plea for equality for the Czech and German languages in Bohemia. Anxiously the Prussian king beseeched the tsar to move troops to his western frontier to overawe the Poles.

But nothing could avert the eruption of social and national desires, least of all regimes which in large measure had lost confidence in their own policies. The meeting of the Lower Austrian diet in Vienna on 13 March was turned into a demonstration by the waiting crowd. Faced by a throng of malcontent bourgeois, students and workers and by the Civil Guard's refusal to restore order, the court accepted the advice of the mayor of Vienna and the university rector and acceded to popular demands. Metternich was forced to resign, and press freedom and a constitution for the monarchy were held in prospect. Meanwhile responsibility for the maintenance of order passed to a National Guard and an Academic Legion representative of the middle class and intelligentsia. Hearing the news, the Hungarian Upper House dropped their opposition to Kossuth's proposals and a deputation set sail along the Danube to

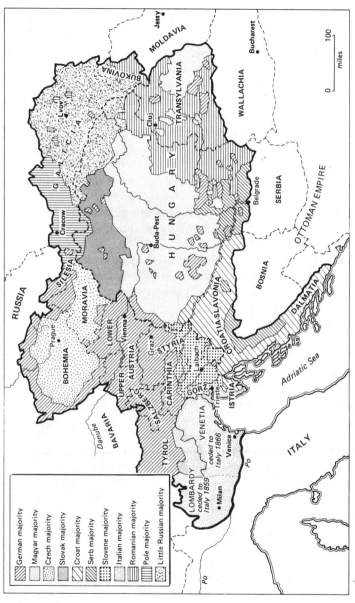

Nationalities of the Habsburg monarchy in 1848

lay demands for a separate Hungarian government before the emperor. Meanwhile, Prussian liberals forced their king to grant a constitution and German patriots gathered in Frankfurt to reshape the confederation set up in 1815 into a German national state. From Paris, Polish and Romanian *émigrés* flocked towards their homelands; Venetians and Milanese declared their independence of Austria, and throughout the remainder of the Habsburg monarchy, spokesmen for the smaller ethnic groups assembled to call for greater or lesser degrees of cultural and national recognition. Even in humble Belgrade, where there was no overt stirring, the Balkan schoolboy Jevrem Grujic felt the contagion of this 'spring-time of the peoples'. 'In the history of the world a new epoch wills itself into being', he wrote to his brother, 'France is first in this, but Frenchmen as you know do nothing for themselves, but for all mankind. And Serbs yonder [in the Habsburg monarchy] wish the same as us. What? That we should found a Serbian Kingdom . . . restore a Serbian Empire.'

Young Grujic's naive euphoria mirrors quite well that of older men emerging from the restrictions of the Metternichian era into the sudden light of freedom. But their position had its dangers. The new leaders had little opportunity to debate in advance either the social or the national implications of the demands which now jostled to the fore. Were the aspirations of Germans, Czechs, Poles and Italians, of Magyars, Croats, Serbs and Romanians compatible with each other or with the maintenance of a stable European polity? Could the wishes of liberal constitutionalists be met without bestirring a deeper social revolutionary current of the masses which would sweep their work away in its turn? Events were to show that the social issue could be resolved, but the national issues could not. In consequence, 1848 was to open up a period of intense instability in Central and East European politics until the late 1860s when national aspirations adjusted or were forced to readjust to the new social balance which the overthrow of feudalism had shaped.

Although posterity has been more interested in the national conflicts of 1848, it is arguable that the social question loomed larger to contemporaries at the outset. After all, they knew well that the revolution of 1789 in France had inaugurated years of mounting radicalism and bloody strife. Only in 1846, Polish nobles rising in Galicia had been cut down by their own peasants, more interested in social emancipation than national freedom. Street-corner socialist agitation alarmed Count Anton von Auersperg as he was fêted by Viennese crowds for his liberal poetry in the first days of the revolution, while the Hungarian diet was electrified by reports of thousands of peasants with scythes, massed outside Budapest where, the Palatine wrote, 'anarchy reigned' – actually they had only come to a fair. Already the peasant petitions (which were to total 886 by the end of the year) were pouring into the authorities in Bohemia and Moravia. Beside a Serbian flag put up in place of a Hungarian one by Serb nationalist students, Serb peasants shouted 'under this banner we will divide the land'.

All this could not but be a challenge to liberal leaders who, as men of property or education, bore in their bones a dread of popular anarchy and licence. This was naturally true of the gentry reformers of Poland, Hungary and the Principalities, and the patrician debaters of the Leseverein. But it was about equally true of the emergent leaders of the smaller peoples: among the Czechs, the historian Palacky, a village boy married into the gentry, the seminarist turned journalist, Havlicek, and the well-to-do millers' sons become lawyers, Rieger and Brauner; for the Transylvanian Romanians, the Orthodox bishop, Saguna, the seminary professor, Barnutiu, and the editor and priest's son, Baritiu; Baron Kulmer and Baron Jelacic with their links at court for the Croat Illyrians, and the assorted parish priests, small-town lawyers and secondary school teachers of the Slovenes, Slovaks and Ruthenians. These men wanted the constitutional freedoms of speech, press and assembly, civic equality, trial by jury and an end to religious discrimination. They stood for the abolition of serfdom, elected assemblies, public budgets, national guardsmen and linguistic rights; but they also wanted order, compensation for nobles, a restricted franchise and guard membership only for 'responsible' elements, and they might have doubts about emancipation for Jews. While squeezing their constitutional and national desiderata out of the numbed authorities, they co-operated with them in defusing potentially broader social unrest.

Thus within three days of the reported peasants' gathering at Budapest in mid March, Kossuth persuaded the Hungarian diet to accept not only the compulsory ending of feudal obligations but also the payment of compensation by the state rather than the peasants. In Austria, the abolition of robota was approved in principle in a series of rescripts to the provinces from late March, followed by a detailed measure undertaken by the Galician governor, Count Stadion, in April. Not emancipation itself, but how much and whether with or without compensation had become the issues. Prince Czartoryski, *émigré* leader of the Polish right, found himself temporarily supporting the stance of the Polish Democratic Society, organ of the Polish left. Installed in power in Bucharest in a bloodless coup in June, the Wallachian revolutionaries abolished gipsy slavery and summoned a conference of peasants and nobles to discuss reform. In the larger cities the abolition or reduction of certain taxes and the piecemeal lowering of working hours and rents helped temporarily to allay urban discontent.

What would have happened if this course had not been followed? It is hard to say. Certainly the landlords made bigger concessions than they would have been prepared to make before 1848. They gave the peasants in Austria and Hungary ownership over the greater part of the land they had previously cultivated, as opposed to the purely civil emancipation without land which the Napoleonic code had introduced into Poland in 1807. But thereby they retained the initiative and could settle other aspects of the matter, like vineyards, forest rights, the use of the common land, or even (in Hungary) the traditional control of inns, mills and hunting satisfactorily to themselves. Moreover, despite Kossuth's urgings, the emancipation applied only to the holders of rustical land, not to peasants settled on the lord's manorial lands, who in Hungary at least, combined with the landless, formed a majority of the population. Actually, rustical peasants were often opposed to concessions being made to the smallholders and landless whom they saw as potential rivals. Patterns of deference and paternalism continued in many places for all the resonance of revolution. 'Brothers,' an edict of the Wallachian revolutionaries assured the peasants,' your enemies are not and never have been the boyars, but bad laws and the errors of Princes.' They requested peasants to continue their labour services for a while, for money, but this reference to payment was absent from their proclamations intended for nobles. In still more peripheral regions even this brand of 'liberalism' was unable to gain a foothold. The prince of Moldavia locked up all signatories of a timid reform petition he could lay his hands on; the Serbian prince prudently summoned a national assembly, in which village patriarchs proved more influential than Belgrade students barely out of their teens.

Thus liberalism dug deeper according to the level of development a society had reached. Baron Jelacic, governor of Croatia, treated the Croatian diet and the Illyrian hotheads with elaborate courtesy and effectively ignored them. In other places, radicals opposed moderate liberals with a fully fledged democratic programme – universal suffrage, emancipation without compensation, even a muted republicanism. In Poland the radical–moderate split was of long-standing, with the radicals including the intelligentsia and a minority of nobles. In Hungary something of the sort developed rapidly in 1848, except that the radicals of the Pest Committee of Public Safety and later the Society for Equality ultimately deferred Kossuth's charismatic reformism, and preferred to pressurize the gentry diet rather than displace it. Only in Vienna were the notables of the Leseverein and the Lower Austrian diet unable temporarily to meet the challenge from men of plebeian origin like the lawyer Bach, the Academic Legion chaplain Füster, or the young Jewish doctor Fischhof, as well as from artisans demanding cheap credit and workers calling for guaranteed work. There popular demonstrations in May gave effective control of the city to a fairly radical Committee of Security and the imperial family fled to Innsbruck. But even in Vienna workers were not a threat by themselves. Without student guidance – except for a number of printers' strikes and a cotton printers' strike in Prague – their activity did not go beyond occasional anti-Semitic and anti-clerical outbursts. The urban risings of 1848 – in Cracow in March, Prague in June, Vienna in October and Lemberg in November – were all initiated by bourgeois and student radicals; and these radicals won only a handful of seats in the Magyar diet (though about fifty noble deputies sympathized) and a small minority in the Austrian parliament elected on near universal suffrage. The monarchy and its neighbours witnessed nothing like the workers' rising of June 1848 in Paris or the peasant movement of Russia in 1917. If the position was somewhat more complicated in Vienna, the overall impression of our area in 1848 is of the success of the educated classes in maintaining social control. This demonstrated that power could safely pass beyond the confines of the absolutist bureaucracy to a broader elite of liberal landlords, intellectuals and professionals.

Unfortunately for the revolution, this success was not matched in the field of nationality. At first, there was little awareness that this would be so. The pronouncements of revolutionary journals, particularly radical ones, breathed a universal benevolence, nourished by the conviction that, among men imbued by the high ideals of modern progress, concord must ultimately prevail. Of all the national groups in Eastern Europe only the Poles fully realized in advance that the fulfilment of their aspirations would entail reshaping of European politics as a whole. Led by Czartoryski from the Hotel Lambert in Paris, their exile propaganda before 1848 had striven to enlist the support of liberal England and France for the mobilization of the oppressed peoples of Eastern Europe against the partitioning powers, particularly Russia. In effect, this meant action by Polish agents to ensure that the Balkan Christians won autonomy under Turkish and Western, not Russian aegis. It was an ingenious scheme to combine Polish interests with progressive principles and *Realpolitik*, simultaneously exploiting Balkan aspirations and the rivalry of Russia and the western powers in the Near East. Moreover, by concentrating on Russia – contacts with Hungarian nationalists, for instance, were slighter than those with Romanians – it minimized the likely upheaval in the European state system. Yet the Polish strategy suffered from divisions in Polish ranks. The 1846 revolt in Galicia was initiated by the Polish left on the quite different premise of revolutionary alliance between patriotic gentry and oppressed peasants. Nor did the Poles have the support of the smaller Slav nations who looked to Russia as a father figure, inspiring vague Pan-Slav dreams of cultural reciprocity and common nationhood. Their plans were also in potential conflict with the burgeoning desire of German liberals for a concerted German foreign policy in an age of mounting economic competition and nationalism. 'Germany's present peace is perhaps only the quiet before the storm', wrote a German patriot in 1842, 'for a new national enemy, in addition to France . . . is arising in the Slav peoples.' Was there here a basis for understanding with the Kossuthites in Hungary, who shared their constitutionalism and hostility to the Slavs?

Nonetheless, the Poles and Romanians made the early running in 1848 with their call for an anti-Russian alliance in the name of European freedom. Czartoryski hastened to liberal Berlin, the returning Wallachian exiles took power in Bucharest; but the illusions in their strategy were soon revealed. Neither Whiggish England nor republican France nor newly liberal Prussia were really prepared to take on tsarist Russia in the interests of the oppressed. German national feeling cumulatively whittled away even the modest autonomy initially promised to the Poles of Prussia. Polish forces in Prussia were easily dispersed and Turkish troops occupied Wallachia in agreement with Russia. It was back to Paris for the exiles. The collapse of the Polish strategy was tantamount to the collapse of the idea of European revolutionary solidarity on which it was based. Hereafter numbers and power held the key.

This shifted the focus of attention to the 45 million inhabitants of the German confederation whose future was under discussion in the Frankfurt assembly. Over 12 million of these came from German-dominated western provinces of the Habsburg monarchy, a constitutional tie reinforced by the traditional primacy of the Habsburgs among German princes, and by memories of Germany's imperial mission to the East. These factors explain the appointment of the Austrian Archduke John as head of the Frankfurt assembly executive and the assembly's October vote forbidding the inclusion of Germans and non-Germans in the same state, except in a personal union. The implication of this vote was either that the multi-national monarchy should cease to be or that its German and non-German parts should be linked only in a loose structure under a common ruler ('personal union'), in effect releasing the German inhabitants for *de facto* integration in a united Germany. German nationalism would outweigh Habsburg tradition in determining the political structure of Central Europe.

This preferred German solution to the region's problems had a certain rationale. Austria's Italian subjects had clearly shown their desire for independence; Galicia under the Poles could go its own way; and Hungary's parliamentary government already conceded in the famous 'April laws' came very close to personal union. Like the Polish plan, however, the Germans' ignored a number of important realities. First of these was the reluctance of the Habsburgs to abandon the centralized monarchy Maria Theresa and Joseph II had built. Driven from Vienna but retaining the loyalty of the army, they had been strengthened by its suppression of a rising in Prague in June and defeat of the Italian rebels and their Piedmontese allies in July. This made it less likely that they would permanently honour the concessions forced out of them by the Hungarians in the April laws. In this attitude they would enjoy the support of many Austro-Germans reluctant to see the emasculation of the empire they dominated. The 130 Austrian delegates in Frankfurt solidly opposed the October constitutional vote.

The second oversight of the Frankfurt liberals was to ignore the 5 million Czechs and Slovenes in western Austria who were to be deemed mere minorities and incorporated into the new German state. German contempt for the minor Slav peoples was rooted in racial antagonism, historical dominance and economic superiority. Italians and Hungarians counted as nations; at a pinch, so did Poles; Czechs did not. 'Germans, be not too just', said Arndt at Frankfurt, 'every particle could not have a national life of its own.' The Czech leader, Palacky, dramatically apprised the Germans of their oversight in a letter rejecting an invitation to attend the Frankfurt pre-Parliament. As a 'Bohemian of Slav race', he called for the reorganization of the monarchy on a federal basis, with full weight to its Slav majority and an independent policy, making it a bulwark against both German and Russian hegemonic schemes. A Slavic congress meeting in Prague issued a manifesto on Slav claims to the nations of Europe. The emergence of this Austro-Slavic federalist movement in place of the vaguer, cultural Pan-Slavism was one of the least expected, yet most significant features of 1848.

The chief impact of 'Austro-Slavism' as it came to be known, was decisively to worsen the relations between Vienna and Hungary. Croat and Czech nationalism developed into an alliance between plebeian patriots and provincial aristocrats hoping to win the court for devolution. The non-Magyar majority in Hungary – Croat, Serb, Slovak, Ruthene and Transylvanian Romanian – was encouraged to prepare to resist Magyarization by force. Limitless scope was offered for Magyars and the court to accuse each other of bad faith in their dealings with the non-Magyars. While Kossuth and the radicals campaigned for an independent Hungarian army to meet the non-Magyar threat, the court denounced the April laws and connived at Jelacic's entry into Hungary at the head of a Croatian army. By October the Magyars and the dynasty were at war.

Thus by the time the Frankfurt assembly voted on Austria's relationship to Germany the premises of the debate had become shaky indeed. Unless the Austro-German and Magyar liberals showed the same militant unity as the dynasty and the Slavs, their cause was lost and the common monarchy saved. The radicals in Vienna appeared to realize this. In October, citizens prevented troops from leaving the city for the Hungarian front, precipitating a crisis which brought the radicals back into control and sent Slav and moderate German members of the Austrian parliament into retreat in the little Moravian town of Kremsier. A Hungarian army appeared in the vicinity but was reluctant to intervene in internal Austrian politics. At the end of October General Windischgraetz subdued the mutinous capital. The fall of Vienna was the first of a series of blows to the revolutionary cause throughout Europe, followed before the end of the year by the dismissal of the liberal government in Prussia, the election of the opportunist Louis Napoleon as president of France and the appointment of a hard-line conservative in Prince Schwarzenberg as prime minister of Austria. The feeble Ferdinand meanwhile abdicated in favour of his 18-year-old nephew Franz Joseph.

These changes portended the final collapse of the revolutionary cause. For a time the rump parliament continued to meet at Kremsier to draft its terms for a constitutional, decentralized Austria, very much under the influence of the Czech politicians, Palacky and Rieger. No sooner was the constitution ready in March 1849 than Schwarzenberg had the parliament dissolved and a centralist constitution imposed from above. The dynasty had no further need for its Slav allies. Their humiliation preceded by little that of German parliamentarians in Frankfurt who, losing hope of a meaningful relationship with a revivified Habsburg Austria, offered the title of German emperor to the king of Prussia – and saw it refused. Their only weapon, their moral authority, gone, by June they had been dispersed by force. This left only the Hungarian revolutionaries, now formally republican, in the field.

In this last act of the revolutionary drama it was fitting that the professionals should return to the stage. In London and Paris Polish and Romanian agents sought to revive the internationalist conscience of the liberal powers, joined now by Magyar emissaries, Teleki in the French and Pulszky in the English capital. The great poet Mickiewicz edited *Tribune des Peuples* in the revolutionary cause. The Polish generals, Bem and Dembowski, fought in the Hungarian independence army and a Polish legion participated in Piedmont's renewed campaign against Austria in March 1849. All efforts were bent to repairing the disastrous national rifts of the previous year. In May Czartoryski, Teleki and the disillusioned Czech leader, Rieger, reached agreement in Paris on a compre-hensive plan for the elimination of the Habsburgs, German and Italian unification, a loose federation in Hungary (to appease the Romanians) and a strong federation in the remains of Austria. It might be said to have been the revolutionary equivalent of the settlement reached a couple of months earlier by moderates at

Kremsier, and like it was doomed to remain a might-have-been in history. Anyway, Kossuth, the real leader of Hungary, was quite unwilling to accommodate the Romanians politically and did not even concede their language claims until 14 July, a month after the Russian tsar had sent troops into Hungary in support of the monarchical principle. It was too late. Three weeks later Hungarian forces surrendered to the Russians at Vilagos and the revolutions of 1848–9 were finally over.

1848: aftermath and post-mortem

Can a general survey justify detailed reference to the tortuous web of unimplemented agreements, failed strategies and revoked constitutions which is 1848? E. H. Carr has warned us not to dally with the failures of history. Yet glorious failures can exert a spell over future generations, as Kossuth and the nineteenth-century Polish revolutionaries were to do in their respective countries. Moreover the complexities of 1848 reflected something of high historical significance – the fracture caused when a long-term social tendency comes of age and encounters the full weight of particular circumstance. No tendency in history is so omnipotent that it may not be checked or distorted at this initial trial of strength. So it was in 1848 with liberalism and nationalism. But the line of fault suggested the way the onward progression would resume after the initial calamitous impact.

Thus the apparently crushing defeat of the revolutionaries was the end of the first act rather than the whole scenario. Its immediate consequence was to swell the number of exiles treading the conspiratorial path along which the Poles and Mazzinians had first ventured. Kossuth became the impassioned spokesman for an independent Hungary in Britain and America, his chief theme the impossibility of restoring the pre-revolutionary *status quo*. Prussia and Piedmont had acquired constitutions and parliaments in 1848, which continued to function and soon inclined again in a liberal direction. By the late 1850s, reform ideas were penetrating areas unstirred in 1848, to tiny Serbia and mighty Russia where Alexander II prepared for the emancipation of the serfs. In the Habsburg monarchy only the aged General Windischgraetz spoke in favour of undoing the peasant reforms that had established the basis for capitalist economic development. Indeed, the decade 1849–59 saw a great acceleration in the tendency observable even under

Metternich in the direction of a conservative modernization. In Hungary the abolition of the customs barrier with Austria crushed native textiles, but the introduction of a modern tax system, and the great inflow of Austrian capital helped establish a railway system and heavy industry in part compensation. Throughout the monarchy, chambers of commerce were founded. Gild privileges fell away in 1859. Most of this was due to the commerce minister, Bruck, a Rhenish businessman in origin who dreamed of a Central European customs union, and together with Bach, the former radical lawyer turned minister of the interior, bequeathed neo-absolutist Austria something of the spirit of bourgeois enterprise. True, Hungary was divided into five regions administered largely by Germans and German-speaking Czechs, the Catholic Church resumed the control over marriage and education it had lost since Joseph II's reign, and independent journalism and autonomous cultural life shrivelled in the hostile climate; but at the same time the clerical-conservative Count Thun, minister of education and cults, gave minor languages a much greater role than before in schools, including the secondary level. In their strange combination of innovation and repression, the 1850s bore all the marks of a period of unstable transition.

How clear was this at the time to the participants of 1848? There are always some who will find their every prejudice confirmed by events. This could be true of the very old, like Metternich, or the very young, like Emperor Franz Joseph. On the other side, the Romanian 'Reds', back in their Paris lodge 'Fraternity of the Peoples' in the snug cocoon of international radicalism, continued to cherish the vision of revolutionary mankind ensnared by reaction. But there was much disillusionment as well. 'Trustworthy and disinterested men are scarce in our fine country', wrote one jaundiced Romanian patriot after a mission in the Wallachian countryside. 'You and I and many others have been the victims of a mirage, an optical illusion.' Many lost their faith in the indissolubility of patriotism and liberty and the moral power of international brotherhood. Appreciation grew for power politics. Should they not have put their own nation first? After all, liberty could always be fought for again, but a dead nation could never be resurrected. In the uncompromising words of the Serbian philologist, Danicic, 'Nationality without liberty can exist upon the earth, but freedom without nationality is unthinkable. . . . The Serbian nation is in the world for no other purpose than to be the Serbian nation.'

Such sentiments were picked upon in other post-mortems to give an exactly opposite interpretation of the revolutionary defeat. In a famous piece of contemporary journalism, written by Engels and published under Marx's name, the founders of socialism denounced the minor peoples of Eastern Europe because they had put nostalgic memories of dying languages and half-forgotten glories before the progressive interests represented by the German and Magyar liberals. Pan-Slavism 'intended nothing less than to subjugate the civilised West under the barbarian East, the town under the country, trade, manufacturers, intelligence, under the primitive agriculture of Slavonian serfs'. In a different key, but to the same effect, Kossuth attacked the 'dastardly role' and 'fictitious pretensions' of the non-Magyars.

Representatives of the smaller peoples hotly denied this indictment. 'You say you want democracy, and at the same time you want the thousand year old Hungarian state. But the two are incompatible', wrote a Romanian of Hungarian opposition to Transylvanian autonomy; Germans and Magyars simply refused to others national rights they claimed for themselves. Were not, asked Palacky, the rights of nations the rights of nature, and could any nation ask of another that it should sacrifice itself for its sake? Their distinction between the 'historic rights' of the larger powers and their own 'natural rights' not only enabled the spokesmen of the 'nations without history' to set their claims in terms of liberal rhetoric, but also exposed a vital question of political organization which 1848 had first raised. Should a revived Polish or Bohemian or Serbian state have the territories of 1772 or 1620 or 1389 respectively, or those currently inhabited by speakers of Polish, Czech or Serb? Should Transylvania belong to Hungary because of historical association, or to Romania because of its Romanian-speaking majority? Marx's stress on German economic progressiveness was designed, as befitted a 'scientific socialist', to cut through the historic–natural antithesis by providing a more practical, clear cut, materialist criterion for the exercise of power. But were his views, too, not coloured by historical presuppositions and traditional German scorn for 'backward' Slavs which blinded him to the economic progress Czech society, in particular, had made in the generation before 1848? Indeed, some modern historians like Namier, influenced by the excesses of Nazism, have reversed Marx's verdict and charged the Germans of 1848 with a nationalistic response to the Slav awakening.

Such contradictory verdicts drawn from the same premises suggest that the premises are false. It is impossible to classify the participants in 1848 into liberal humanist and narrow nationalist groups, or even to explain the revolutionary failure in terms of a clash of liberal and nationalistic principles. Liberalism and nationalism represented different but related responses to the situation of modernizing Europe in the nineteenth century, neither in itself adequately expressing all the facets of this situation, but both shared by all participating in it. Liberalism was in origin an individualistic creed, promising man progress and harmony in the event of his liberation from the institutional constraints of feudalism, absolutism and a dogmatic Church. It prospered best where socio-economic development was furthest advanced, which lends point to Marx's and Engels's criticisms of the Slavs. But this liberalism had two inadequacies: it ascribed Slav backwardness to racial character rather than different levels of development which could be compensated for and, by proposing a liberal society operating through existing educated and propertied groups with at best local recognition for minor languages, it threatened to freeze the differentials and foreclose the prospect of compensation. Slavs and Romanians therefore were right to sense that their emancipation as individuals, at least on a modern scale, could only come through asserting their solidarity as a group, through nationalism. This nationalism presupposed liberal objectives, just as the liberalism of their opponents was filtered through national lenses. Before 1848 the complexity of the relationship between liberal and national ideals had not been realized. All had fought a common absolutist foe and a pervasive idealism had rejected the notion that there could be a conflict between the rights of individuals and the rights of groups. Now awareness of this potential conflict envenomed the relations of German and Slav and lent a darker tone to European politics, enhancing the prevalent uncertainty.

Uncertainty resulted from the fact that the German, Italian, Polish, Romanian and Hungarian questions remained on the agenda, giving diplomatic alignments a complexity previously unknown. Piedmont pursued her claim to Italian leadership on the battlefields of the Crimea and Napoleon III his claim to his uncle's mantle by uniting the Romanians. Prussia schemed in Belgrade, Kossuth in London, the Poles in Constantinople. But before these entanglements can be fully appreciated a final twist must be introduced into the design, for these post-revolutionary years also saw the integration of the Balkan question into European politics as one of the major issues of the age.

The Balkans

For many years the Eastern question or contest for the succession to the declining Turkish empire had held the attention of the powers. The Balkan question, as such, emerged only when the native peoples of European Turkey, under the stimulus of new ideas, began to develop nationalisms of their own. Internal modernization produced nationalism which in turn called into question the region's political structure. The themes of Balkan politics for the first time equated with those of the lands north of the Danube. Whereas, however, Hungarian nationalism created a fresh problem for the European body politic, Balkan nationalism transformed the essence of an existing problem. Through its relationship with the vital Eastern question it touched a live nerve of European politics. In the longer term the aspirations of southern Slavs were to prove far more disruptive than those of Magyars or Poles.

Balkan modernization differed also in a further respect. The reforming impulse came too late and too feebly to the Balkans for their societies to hope to stand alone as wholly autonomous powers, as Austria and Poland had striven to do in the Enlightenment. Almost the most important part of their efforts at modernization was to impress prospective patrons with their fitness for sponsorship as bona fide members of the European comity of nations. It is important to realize that this was nearly as true of Turkey herself as of her vassal peoples: from the mid nineteenth century both the Turks and their Christian subjects were competing for European legitimacy. Although Balkan nationalism ostensibly had European models, at the grass-roots level it often related to Ottoman modernization in the same way that Czech or Magyar nationalism had responded to the centralizing policies of Joseph II.

Given this analogy, the Ottoman reformers had many cards on their side. First, Britain, France and Austria all had a strong material interest in the integrity of the Turkish state as a barrier against Russia. But there was more to it than this. Turkey was an empire which had not lost all its former glamour; adventurous Europeans still converted to Islam, like Czartoryski's agent

Czajkowski or the general, Omer Pasha, born a Serb. True, the Muslim Sultan ruled over millions of reluctant Christian subjects, but Franz Joseph was in similar boot with millions of Magyars and Slavs, the Russian tsar with Catholic Poles, the queen of England with Catholic Irish and Muslim and Hindu Indians. Could aristocratic diplomats side with Balkan peasants, Christian or no? Actually, religious and racial prejudice in the European camp was considerable, and before 'the Turk', as he was known to the nineteenth century, could benefit from European support he had to demonstrate that he was putting his house in order. Hence the strange dialogues between the Ottomans and their European confidants – Palmerston in the 1830s, the Polish *émigrés* in the 1840s, the Russian ambassador, Ignatiev, in the 1860s and 1870s – part genuine, part charade on both sides, in which Turkey's candid friends urged her to save herself by reform.

This line of thinking required considerable adaptability from Ottoman statesmen who in the eighteenth century had still been wholly isolated from and scornful of the infidel West. It prevailed because of the pressure of events; the lives of prominent reformers show many personal experiences of the superiority of Western arms in formative years. Mahmud II (1808–39), nephew of the murdered Selim III, was as convinced as his uncle of the need for military reform but bided his time, steadily weakening the reactionary alliance of janissaries and ulema until he was able to destroy the former in a coup (1826). From this point the transition to Western dress and styles (compare eighteenth-century Poland and Hungary) proceeded apace in Mahmud's court. The sultan abandoned the traditional remoteness of his predecessors, toured frontier fortifications, sent young men abroad for officer training, signed trade treaties which swelled the European colony in Constantinople, even made the brother of the opera composer, Donizetti, director of the reformed army's regimental band! Henceforth the dominant statesmen of the Turkish reform period or Tanzimat – Reshid Pasha (1800–88), Ali Pasha (1815–71) and Fuad Pasha (1815–69) – were to gain power for their knowledge of European languages and European diplomacy; the Tanzimat's main documents, the Hatisherifs of 1839 and 1856, were to be issued at points of maximum European pressure on Turkey; and great reputations – witness Midhat Pasha in south-east Serbia and Bulgaria in the 1860s – were to be made combatting separatism in provincial governorships which would have been dead-end jobs half a century earlier.

The Tanzimat had four main aims: first, to establish an efficient bureaucracy operating by rule and ensuring equal rights to Muslims and non-Muslims; second, to bring the traditionally wayward provinces of the empire firmly under central control; third to finance this expanding state role by replacing tax-farming by a modern tax system based on census information, and collection by paid officials; fourth, to shift the basis of law and education from Islamic to European principles. How far were these achieved? By the 1860s a fairly modern central administrative machine existed in Constantinople which had broken the back of most die-hard provincial reaction, notably in Bosnia in the campaign of 1850–2. The capital had a burgeoning press, a fledgling intelligentsia, even something of a liberal opposition in the form of Paris-based exiles, the young Ottomans. But only 3371 Muslim boys attended European-style secondary schools in 1855; educated officials were too few to make the reforms a reality in the provinces. There, Muslim evidence still outweighed that of the Christians in the courts, tax-farming continued, Muslims led backlashes against the introduction of bells on Christian churches, and Christians resisted educational reforms which threatened their traditional cultural autonomy. Moreover, the Tanzimat was socially conservative. In encouraging a new landed class as an ally against Muslim traditionalists, it hit the interests of the peasant majority. Under the Tanzimat, Christian peasant revolts increased in number, in southern Serbia in 1841, in west and north Bulgaria in 1847 and 1848, in Herzegovina in 1858 and 1862.

This situation was the more serious for the Porte because Balkan Slavs now had a focus for their aspirations in the autonomous principality of Serbia. Emerging as a statelet of some 12,000 square miles and 400,000 inhabitants in 1817, Serbia initially diverged far from European norms. When her first prince, Milos Obrenovic, an illiterate pig-dealer in origin, bought himself a bed in 1834, he was probably only the second non-foreigner to use one. Europeanization began to make headway with a switch to the rival Karadjordjevic dynasty in the early 1840s, assisted by a group of notables calling themselves the Defenders of the Constitution. More schools and scholarships abroad (about ten a year) quadrupled judicial officials between 1844 and 1853 and reduced illiteracy among them from 35 per cent to 6 per cent; the civil code of 1844, by stressing individual at the expense of communal property rights, also helped foster a small middle class. A national library, national museum, national theatre and Learned Society appeared and with them the first stirrings of nationalism and liberalism; the former expressed in the secret 1844 plan to recreate the Serbian medieval empire, the latter somewhat later in criticism of the bureaucracy by educated youth who had failed to get a job in it (there was nothing else to do) or who realized that Serbia's conservative development might prejudice her image among 'unredeemed' Serbs in Austria and Turkey. For the aspiring Serbian state matched Turkey in the priority it gave to establishing a prestigious bureaucracy rather than developing the economy or making education generally available. 'The people should not get it into their heads that they can express an opinion about their judges or officials', wrote Garasanin, leading statesman of the period. Officals wore uniforms and high boots, carried swords, had pension rights, and generally formed a tiny elite with the wealthier Belgrade merchants in a 97 per cent peasant society which liberalized property laws were steadily bringing into debt. Three quarters of all court cases in 1858 concerned debt, but non-usurious credit was available only to the elite. By the 1860s opposition was coming from liberals stressing the customary freedoms and from the remarkable Russian and Swiss-educated socialist Svetozar Markovic (1848–75), who advocated replacing the bureaucracy with a network of peasant communes in a Balkan federation.

Bulgarian national development followed a somewhat different course for Bulgaria was nearer to Constantinople and more easily subordinated to Turkish political and Greek cultural power. On the other hand, Bulgarian merchants benefited economically from closeness to the metropole; the first modern Bulgarian textile mill went back to 1836. This prosperous urban class was the backbone of the movement to replace Greek by Bulgarian as the language of Church and school and got under way in the 1830s. For a generation Bulgarian nationalism expressed itself chiefly in the struggle for a Bulgarian Orthodox hierarchy or exarchate, free from the Greek-dominated ecumenical patriarchate in Constantinople. This was achieved when Ignatiev persuaded the Turks to agree in 1870. But by that time it was too late to head off an explicitly political movement led by *émigrés* operating from Serbia and Romania and sharing the techniques, slogans and some of the divisions of European radicalism; Rakovski, Karavelov, Levski and Botev are the famous names.

Ultimately, Balkan backwardness prevented the Ottoman reformers from creating a significant body of Slav collaborators comparable to the Habsburg party in Hungary or even the non-nationalists in Russian Poland. The government resources were too limited, atavistic cultural prejudices too deep and the undeveloped native populations too socially homogenous. Thus Balkan nationalism ideologically had the field to itself, though hampered by the same backwardness in its turn. Strangely mixing Orthodox Christianity, heroic folk poetry and the rights of man, borne by the literate and mobile – priests, merchants, itinerant teachers – Balkan nationalism preached that the Slavs were the rightful heirs of European power and progress against barbarous, Asiatic Turks. From the time of the Serb revolt of 1804–13 and the Romanian revolt of 1821, detachments of the various Balkan peoples had assisted each others' causes. In the 1860s this co-operation took on a more formal character under the auspices of Prince Michael of Serbia, who concluded agreements with Greece, Romania, Montenegro and the Bulgarian *émigrés*. The aim was the destruction of European Turkey. European politicians now took the Balkan peoples very much into their calculations, whatever their reservations about Balkan civilization. 'It is inadvisable to call the Serbs a nation of robbers,' wrote an agent of Kossuth, 'though that is what, historically, they are!'

The 1860s: the collapse of revolutionary politics

Prince Michael and Kossuth both assumed that there was a tide in the affairs of Europe which would carry their causes to victory. The Crimean War (1853–6) which opposed England and France to Russia had been a sad disappointment to radicals. Ostensibly it was the clash between tsarism and the Western powers they had always wanted. Yet all the efforts of Poles and Magyars, including two Polish Cossack regiments in Turkey, could not persuade the allies to broaden their limited war in the Crimea; support for the Polish cause might have jostled Austria, a partitioning power, out of her benevolent neutrality.

However, the outcome of the Crimean War appeared much more favourable to the forces of change. Russia was humiliated and Austria weakened, both by Piedmont's help to the western allies in the Crimea and Austria's failure to reciprocate Russian help in Hungary in 1849. It was at this time that Austria began her ultimately disastrous policy of seeking influence in the western

Balkans through favours to the local Catholic minorities. The peace treaty which closed the war also ordered constitutional conferences in Wallachia and Moldavia to consider the future government of the Principalities. What none anticipated was that, under the influence of returning exiles, both conferences would not only vote for union of the Principalities but elect the boyar Alexander Cuza as their common prince. Louis Napoleon threw his weight behind the Romanians, smoothing the path for what was in effect a united Romania (1859). The first of the defeats of 1848 had been reversed.

Louis Napoleon, an adventurer who had attained quasi-absolute power, embodied the contradictions of the post-1848 years. His attempt to transcend them by imitating his uncle's style of demagogic grandeur precipitated the crisis which radicals were expecting. In 1859 France and Piedmont provoked Austria into a war which was intended to drive her out of a revivified and reunited Italy. As in the Crimean War, the exiles strove might and main to broaden the theatre of operations so that the Hungarian and even the Balkan questions could be brought into play. Kossuth won a promise in principle from the French emperor of support for independent Hungary if England could be reconciled to the collapse of the Habsburg monarchy. While Kossuth campaigned successfully for English neutrality, his agents conferred with Cuza of Romania and Michael of Serbia over the logistics of support for a Hungarian rising. Romanians speculated about a greater Daco-Romania, Serbs about a general Balkan movement and resurrected empire, Kossuth about a Danube confederation of all three peoples under Magyar leadership. Prince Michael consulted Louis Napoleon in Paris and visited London. But again the best laid plans foundered on the great powers' ultimate reluctance to endorse such sweeping changes. Without warning Louis Napoleon concluded an armistice with Austria which left even the unification of Italy incomplete.

The next upheaval came in Congress Poland. A typical assortment of students and bourgeois in Warsaw managed to pressurize representatives of the gentry into calling for peasant and other reforms. The tsar's response was to appoint as head of the civil administration a rather conservative Polish aristocrat, Wielopolski, who proceeded to try to split moderates from radicals by a mixture of coercion and kindness. Unfortunately, this seemingly deft approach underestimated the emotive power of the leftist insur-rectionary tradition even for the Polish right. The left rose in revolt in January 1863, dragging the whole national movement along with it. Once again Britain and France confined themselves to verbal protests and the rising was crushed.

The continued failure of strategies based on international co-operation told the same story as in 1848. It was the Germans who really held the key to the region's future. After the defeats in Italy in 1859 Emperor Franz Joseph had been forced to create a form of parliament, the Reichsrat, which like the Prussian diet had a liberal majority. This revival of liberalism in the German-speaking world was due to lack of money, the Achilles heel of authoritarian regimes as surely as lack of power had been that of the liberals of 1848. A state which devoted 52 per cent of its expenditure to the army, as Austria did in 1854 and anticipated outgoings – for 1860 – more than twice the likely revenue, could not afford to forgo the financial skills of the bourgeoisie. If Emperor Francis had effectively declared state bankruptcy in 1811, Franz Joseph in 1860 had to swallow his pride and accept the capitalists' request for constitutional government in return for a loan. Not that the first Reichsrat was directly controlled by financial interests. With sixty-eight landlords and property owners, thirty-seven state officials, thirty-eight lawyers, twenty-three industrialists and businessmen, eighteen clergy, eleven professors and five members of the professions, it had much the same mix of liberal noble and upper bourgeois as the reform movement of March 1848 and showed the same combination of Josephinist and modern liberal principles. Nonetheless, the Reichsrat was united in demanding that ministers should be responsible to it, which the emperor still denied.

In other parts of the monarchy the reintroduction of constitutional life similarly restored the configurations of 1848. In Hungary the majority of Magyars took their stand on the continued validity of the April laws; in Bohemia Palacky reiterated his federal views and denounced any possible deal between the dynasty and Magyars at the expense of the Slavs. Both Magyars and Czechs boycotted the Reichsrat. Things were not, however, quite the same as in 1848. Without a revolutionary ambiance the masses were mute. The acknowledged Hungarian leader was not the impassioned Kossuth but Istvan Deak, a sober and taciturn lawyer. Neo-conservatism, obliterated in 1848, was an influential force and the middle gentry, who had been hard hit by the emancipation of the serfs, were eager for economic reasons for a settlement. Finally, the Czechs were alone in their Austro-Slavism, for after their previous betrayal by the dynasty the non-Magyars of Hungary were willing to bargain with the Magyar liberals. The upshot of all this was to undermine Slav federalist prospects, and to enhance those for a settlement between Austrian and Hungarian liberals along 'dualist' lines, with minor settlements thereafter between the Magyars and non-Magyars in Hungary. This was the olive-branch offered by Deak in the famous Easter article in 1865, when for the first time he envisaged a closer union between Vienna and Budapest than that implied in the April laws. This left the ball in the emperor's court, for it was the dynasty that had stuck fast to a centralized monarchy seventeen years before.

Then the Habsburgs had been able to maintain their pre-eminence in Germany. This time they faced a sterner foe than the Frankfurt liberals in the person of the Prussian prime minister, Otto von Bismarck, who had decided that the German question should be solved without the participation of Austria. Franz Joseph and his ministers were no match for the Prussian's diplomatic skill. In 1866 he inveigled Austria into war, blamed her for it, and after victory forced her to renounce all interest in the restructuring of Germany which he then undertook under Prussian aegis. This catastrophe left Franz Joseph no alternative but to accept the Hungarian terms and transform his monarchy into two equal constitutional states – Austria–Hungary – sharing in addition to the same sovereign, a common army, tariff and foreign policy. By this famous 'compromise' the Dual monarchy came into being.

The Prussian victory in 1866 quickly unravelled the tangled skein of mid-European politics. By 1871 the unification of Germany and Italy was complete. In the Habsburg monarchy the Slav question resolved itself into 'little local difficulties' once Magyars and Germans agreed to share power, with martial law in Prague stifling Czech protests and the Magyars fobbing off their Croat and Serb allies on less than generous terms. Dropped by the Magyars and no longer in hopes of a Garibaldi landing in Dalmatia, the Serbs found the orchestration of a Balkan rising beyond them. Even the Poles were finally ready to switch their energies from insurrection in Russian Poland to winning the same kind of autonomy in Austrian Galicia as the Magyars had in Hungary. The era of upheaval was over.

The outcome, except for the luckless Congress Poles, who found themselves directly subjected to tsarist absolutism, was a wave of constitutional laws (Austria–Hungary 1866–7, Rumania 1866, Serbia

1869) establishing a moderate liberalism through the greater part of the region. Henceforth regular parliaments became the ostensible focus of political life – 'nothing concerning the people without the people', in the Serbian statesman Ristic's phrase. Military and diplomatic matters, however, remained the prerogative of sovereigns, while declarations of ministerial responsibility left open whether in practice they or the elected representatives could control the rise and fall of governments. The liberal parliament differed also from its modern counterpart in that it was not elected by universal suffrage, except in egalitarian peasant Serbia, where, however, one-third of the deputies were actually nominated by the prince. About a quarter of adult males had the vote in Hungary, and in Austria and Romania a system of voting in separate electoral colleges according to income heavily favoured the wealthy, so that the Austro-Germans had majorities both in the Viennese Reichsrat and in the diet of Czech Bohemia. Against this were significant breakthroughs in the field of personal rights. The Austrian Catholic Church finally lost its control over marriage and education; for the first time Protestants, Orthodox and Jews were fully equal citizens, endowed in Hungary at least with a remarkably democratic system of church government under lay control. Citizens' rights to education and local administration in their own language were specifically guaranteed. Serfdom vanished from its last European stronghold with the Romanian emancipation law of 1864. Of course, qualifications, major and minor, are necessary. Jews still lacked full rights in Romania and non-Orthodox were more equal in law than fact in Serbia, where proselytism among the dominant Orthodox was expressly forbidden. More significant, the nationality rights in the Habsburg monarchy, in keeping with liberal principles, applied only to individuals and did not mean equal status for all language groups or shake the dominant position of German and Magyar as state languages in their respective countries. Similarly, economic freedom was likely to mean more to the prospective entrepreneur than to the illiterate peasant or farm labourer; railway mileage went up by 150 per cent in Austria in the years 1867–73 and 682 joint-stock companies were founded, but the right of association did not extend to working-class political organizations. In the liberal creed, the full emancipation of the masses was to be prepared by education, and compulsory primary school attendance was written into the constitutions of

Austria, Hungary and Romania; Serbia did not take the plunge till 1882.

In its comprehensiveness, its inner consistency and its subtle course between absolutist dogma and popular demagogy mid nineteenth-century liberalism had about it an air of historical inevitability. Originating in a more mobile, urban and literate society than Eastern Europe knew, it unerringly picked out and fortified those groups which showed all or some of these features – Austro-Germans rather than Czechs; Magyars rather than non-Magyars, bourgeois and bureaucrats rather than peasants and workers. Why had its triumph been delayed for twenty stormy years? The answer does not lie primarily in its clash with a decaying absolutism; although no old order lightly yields up its power. The liberal elites of Central Europe were divided among themselves by nationalism, a force with a different emotional charge, which sought to right the wrongs not just of late bureaucratic absolutism, but of long centuries gone by. Whereas with the maturing of liberalism, it became easier to see the lines of an accommodation between it and existing forces, such as eventually brought ex-academic legionaries from 1848 into Franz Joseph's Dualist cabinet, in nationalism's progression from cultural antiquarianism to dreams of independence and empire, the opposite was the case. Internally, it veered towards radicalism, the unacceptable face of liberalism, for as Kossuth and the Polish left agreed, only thus could the people be mobilized to resist alien rule. Externally, it challenged the whole European state system.

The background to the sudden collapse of revolutionism in the 1860s is the growing rejection by contemporaries of nationalism's disruptive implications. They saw the impracticality of the international strategy, whether based on Mazzini's revolutionary idealism or the purportedly more realistic 'sacred egoism' of a Czartoryski and a Kossuth, who would have accepted narrower deals at their allies' expense, (thus the Poles once proposed to Austria that she should take the Romanian principalities in return for restoring Galicia to themselves). They saw, too, the danger that a radical appeal to the masses would alienate more conservative nationalists and that, when aroused, the masses might well opt for a different ethnic cause, as the Magyars found with Slavs and Romanians, and the Poles with Ukrainians. On these terms, mass politics were simply too risky. Besides, with newspaper circulations in the thousands in the Habsburg monarchy and hundreds in the Balkans, as against the 250,000 of leading English, French and German publications by the mid 1860s, the means of communication necessary for mass politics did not exist. Had not Polish nobles been cut down in 1846 by peasants they were pledged to emancipate? In his Turin exile, Kossuth refused to draw. the conventional conclusions and seek a pardon to return home, but the majority of his collaborators eventually capitulated. So it was that by 1857 the Romanian '1848ers' had adopted the anaemic slogan, 'Autonomy, union and a foreign prince', that Serb government agents in Turkish Bosnia preferred winning Muslim landowners' co-operation with guarantees of their estates to preaching agrarian revolt among the Christian peasantry, and that Deak tacitly supported Vienna's campaign to keep the 'lower orders' out of the politics of the Austro-Hungarian compromise. Expedient liberalism had won out over romantic radicalism. This is the story of the 1860s.

In his famous *Leading Ideas of the Nineteenth Century* (1851) Baron Eötvös, a Tocquevillian liberal, colleague of Deak and Eastern Europe's most ambitious contemporary thinker, lent an idealist gloss to this transition. The leading ideas – liberty, equality and nationalism – were mutually contradictory, said Eötvös. Taken to extremes, liberty impinged upon the liberty of others; equality, by denying the competitive urge, could be enforced only by a despotism which would seek to justify itself through nationalism, the strongest force of the age. Yet nationalism recreated the privilege of birth. The solution was not to deny these vital impulses of modern life, as conservatives argued, but to harmonize them by tempering them with the spirit of Christianity. Christianity's great enemy, Eötvös concluded, was not science or rationality, but the industrialism which herded men together, creating social evils and sapping the moral fibre with which alone they could be overcome.

Eötvös's elitist idealism, his fear of equality and mass society, show how much East European liberalism derived from enlightened paternalism rather than the dynamic spirit of a rising bourgeoisie. They also reflect the concern of a Magyar patriot, seeing the threat posed by mass democracy to his own nation's traditional role in Hungary, as indeed to the other culturally dominant nations of the region. But even in its diluted form East European liberalism also stood for things which pointed, ultimately, to the mass society Eötvös feared: communications, capitalist development, education and common citizenship. Here lay its dilemma. The extent to which this mass society can be said to have come into existence in the half century preceding 1914 and the impact of social change on the political settlement reached in the 1860s will be the themes of Chapters 5 and 6.

5 Economics and society, 1850–1914

By the 1870s, the lands of Eastern Europe had been drawn within the orbit of Western liberal capitalist society, responded, however faintly, to its pulse, and aspired to still closer association. The forty or so years that followed till the First World War, the longest period of peace between major powers in modern times, provided the ideal background for the aspiration to become reality. When they began, the majority of inhabitants of our area still lived in a mental world shaped by age-old patterns of absolutism, serfdom and religion; at their end, a generation had been born which is still alive today. The present communications network and school system, the modern city with its sprawl of working-class tenements, the contemporary nation possessing its mature historical awareness and mass support, even our familiar patterns of sport, entertainment and popular journalism had all taken recognizable shape by 1914. At no time before, or in many ways since, did the region have a more commonly accepted code of values than the constitutional monarchy, capitalism and nationalism of these years, or a more widely understood medium for inter-communication than the German language, which was the window on the wider world for its entire intelligentsia, with the exception of some Francophile Poles and Romanians. For all this, and notwithstanding the considerable progress that was made, liberal capitalism failed to remould Eastern Europe in its own image and did not diminish the great differences in cultural and economic development between its various parts.

The most advanced sector of the region remained the German-speaking Alpine provinces of Austria and the mixed German-Slav lands of the Czech Crown, with relatively industrialized portions of Poland and Hungary marking a transition to the less developed east and south. Even in these more favoured zones recent historical research rejects the idea of a dynamic breakthrough to self-sustaining industrial growth on the lines of Rostow's take-off model.* The Habsburg monarchy lacked the conjunction of plentiful coal and iron and the contacts with major routes of international commerce which enabled great industrial concentrations to spur leading sectors like the heavy industry of the Ruhr or the textile mills of Lancashire. If a modern industry did develop it was because of the Bohemian and Alpine regions' traditions of manufacture and domestic industry from the late seventeenth century, allied to an educated workforce and close links with industrializing Germany. The result of this balance of positive and negative forces was an Austrian industrialization which was an exemplar of delayed but steady growth over an extended period, qualitatively comparable to English, French and German industrialization, but quantitatively smaller in scale.

Development and under-development in industry

The basis for a modern industry was laid in the 1850s. Its immediate stimuli were the emancipation of the serfs, abolition of the Austro-Hungarian customs barrier and gild restrictions and the foundations of banks prepared, like the French *Crédit mobilier*, to invest in industry. When constitutional government was added in 1867 the remarkable *Gründerzeit* (founding period) followed until 1873, during which time 138 new banks appeared, joint-stock industrial share capital rose eightfold and the railway network increased from 4000 to 10,000 kilometres. Heavy industry benefited most, but the mechanization of cotton-weaving also made great strides and Bohemian sugar-beet production, in which landlords invested much of the compensation they received for the emancipation of their serfs, spurted forwards. Meanwhile, the break with the past was underlined by the dismantling of the fortifications around old Vienna and the building of the famous Ringstrasse in their place, a chain of majestic boulevards encircling the inner city, soon to be flanked by symbols of the new age in neo-classical style, the Austrian Parliament, the Vienna City Hall and the palaces of Vienna's leading entrepreneurs.

The upswing of the economy, suddenly halted by the financial crash of 1873, resumed at the start of the 1880s. From this time steady progress on all fronts was enabled by rapid adaptations of

*See W. W. Rostow's influential *Stages of Economic Growth* (1960) which explains the British Industrial revolution in terms of the 'take-off' of the British cotton industry in the years 1783–1802.

foreign techniques and by supportive policies of the state. Railways, which had doubled in length in the 1860s and 1870s, doubled again (now under state ownership) between 1880 and 1913; Austria returned to protective tariffs in 1879, and in 1892 finally stabilized her currency by adopting the Gold Standard. Electrification, mine lines and better boring techniques helped 126,000 miners to produce five times more coal in 1913 than 62,000 had in 1872. The Thomas process was successfully adapted to the smelting of Bohemian iron ore. In the textile industry cotton established its supremacy over wool, linen and silk. New technologically advanced fields were also opened up in chemicals, electricals and petrochemicals. All in all, the increase of coal production from 1 million tons in 1851 to 9 million in 1872 and 44 million in 1913, of pig iron production from 160,000 tons to 370,000 and 1,750,000, and of cotton spindles from 1,370,000 to 1,500,000 and 4,700,000 over the same periods sufficiently reflects the substantial progress that was made.

Who were the men behind this significant expansion? Already in the 1860s a powerful capitalist class was developing in Vienna which, like its counterparts elsewhere had a variety of origins. The Rothschilds and Sinas made their wealth originally in merchant-banking; men like Dreher and Mautner in brewing, Mayr in metallurgy, Hornbostel in textiles and Drasche in bricks built up and modernized pre-industrial family enterprises; the great textile manufacturers Haas and Reithoffer had an artisanal background, like the locomotive builder and former apprentice locksmith, Sigl. Later on, when family businesses became less common, company management could be the launching pad for an independent career. On the whole, it is clear that the story was not one of rags to riches and that capitalists emerged from a set of related previous occupations. Their new status was, however, quite different from that of their forefathers. The leading architect of the day was commissioned for the safe manufacturer Wertheim's Ringstrasse palace, the leading designer for the interior of Baron Anselm von Rothschild's. Wertheim had his own theatre for which Joseph Strauss composed the polka 'Feuerfest' to celebrate his patron's twenty thousandth safe in 1869. From 1860 the ennoblement of industrialists and bankers began in earnest. This new elite of wealth quickly displayed the social and philanthropic pretensions of its kind. Mautner and Rothschild founded hospitals named after them. Drasche, owner of 200 acres of rented property in south

Vienna, began the custom of providing special accommodation for his workers, alongside scholarships, and pensions for officials. He died a knight and his son a baron for their pains.

Paternalism was no doubt reinforced by the fact that entrepreneurs, including the many assimilated Jews, came almost entirely from the traditionally dominant German speakers, though the workforce in the Czech lands and even in Vienna itself contained many non-Germans. Ultimately, the continued association of industrialism with the Austro-Germans, whether for socio-ethnic reasons or because of the conservative attitudes of bankers and bureacrats reflected the failure of industrialization in Austria to permeate and transform the society as a whole. Vienna, with 1,651,000 inhabitants in 1900, remained the only really large city, with Prague at 201,000 (including suburbs, 360,000) in second place. The regional distribution of industry changed little, though the Czech lands' sugar, coal, iron and steel gradually gave them the edge over the Alpine provinces and helped shift the balance within Bohemia itself somewhat from the German-speaking periphery to the metallurgical and food industries of Prague. But Galicia, with more than a quarter of the population, had only 6 per cent of the industrial workforce and a *per capita* income one third of that of the Alpine provinces. Not much better off at the other extremity was beautiful but barren Dalmatia, ruined by the decline of sailing ships and a wine industry blighted by disease. Hence aggregate Austrian economic statistics disguised West European levels of performance in the advanced provinces and extreme retardation in other areas, which unbalanced the internal market and hampered overall growth. Faster proportional growth than the older industrial countries, Britain and France, in the half century before 1914 must be set against slower progress than Austria's neighbours, Germany and (generally) Russia. Lower living standards are shown by a *per capita* consumption of meat and tobacco three-fifths that of Germany's in 1913, of cotton a half and pig iron and coal only a quarter. The Austrian novelist, Musil, has amusingly parodied his country's lack of dynamism in comparison with the other powers.

There, in Kakania*, that misunderstood state that has since vanished . . . there was speed too, of course, but not too much speed . . . . The conquest of the air had begun there too, but not too intensively. Now and then a

*A satirical term for Austria based on the fact that all Austrian institutions were dubbed k.k. standing for *Kaiserlich–Königlich* (imperial–royal).

ship was sent off to South America or the Far East; but not too often . . . .
There was some display of luxury; but it was not, of course, as over-
sophisticated as that of the French. One went in for sport; but not in
madly Anglo-Saxon fashion. One spent tremendous sums on the Army;
but only just enough to assure one of remaining the second weakest
among the great powers . . . .

This somewhat chequered record explains the readiness of the
Austrian bourgeoisie to look for support to the state in certain
spheres, for all its *laissez-faire* stand on matters like gilds, factory
legislation and working-class combination. The relative free trade
of the 1850s and 1860s was the result of high policy rather than
business pressure and its knell was sounded by the financial crash
of 1873 which increased suspicion of unrestricted capitalism. In
later decades through its protective tariffs and heavy investments
in communications and education (24 per cent and 3.2 per cent of
the national budget respectively in 1913), the state played an
increasing role in creating the infrastructure of a modernizing
society. The dependence of Austrian industry on bank investment
– though Rudolph believes it has been exaggerated – confirms the
picture of a society whose tardy industrialization required institutional support. Banks, too, were the prime movers in the development
of cartels, by which different concerns in an industry banded
together to regulate competition. Austria's complex cartel structure
– more than 200 in 1912 – was thus a sign of insecurity as much as
industrial maturity.

The same amalgam of state and private initiative, liberal and
monopoly capitalism, can be seen in Congress Poland and Hungary,
the only other areas of Eastern Europe to record significant
industrial progress before 1914. As in Austria, a distinctive capitalist
bourgeoisie developed in the Congress Kingdom and came to play
an important role in national politics, though it numbered many
assimilated Jews and Germans in its ranks. Kronenberg and Bloch
were the most prominent representatives of the entrepreneurial
class which, in the 1860s and 1870s, laid the foundations of a
modern banking and railway system, bought up the iron and
metallurgical works successively relinquished by an economically
liberalizing state, and contributed to the intellectual struggle
against Russification, as in Kronenberg's commercial college and
the museum of agriculture and industry, privately founded in 1875.
It was, however, the Russian state that provided the chief spur to
Polish economic development by its return to a strictly protectionist

policy from the late 1870s. Benefiting from better educated workers and relative closeness to Western sources of supply, Congress Poland developed rapidly in the last quarter of the nineteenth century into an industrial centre of the sprawling Russian empire. Where Russian industrial production merely doubled between 1867 and 1889, in the Congress Kingdom it quintupled and in the case of cotton went up fortyfold. By the turn of the century the value of industrial production was half as great again as that of agriculture, and 250,000 people were industrially employed; Warsaw and Lodz had become great industrial cities with 900,000 and 500,000 inhabitants respectively.

In Hungary, middle-class traditions were weaker than in Poland and fledgling capitalists were united in a customs union with economically stronger Austria, which had largely disposed of the native textile industry in the 1850s. Yet, like the Poles, the Hungarians benefited from the assimilation of numerous urban-based Germans and Jews into a nationally minded bourgeoisie, while the customs union encouraged the inflow of Austrian and other capital and expertise, and facilitated the emergence of a Budapest financial market. Moreover, the Hungarians had the boon of an autonomous government which could channel national energies to the modernization process. Budapest itself, its broad avenues radiating out from the Danube bridges and intermeshing with concentric boulevards, became an elegant symbol of Magyar resurgence and a metropolis of 800,000 people in 1900, of whom 80 per cent habitually spoke Magyar, a remarkable advance on the largely German-speaking town of fifty years before. The Hungarian government spent 240 million Krone (£10 million) on aid to industry in the Dualist period, only 5.9 per cent of the increase of joint-stock investment but a significant departure for the nineteenth century. It was rewarded by a sixfold rise in the Hungarian national product between 1850 and 1913, though Hungarian industry remained closely tied to agrarian products, as in brewing, sugar distilling, flour milling, agricultural machinery and the like.

By contrast to these developments in Austria, Poland and Hungary the agrarian societies of the Balkans did not achieve any significant industrialization before 1914. This was not for want of trying. Laws for the encouragement of industry were passed in Romania in 1887, in Bulgaria in 1894, 1897, 1905 and 1909 and in Serbia in 1873, 1898 and 1906. The small-scale Balkan intelligentsias lacked the independence to denounce the dominant liberal capitalist trend of European society as the Slavophiles and Narodniks did in Russia. Yet the results were minuscule. Romania, with 18.5 per cent of her national product from industry in 1912–13, did twice as well as Serbia and Bulgaria, largely because of her oil deposits. Her industrial work force of 58,000 in 1913 compared with 16,000 each in the other two countries. Even this represented quite a sharp spurt forwards in the new century. The bulk of what industry there was bore an agrarian character.

The absence of Balkan industrialization and the partial or non-industrialization of large areas of the Habsburg monarchy and Poland pose something of a problem for conventional theories of economic development. Karl Marx was merely echoing nineteenth-century liberal assumptions when he wrote that 'the industrially developed land shows the less developed the image of its own future'. As it was drawn into the world-wide capitalist market so each society would duplicate the stages through which others had passed till a common international order would emerge – whether peacefully or through struggle, on this alone liberals and socialists parted company. How, then, is non-industrialization to be explained? Was the liberal vision illusory? Many late twentieth-century commentators, witnesses of similar, much greater developmental disparities today, would answer yes. Under-development theorists have argued that capitalism of its nature cannot spread its benefits, such as they are, over all the world. Extensive areas must remain captive to the wealthy metropoles, the reservoir of raw materials and cheap labour, in Aristotelian terms the sacrificial means for the attainment of the prosperous Western life-style. Is the fate of Eastern Europe before 1914 the earliest demonstration of this bleak analysis?

An affirmative case can be made. Even Austria, the most advanced part of the region, still imported much of its industrial materials in 1914, while its two chief exports – sugar and wood-products – were agriculturally based. Foreign capital totalled 36 per cent of its capital investment (6.8 billion Krone) against only a half a billion Krone of Austrian investment in the West. In turn, Austrian capital dominated the weaker economies on its eastern flank. Austrian investments in 1900 amounted to 40 per cent of Hungarian capital and 73 per cent of Austrian industrial exports went to the captive Hungarian market. On the other hand, more than half Hungary's exports were of agricultural raw materials. The Balkan countries stood on a lower level again, for here, alongside Austrian and Western capital, Hungarian capital participated significantly in leading banks in all three countries. Three of the five main banks of Bucharest were controlled from the monarchy; under Austrian pressure the Andreevits bank in Belgrade even refused Serb businessmen credit during the Austro-Serb diplomatic crisis of 1908. Through trade treaties with Romania in 1875 and Serbia in 1881, the monarchy opened the smaller countries' markets to her industrial products in return for receiving her agrarian goods, a process which, around the turn of the century, made it the recipient of about five-sixths of Serbia's exports. The pattern appears to be one of a chain of increasingly dependent economies, each one in turn more heavily fettered to its more powerful Western neighbours.

The work of the American Gerschenkron on economic backwardness offers a somewhat more optimistic perspective. Laggards in industrialization face great difficulties in raising the capital to finance increasingly complex technology, but should they succeed they benefit from possession of a more up-to-date industrial infrastructure than that of their more established rivals. Moreover, capital accumulation may be possible through the mobilization of corporate institutions – banks, joint-stock companies, the state itself – which can pool individual resources and devise means of substituting for factors present in earlier industrializations but no longer repeatable. Thus, while delayed industrialization cannot just be an image of the original process, it is by no means impossible.

Gerschenkron's thesis appears to fit certain East-Central European regions better than the theory of under-development. Even in fairly backward milieux, late nineteenth-century industry showed a capacity to benefit from technological backlog and establish itself in sophisticated form. Large-scale industry increased much more rapidly than small, absorbing the majority of workers in centres like Lodz and Budapest. Again, foreign capital did not just involve the draining away of profits to foreign bond-holders, but could play a positive role in initiating industry, later becoming domesticated or declining in importance. Thus the greater part of the 39 per cent of foreign industrial capital in Congress Poland at the turn of the century was held by incomers who had effectively settled in the country or by autonomous enterprises founded in Poland by foreign concerns. Similarly, the share of foreign capital in the Hungarian economy declined from 60 per cent in the 1867 period to 25 per cent on the eve of the First World War. The great bulk of this foreign capital, both in Hungary and Austria, was no longer invested directly in the dynamic parts of the economy but in government and other official securities. Hungarian historians, who in the 1950s adhered to a colonialist interpretation of their country's position in the nineteenth century, have come to acknowledge the customs union's role in raising Hungary's national income faster than Austria's in this period and giving her an industrial growth rate arguably the highest in Europe after 1890. They qualify this only by arguing that, in encouraging food industry at the expense of textiles, Habsburg tariff policy gave an unbalanced twist to Hungary's economic development, and helped shore up the baneful role of agrarian conservatives in the state.

This balanced verdict is harder to sustain for the Balkan countries. There, as the historian of banking Feis has written, when the new-born Serbian state first opened its eyes, its glance fell on the creditors surrounding its cradle. Too weak to insist on protective tariffs, lacking direct control over what industry they had, often circumscribed in their economic policies by international law* – or by international debt commissions – the Balkan states found themselves forced into a series of international loans at very low rates of issue, which went mainly on the army and debt interest payments and only minimally to industrial investment. Thus Serbia declared state bankruptcy in 1895; in 1914 Romanian oil was 95 per cent foreign owned. Gerschenkron argues that the unfruitfulness of foreign loans stemmed from the economic illiteracy of national-istic Balkan leaders; but the criticism is somewhat one-sided. International finance did not exert itself to instruct its clients about priorities, it simply pocketed its interest. Liberal capitalism's progressive role finally petered out in the Balkans.

The failure of liberalism in the countryside

The most obvious symptom of under-development was the continuing preponderance of peasants, living at or near subsistence level in a traditional cultural milieu without the means or inclination to provide a market for native industry. 86 per cent of the population in Serbia and Bulgaria in 1900 were peasants, but the proportion was two-thirds in Hungary and Congress Poland and

*The Treaty of Berlin, for instance, bound Serbia and Bulgaria to build through-railways for their more advanced neighbours' benefit.

over half in Austria also. More than anything else, these figures disclose the failure of liberalism to remould East European society, for the subsistence peasant, with his local loyalties, self-sufficiency and distinctive life-style represented the antithesis of the liberal citizen ideal. What had gone wrong?

It is arguable that, in Serbia and Bulgaria, liberalism had not influenced the countryside because it had not been tried. There, special laws protected peasants from eviction from their homesteads for debt. To this extent, Balkan politicians deliberately inhibited differentiation among the peasantry into a class of successful farmers producing for the market and a sub-layer of landless labourers and potential factory workers. Yet the argument is somewhat strained because in other respects Balkan legislation followed the line of economic liberalism. Serbian peasants were free to divide their holdings if they chose and the civil code favoured individual over communal property, so contributing to the gradual disintegration of the zadrugas. Besides, subsistence peasants also survived in large numbers north of the Danube where the emancipation decrees of 1848, 1861 and 1864 preserved the large estates and were not so solicitous of peasant interests. However applied, liberal capitalism was simply ill-adapted to rural society. Nineteenth-century liberalism's fundamental paradox, whereby equal civil rights for all became the basis for the economic advancement of the entrepreneurial few, had a certain plausibility in the urban milieu in which liberalism first took shape. The future capitalist and his future employees could, at least in some cases, start from the same point in the *tabula rasa* of industrializing society, and the expanding enterprise of the former could multiply work opportunities for the latter. But individual enterprise was much less easy to operate on the land, with its centuries-old pattern of common pastures and forests, its strip system and communal cultivation. Again, land, not being an elastic asset like industrial capital, could not provide an ever increasing number of jobs, and could be more easily monopolized by traditional elites. Capitalism in the countryside would merely impoverish the weaker peasants without a background of industrialization in the towns; but industrialization in the towns could not proceed without the market provided by prosperity in the countryside. This vicious circle bedevilled all questions of East European economic development.

The cycle began in the emancipation decrees themselves. Only rustical peasants acquired property rights in their land, for the numerous landless and dominical peasants were untouched by the reform (see Chapter 4, p. 88). In the division of common lands and lands of disputed status, the nobles customarily gained the lion's share. Where the state was relatively neutral, as in Hungary after 1848, peasants secured 10–15 per cent of the common land; where the state favoured the nobles, as in Galicia, their share was less than 1 per cent. Only in the Russian western borderlands, where the authorities sided with non-Polish peasants against Polish landlords, did the peasants acquire ownership of almost all the land they had formerly cultivated as serfs. The upshot of the whole complex process was that about two-fifths of the land fell to peasants in Hungary and the Congress Kingdom, somewhat more in Austria and somewhat less in Romania. This was insufficient to provide an adequate plot to all the new proprietors, particularly the smallholders hit by the division of the common lands on which they had formerly relied.

For some time after emancipation, transitional forms hindered the introduction of fully fledged capitalism. Rather than sell up their tiny plots and move into rural or urban labouring, small peasants often rented part of the manorial demesne, discharging their rent by working the lord's land. Elsewhere this neo-feudalism eventually declined, but in Romania it consolidated into the system of labour contract between landlord and poor peasant which, as Mitrany has argued, combined for the latter all the disadvantages of feudalism and capitalism. Outside Romania, population increase and sub-division of plots disproportionately swelled the ranks of the agricultural labourers. By 1900 they numbered 39 per cent of the rurally employed in Hungary and 36 per cent in Bohemia. The real wages of these workers, after an advance in the generation following 1848, appear to have declined, if anything, after 1880. Many were women, some 45 per cent of the total in Bohemia. Increasing numbers were seasonal, tramping the countryside in search of all too intermittent employment. Worst off were the farm labourers, still often subject to their masters' discipline rather than the civil law. In Galicia they worked up to thirteen hours in winter, seventeen in summer, slept in stables and were paid mainly in kind. The Hungarian writer Illyes, himself born on an estate, has left us a vivid picture of farm servant discipline.

Up to the age of thirty to thirty five, the people of the Pusztas are generally struck on the face. After this they usually receive blows on the back of the head or the neck and then just one blow as a rule .... With old folk such direct disciplinary methods are used sparingly. Over the age of sixty most of them will begin to cry at the mere sight of a hand raised to threaten them — not because they are afraid, but because of the humiliation. By that time they have gained some idea of human dignity.

It was the great estates which benefited most from the introduction of capitalism in agriculture, substantially increasing their share of the land at the expense of medium-sized farms. While investment did not match that in Western Europe (mortgage credits represented 33–40 per cent of the arable land value in Hungary in 1900, only some 10 per cent in Romania), it permitted some improvement in yields. There was a sharp increase in cultivated land and the proportion of land under grain throughout the region, and a widespread transition from the three-field system to permanent crop rotation with elimination of fallow. Machinery, except in Prussian Poland, remained largely a landlord preserve; 9 per cent of Austrian farm units used it in 1902, mainly animal-powered. In the Balkans even the wooden plough was not seriously challenged until after 1895. Still, wheat production nearly doubled in Hungary, trebled in Romania and quadrupled in Serbia in the thirty years before 1913 and the region became one of the more significant grain exporting areas in the world. Eastern Europe had not lost its preponderantly agrarian character.

This economic fact necessarily had social consequences. Even in the most industrialized areas the capitalist class continued to play second fiddle in high society to the landowning aristocracy. Access to Franz Joseph's court was restricted to those who could claim sixteen-quarters of nobility or noble ancestors on all sides for four generations. Below the court, a second circle, slightly less select, grouped aristocrats with a few of the very richest, nearly always ennobled, members of the commercial world, of whom the Rothschilds may be taken as examples. Only at a third level did the businessmen, lawyers, writers and academicians of successful bourgeois society create the effervescent social world which has since come to be thought of as quintessentially Viennese. Yet the distinctive feature of this society was its desire to assimilate the classic forms of Austrian aristocratic culture. Unable, with the partial exception of the Czechs, to expand beyond the bounds of the German and German-Jewish ethnic group, doomed therefore to remain the creed of a minority, liberal capitalism shed its dynamic character and guided its offspring away from public endeavour to seek fulfilment in artistic and contemplative courses. The pursuit of culture which to the fathers in the 1860s, had been the reward for an energetic life, a means of self-examination for the earnest moralist and of regeneration for the masses became, for their sons in the 1890s, a matter for subjective aestheticism and privatized enjoyment, shielding them from the coarser passions of the world about them. It is no chance that the psychological theories of Sigmund Freud were first developed in this rather introverted milieu or that the leading objects of popular attention at the.time were not statesmen or sportsmen but designers, actors or musicians, like Gustav Mahler, whose stormy artistic life as head of the Viennese opera mirrored the preoccupation of the Austro-German middle classes with cultural rather than political disputation. Little time was left over for radical politics. Unlike many of their German counterparts Austrian businessmen from the start of the constitutional era enthusiastically accepted ennoblement and its attendant life-style.

In Hungary and Poland the capitalist bourgeoisie compromised even further with pre-existing social norms. The aristocratic figure-head adding lustre to a board of directors was well-nigh universal. Ennoblement became almost the concomitant of commercial success; half the important Jewish capitalist families in Hungary had had members ennobled by 1914, a total of 346, all but eight after 1860. Society's aristocratic tone was further strengthened by the fact that the bureaucracy in Dualist Hungary and the intelligentsia in Congress Poland were largely formed from impoverished gentry who had migrated to the towns. In an atmosphere of mounting nationalism, exclusive gentlemen's clubs, black-balls and even duels (Tisza, the Hungarian Prime Minister, fought several in 1913), parvenu German and Jewish businessmen who made up a large part of the capitalist class were hardly likely to throw their weight around. Thus the partial integration of wealth and birth which took place did so very much on the latter's terms as the following quote from a Budapest paper shows: 'Distinguished 45-year-old landowner is thinking of marrying. With ladies of good family a dowry of 40,000 to 60,000 F. is required, with ladies of bourgeois origin 100,000 to 200,000 F.'

The hegemony of classical liberalism which had appeared so unassailable in the 1860s could not survive unscathed in such a climate indefinitely. In Austria it lasted just from 1867 to 1879, when

Franz Joseph dismissed his liberal ministers for opposing him on a foreign policy matter and replaced them with a coalition of German-speaking clericals and Slav nationalists presided over by a boyhood friend, Count Taaffe. It was the clericals, led by aristocrats like Taaffe himself and backed by Catholic Alpine peasants, who gave the tone to this coalition's anti-liberal programme: a lowering of the franchise qualification to swamp the liberals' professional and business clientele with shopkeepers, artisans and farmers; social welfare legislation to mitigate the effects of *laissez-faire*; greater clerical influence in education; heavier taxation of capital and the partial restoration of gilds to protect small-scale producers against big business. Taaffe's administration fell in 1893. By this time a more dynamic but related movement had developed, fusing conservative clericalism with the populist and anti-semitic aspirations of the Viennese lower-middle class to create the Christian Social Party, whose leader, Lueger, was to be mayor of the Habsburg capital from 1897 till his death thirteen years later. Its success demonstrated the unpopularity of large-scale capitalism in a country where 39 per cent of the textile workers in advanced Bohemia were home workers as late as 1902 and where unsympathetic tax laws appropriated two to four times more of the profits of industrial capital than in neighbouring Germany; as a result, there were fewer joint-stock companies at the start of the new century than there had been in 1873.

Anti-Semitism was not confined to the Christian Social Party. It appeared in stronger form in the German nationalist movement in Austria which began to branch away from conventional liberalism from the beginning of the 1880s and had intermittent success in Austro-German politics. An anti-semitic party advanced briefly in Hungary too, in the 1880s, and anti-semitism was a key plank of the National Democratic Party founded in Romania in 1909. The defence of Christian labour against alien capitalists, the widespread belief in tales of Jewish ritual nurder of Christian children (ritual murder trials actually took place in Hungary in 1882 and Bohemia in 1899), the exaltation of an idealized Christian peasant and artisanal culture was more than a reaction against the important Jewish role in the economy and free professions, in village money-lending (Galicia) or estate-management (Romania). It was an attempt, through the Jews, whom Enlightenment had emancipated, to repudiate the whole universalist, rationalist heritage of enlightened and liberal thought.

Social movement before 1914

It is possible to overplay the strength of this reaction in the decades before 1914. Anti-semitism declined as a political force in the early twentieth century. It was precisely liberalism's pervading presence which produced countervailing tendencies which, however, never looked like restoring the clerical–artisanal–agrarian society some of them postulated. If the East European bourgeoisie had conpromised with the older social elite, the reverse was also true, as the galaxy of Jewish nobles bore witness. So, in a different way, did the Christian Social Party, for this was a mass party led, not by the aristocratic clerical Count Hohenwart, but by the polytechnic caretaker's son Lueger, whose progress both the Vatican and Franz Joseph had originally tried to block.

Outside the Habsburg monarchy, even where economic development was limited, bourgeois values faced less of a challenge because a nobility was either absent or politically weak. With Prince Czartoryski's death in 1861 and Prince Wielopolski's failure to prevent the 1863 rising, the great magnate families ceased to play an influential role in Congress Poland. While Hungarian literature continued to centre round the gentry, whether in the historical novels of Jokai or the drawing-room comedies of Molnar, Polish prose began to take up bourgeois themes, espousing Jewish, sometimes even female, emancipation. In Romania the status of boyardom had always been more loosely defined than that of other East European nobilities, which facilitated a merger of birth and wealth in Bucharest, a town aping what it liked to see as its Latin sister-city, bourgeois Paris. Most interesting of all was the emergence of urban elites in the egalitarian peasant societies of the Balkans, composed of merchants, lawyers, educationalists and civil servants. 'How can one live outside Belgrade', exclaims a character in one of the comedies of Nusic, the most penetrating satirist of Serbian mores. The very backwardness of Balkan society lent a glamour to the few towns that did exist, particularly the capitals, on whose architecture and cultural amenities sovereigns like Charles of Romania and Ferdinand of Bulgaria, both German sophisticates by origin, lavished attention for prestige purposes. Enterprising Balkanites readily followed the fashion. What chance would a parish priest in national dress, wrote a Bosnian Orthodox clergyman in 1891, have of being received by the Bosnian Serb nationalist leader, Gligorije Jeftanovic, a frock-coated merchant, hotelier, factory-owner and bank shareholder?

Over the region as a whole the threat to bourgeois liberalism came as much from its successes as its failures. The growth of communications, the expansion of education, the development of the habit of association were sufficiently far-reaching to facilitate the emergence of mass movements which challenged liberalism from the left as well as the right. Let us see how this had come about.

For all its modest achievements through the greater part of the region, the onset of industrialism had provoked a mobility previously unknown in times of peace. Czech peasants streamed to Vienna and German-speaking Bohemia, Slovenes to Trieste, Poles to Warsaw and Lodz, Hungarians to Budapest. From the 1870's a mounting tide of emigration to the United States of America set in which was to total more than 5 million by 1914. These outlets enabled the population to continue expanding rapidly, for although the birth rate fell, medical improvements brought down the death rate still faster. Nor was migration only industrial. There was increasing call for Polish labour on the capitalist Junker estates of East Germany and for Slovaks and Romanians from the uplands to work in the Hungarian latifundia in the plains. Dinaric mountaineers from the barren west Balkans, particularly Montenegro, continued to migrate into more fertile Serbia. Jews moved west from the Russian pale of settlement into Galicia and from there to Hungary, where their numbers rose from 247,000 in 1840 to 830,000 in 1890. Migration enlarged awareness and in the case of American remittances financial means as well.

In an age which liked to speak of the 'thirst for knowledge' education could also be a spur to mobility – in the most literal as well as the general sense. Karl Renner, son of a struggling peasant family and twice to be socialist president of the Austrian Republic rose at 6 a.m. in summer and 5.30 a.m. in winter to walk the long miles to the grammar shcool in the local town. Princip, the ill-fated assassin of Archduke Franz Ferdinand in Bosnia in 1914, tramped all the way from Sarajevo to Belgrade for the sake of a Serb nationalist education. The educational achievements of the half century before 1914 should not be underestimated. Literacy rose from one-third to two-thirds of the population in Hungary and reached 98 per cent in the Czech lands. 75 per cent of the Bulgarian recruits in the Balkan wars (1912–13), 59 per cent of the Romanian and 50 per cent of the Serbs could read and write. This must be set against a general literacy of 7 per cent for Serbia in 1874. The area showed substantially the same educational structure, of German origin, with a large range of schools at secondary level, from classical to commercial, technical and agricultural to suit people of different tastes, but also of different social stations – liberalism was not yet democracy! Two features of the time were the expansion of girls' secondary education, and of university education in the more backward areas of the region. Three new universities appeared in provincial Hungary and five in Romania and the Balkans after 1860, as well as a Czech-language university in Prague.

With a majority able to read and write for the first time in the region's history, there was naturally the emergence of a more popular press. Although this was still a feature of urban rather than rural life – two-thirds of the copies of Budapest's dailies were sold inside the capital in 1896 – circulations could be quite different from earlier times: the Hungarian evening paper *Az Eszte* could reach 400,000 during the First World War as against the 5,000 subscribers to Kossuth's famous *Pesti Hirlap* in the 1840s. Popular entertainment was also beginning to take on a more modern form. While the famous spas of Bohemia continued to be the preserve of European high society, excursion trains provided outings for city workers; the first football international between Hungary and Austria was played in 1902, cinemas became popular, too, in the new century; and gymnastic clubs, choirs and reading rooms appeared even at the village level. At the same time that liberal capitalism dealt the masses harsh economic blows, liberal education and association provided them with means for a broader life and, ultimately, self-defence.

The most striking illustration of this was the socialist movement. The ills of industrialism were not less in Eastern Europe for being more localized. 'Here, squeezed into stinking dwellings are living the most marginal and most miserable part of Warsaw's working classes, hopeless and near to despair', wrote the Russian Governor of Warsaw's slums in 1864. Overcrowding was the scourge of urban development everywhere. With 72 per cent of its population living more than two to a room, Budapest was the most overcrowded city in Europe after St Petersburg; one-fifth of Serbia's metal workers slept in their factories. Despite general tax incentives encouraging employers to provide housing for their workers it was only because almost all householders in larger centres like Vienna took lodgers that the situation was kept in control at all. As it was, Adolf Hitler's early life in the doss-houses and boarding-houses of Vienna reflects the formative experience of scores of thousands of migrants to the cities. Hours were long – eleven in Austria not counting breaks by the law of 1883 – and pay low, because low pay was the universal answer of employers to the technical superiority of the West and the even lower wages of Russia to the East. The average pay of a Hungarian worker at the start of this century was 40–55 pence a week. True, in the Habsburg monarchy and the Congress Kingdom the worst abuses of early industrialization had been removed in the 1880s and 1890s, with restricted working hours for youth and women, Sunday rest and the abolition of truck (payment through credit in company shops), and the Habsburg monarchy at least had adopted a system of accident and sickness insurance. But these benefits did not extend to the large numbers engaged in domestic industry or farm work, nor did they reach the Balkans till the twentieth century, and then more from imitation of developments elsewhere than from a genuine maturing of native opinion. In these latter societies the weight of legislation still lay in a vain attempt to prop up the native artisanal gilds which were being undermined successively by competition from foreign artisanal products, foreign industry, village crafts and, after 1900, native industry itself.

For all the evident grievances, working-class mobilization was not easy at first. Elements of a working-class organization emerged both in Austria and Hungary in the late 1860s and early 1870s, influenced variously by the pro-liberal workers' educational movement in Germany, by Marxism and by Ferdinand Lassalle. In less open circumstances, Congress Polish workers were organizing factory funds. But the hostility of the authorities and confusion between the prescriptions previously mentioned proved too strong, so that the story of socialism in the 1870s and 1880s is one of splits and ineffectiveness, worsened by national tensions. The question as to whether socialists should embrace national goals divided Polish socialists as early as 1881, cooled relations between Czechs and Germans and threatened to embroil the multi-national workforces of Budapest, Trieste, Vienna itself.

In the event, the national mix in the cities of Eastern Europe proved as much a help as a hindrance to the emergence of a clear-cut socialist idea. The Marxism which had triumphed in the prestigious German Social Democratic Party was carried throughout the region by German workers; German-language socialist material was published as far apart as Lodz in Poland and Sarajevo in the Balkans. Social democratic parties on a Marxist basis were founded in Austria in 1889, Hungary 1890, Bulgaria 1891, Romania 1893 and Serbia in 1903. Congress Poland acquired two, one for and the other against national separatism. The speed of response from the more backward regions need not surprise. For two generations educated Balkanites had been assimilating the latest ideas from the West, often by the classic detour of Russia and Switzerland, followed by the Bulgarian Marxist leader, Blagoev, as it had been by his Serbian predecessor Svetozar Markovic. Marxism's revolutionary iconoclasm suited their traditions of revolt as it did that of many young members of the Polish intelligentsia, while the expiring artisanry of their own countries furnished them with just as vivid proof of the ineluctability of economic forces as the plight of the English hand-loom weavers had to Marx.

So, in the generation before 1914, a widespread socialist tradition developed, possessing much common doctrine and symbolism, particularly in the great street marches on May Day which frequently recalled the religious processions of an earlier, more deferential age. The 200,000 workers who tramped past his window in the first Viennese May Day celebrations in 1890 astonished the young bourgeois and later novelist, Stefan Zweig, by their discipline and resolution. Well might his class have been astonished when its patronizing homilies to the workers, even in the heat of 1848, are recalled. The organizers of the only precedent, the demonstration of 20,000 Viennese workers for universal suffrage in 1869, had been tried for high treason for co-operating with German socialists. The 200 who assembled peacefully in Warsaw's main square in 1884 constituted Poland's first ever workers' demonstration, and 146 of them were arrested. Trade unions gained only very limited rights in Austria in 1869 and Hungary in 1875, and were not recognized till 1906 in Russian Poland and 1910 in Serbia. Strikes, too, were initially met by the regular drafting in of troops or the state backing of blackleg labour. But their number grew; twenty-eight were reported in Austria in 1885; there was a famous victory in the Zyrardow textile factory near Warsaw which employed 8000 workers in 1883. Usually small strikes were more successful than large ones. By the twentieth century the authorities for the most part had given up direct repression, and trade unionists were becoming quite numerous – 450,000 in Austria, 130,000 in Hungary (in 1907); against this, Romania had but 9,000 unionists in 1909, the Bulgarian Social democrat party a total of 2507 members in 1902.

Political ideas were beginning to penetrate the peasant masses as well. The Hungarian farm labourers' strike for higher pay in 1897, the demonstrations against the state tithe in Bulgaria in 1899, the bloody revolt of the Romanian peasantry against the labour contract system in 1907 testified to the recrudescence of peasant activism after decades of passivity following emancipation. Initially, peasant thought was strongly influenced by socialist ideas: socialists participated in the Hungarian labourers' strike, in the foundation of the Bulgarian Agrarian Union and in the 300 or so socialist circles established in Romanian villages in the 1890s. A 'primitive socialism', such as the later Czech national leader Thomas Masaryk ascribes to his childhood years was, after all, a fairly natural response to the difficulties of all but the better off peasantry under the liberal dispensation. The memoirs of Karl Renner, like Masaryk, of Moravian peasant stock, show how contact with socialist ideas could explain to a thoughtful youth the decline of village solidarity under capitalism as the rich peasants grew richer, bought up the poor and became a snobbish elite with the blessing of the local clergy. This was the process that turned the adolescent Renner, an eighteenth child, and his brothers and sisters, out of the family home and scattered them to sordid apprenticeships, blighted small businesses and makeshift marriages in the towns.

Over time, however, fewer peasants followed Renner along the socialist road. For one thing, orthodox Marxism was suspicious of what Marx had called the 'idiocy of rural life' and lumped peasant proprietors along with small shopkeepers and artisans in the *petit bourgeoisie*, a class doomed to be displaced by large-scale production. For another, peasants developed a capacity for independent organization; pre-war Austria had over 8000 credit associations and 2000 other rural societies; Romania in 1913 numbered 2901 'popular banks' whose members included half the country's peasant families. In tandem with peasant credit and marketing associations, developed peasant leagues and parties reflecting traditional values of peasant life, particularly ethnic and religious ones. The title 'People's Party', as in Slovenia, Hungary and among the Poles of Galicia, generally bespoke a clerical appeal to Catholic peasant sentiment. On the other hand, the Czech Agrarian Party (founded in 1899), the Bulgarian Agrarian Union (1899) and the Croatian Peasant Party (1904) explicitly proclaimed their peasant character and Varkonyi's short-lived Independent Socialist Party in Hungary was in fact a peasant-orientated organization; only oligarchic Romania, for all the strength of its co-operative movement, failed to develop a peasant political organization. More equitable taxation, better facilities for credit, education and the co-operative movement, measures in favour of medium and small rather than large-scale property: such were the staple prescriptions of these movements which, however, could vary considerably among themselves, from kinship with traditional conservative clericalism to sympathies with the democratic secularism of the socialists.

These widely divergent elements in peasant movements mirrored a tendency which can be ascribed to Eastern European society as a whole. If in the pre-1848 period, and even more so in that of enlightened absolutism, the innovative tendencies, however crucial, were still plainly confined to certain sectors of life and social groups, this was just not so by 1914. Old and new, enlightenment and tradition met in every sphere. Balkan peasants might still use wooden ploughs, farm scattered, unfertilized plots and buy only salt, tobacco, kerosene and matches outside their villages, but they might also mount the train to take their goods to market. There was an even chance they could read and write and they could well have a cousin in America. Similarly, although the ruling elite had been enlarged to include, alongside the scions of nobility and Church, representatives of business, academia and the free professions, the response of this 'constitutional' authority to claims from social groups outside its charmed circle was still likely to be the resort to force, as striking miners and farm labourers found to their cost. Modern democracy was a long way off when Masaryk could be denied a professorship for fifteen years because the archbishop of Prague disliked his research into suicide, or Renner's candidature for the post of parliamentary librarian necessitated a police check that he was of 'unblemished' character. Nevertheless, Masaryk's and Renner's careers demonstrated that, to the able and energetic youth of whatever background, mass education with a slice of luck now offered a way to advance; and the consolidation of the trade union movement and the electoral progress of Social Democracy suggested that fuller democracy could not ultimately be denied. Hence the number and vigour of the movements in the immediately pre-war period which looked expectantly beyond a tarnished liberalism to the future, whether for socialist, nationalist or peasantist goals.

Such optimism was no longer based on the romantic, idealist habit of thought, which had accompanied the rise of liberalism in our area. In an age of unparalleled material growth this had yielded to a sober positivism, or the conviction that, as the realms of reason, science and technology expanded, so men could successively improve the organization of their society. First appearing in Poland in the wake of the definitive defeat of romantic revolt in 1863, this positivism later fuelled the anti-gentry campaign of Hungarian bourgeois reformers around Oszkar Jaszi and his periodical *Huszadik Szazad* ('Twentieth Century'), founded in 1900. It can be seen also in the influential literary criticism of the Serb Jovan Skerlic, with its rejection of a vapid romanticism, and in the toughly realistic programmes of the Polish bourgeois nationalist Dmowski, and the Bulgarian peasant leader Stamboliski, which built on social Darwinist ideas of struggle and competition to ground movements on the untapped strength of the people rather than liberal rhetoric. Masaryk's 'Realist' school in Prague, Supilo's 'New Course' in Dalmatia, even the interpretations of Marxism by the Prague-born Kautsky, and the Austrian Jew Otto Bauer, reflect the same positivist spirit of the age. The urge to give democratic aspirations a pragmatic basis, to develop in new forms the Enlightenment vision of an Eastern Europe about to be won for European civilization was one of the most widespread and interesting features of the region's social thought before 1914.

Yet it is possible from hindsight to posit a bleaker perspective. Is there perhaps something disturbing in an Eastern Europe increasingly glutted with imported social philosophies? Liberalism had gailed to galvanize the region as a whole, and the response of many was to turn to yet more radical Western remedies. Thus Dobrogeanu-Gherea, the leading socialist ideologue of pre-war Romania, was brought to Marxism by his realization that, despite the liberal 1864 emancipation, Romania's countryside remained essentially feudal. The Austrian and Hungarian socialists led their countries' campaigns for universal suffrage because radical democrats were too weak to do so. By a paradox of the modernization process a society's very backwardness made extreme radicalism seem the only way to overhaul it. Traditionalists, liberals and radicals, all strongly represented because their nostrums corresponded to different aspects of the region's heritage, competed in a way unknown to the West; the social and political order was in danger of overloading. Seen in this light, anti-Semitism appears as the virulent response of some elements of society to the stresses and strains of modernization. Emancipated Jewry, the symbol of the modern movement to the anti-Semite, was to pay for this movement's deficiences, as perceived by Viennese shopkeepers failing to keep up with big business, sectors of the Catholic clergy obsessed with secularism or nationalists bemoaning the indebtedness of the national peasantry to Jewish middlemen and money-lenders. To the school of thought that urged the society forward there corresponded one which urged it to go into reverse. The Eastern Europe that entered the twentieth century was a deeply ambivalent society, whose ambivalence reflected its incomplete absorption into the framework of Western capitalism. The masses had begun to speak but their ultimate allegiance was unclear. More than anything else this fact accounts for the extreme unpredictability of the region's political evolution in the crucial years before 1914.

6 Politics, 1870 – 1918

The political history of Eastern Europe between 1870 and 1918 falls neatly into two parts. For about a generation the system arising from the collapse of revolutionary hopes in the 1860s was consolidated and strengthened. Then, from the 1890s, as new social forces appeared, increasing signs of tension accompanied them until the whole region was thrust into a great war which shattered its political structure for ever, replacing the great empires by a pattern of small and medium-sized nation states, approximately as they are today. The events of this period, therefore, still retain their resonance. Why did such diverse social tensions resolve themselves in the issue of national self-determination, and was this outcome an adequate response to the problems they raised? These questions are perhaps almost too loaded for academic discussion, but they must be faced because so much historiographical discussion implicitly revolves around them.

A generation of stability

An understanding of the final denouement requires a brief summary of the period of stabilization which preceded it, since these years shaped the assumptions that guided governing circles right up to 1918. On the international level, stabilization owed much to the diplomacy of Bismarck who, till his fall in 1890, was concerned to safeguard the new balance of power he had created by the establishment of the German empire and the annexation of French Alsace–Lorraine. Assured of the rancour of France, Bismarck sought successfully to dispel that of Austria–Hungary and bind her in an alliance of the so-called central powers. The Near Eastern crisis of 1875–8, a late ironic echo of the revolutionary hopes of the previous decade, gave him his chance.

In Bosnia and Herzegovina a spontaneous Serb revolt pressurized the little Serbian state into the long-planned national liberation war against the Turks. With only Montenegro for an ally, she failed disastrously, until Russia intervened and dictated the Turks a humiliating peace. However, Russia was isolated internationally, and in the Congress of Berlin in 1878 Britain and Austria forced her to disgorge her gains. European Turkey remained largely intact, subject to the creation of a small autonomous Bulgarian principality and an Austrian occupation of Bosnia – Herzegovina intended to forestall Greater Serbian dreams. Profiting from Austrian–Russian tensions, Bismarck negotiated an Austro-German alliance in 1879, before skilfully merging this into the Austro-German-Russian alliance of 1881 and thereby restoring the conservative accord of the Eastern monarchies for which Metternich had striven.

Bismarck realized that the stability of this combination depended on Germany's refusal to take sides in her partners' Balkan disputes. He once said that the Balkans were not worth the bones of a Pomeranian grenadier. In the longer term he hoped that a division of the Balkans into spheres of influence, with Austria taking responsibility for the western half, including Serbia, and Russia for the eastern half and Bulgaria, would deprive the whole problem of its disruptive force.

To some extent this took place. A decisive factor for stability in the region was the transfer of Russian preoccupations from the Balkans to the Far East after the humiliation of 1878. Deprived of Russian patronage Serbia had little choice but to accept that of Austria. Her dependence on the monarchy was underlined in the Austro-Serb trade treaty of 1881, and in the secret political treaty of the same year, by which she accepted the *status quo* in Bosnia and promised to consult Austria over any relations she entered into with third powers. In 1883 another secret treaty bound Romania to Austria and Germany. Bulgaria, however, remained generally in the Russian sphere of influence. This system of tutelage reflected the great powers' willingness to permit what the Austrian foreign minister Andrassy called *Volkspersönlichkeiten* or ethnic identities in the sensitive Balkans, provided these did not aspire to play an autonomous political role. In this sense Serbia was, according to a successor of Andrassy's in 1881,

our pillar in the Balkans not only in the political, but also in the national sense; she is the natural ally of the general ideas we apply for national development, particularly with regard to Yugoslav tendencies, to which she is strongly opposed.

Indeed, by occupying Bosnia, Austria had succeeded in shattering the Yugoslav tendencies of the 1860s – the end of Muslim rule in the province unleashed bitter rivalry between its Orthodox Serb and Catholic pro-Croat communities which could only exacerbate Serbo-Croat relations elsewhere. From 1883 to 1903 the Hungarian Governor of Croatia, Khuen-Hedervary, played the Serb minority off against Croat nationalist opposition to his rule, while his compatriot Kallay played off Catholics and Muslims against the relative Serb majority in Bosnia.

Thus by the 1880s the principal threat to international stability had been defused. To the external settlement corresponded an internal one, by which ruling elites, broader and more flexible than in the days of absolutism, found ways of coping with the exigenices of constitutional government. In the conservative atmosphere of late nineteenth-century Europe it was possible for ultra-traditional regimes to dispense with constitutionalism altogether, as did Turkey, after the abortive parliament of 1877–8, and Russia, which had never tried it. Sultan Abdul Hamid (1876–1909) and Tsar Alexander III (1881–94) shared a hatred of revolutionaries that turned them against even the mildly reformist courses urged on them by their most experienced statesmen, Midhat Pasha and Milyutin respectively. The administrative and educational systems of Congress Poland, renamed Vistula Land, were wholly Russianized; the local self-government introduced in Russia denied; and the Orthodox Church favoured over the Catholic and Uniate. Despite the constitutional facade, things were little different in Prussian Poland. Besides withholding the local self-government granted in 1872 from Polish districts, Bismarck launched first a cultural and then an economic attack on the Polish population. The former involved restrictions on the Catholic Church and the use of Polish in schools, the latter the establishment of a Colonization Commission (1886) to buy out Polish landowners and replace them with Germans. Only in Austrian Galicia did Poles continue to enjoy recognition of their language and a share in the local administration. Meanwhile, to the south, Macedonia, Albania and Thrace, which alone of its once vast European lands remained under the Porte's direct control, were divided up into six vilayets without regard for their ethnically mixed populations. Although the elective provincial councils of the Tanzimat remained, they had little significance, caught as they were between Hamidian centralism, Balkan nationalist movements, and the consuls of the powers. Where mid nineteenth-century Turkish statesmen had hoped to reinvigorate Ottoman authority, Abdul Hamid's regime was content to rely on the divisions among its Christian subjects. Still, Turkish liberalism remained weak enough for the sultan to win over some of its leaders in 1897, and the first half of his reign brought the longest period of internal peace that the Ottoman empire had known for more than a century.

In the Balkan states, with their revolutionary origins, sovereigns had to adapt to the elections, parties and ministerial responsibility of constitutional life. This did not come easily to German princes like Charles of Romania (1866–1914), and Alexander von Battenburg (1879–86) and Ferdinand von Coburg of Bulgaria (1887–1918), or to King Milan of Serbia (1868–89) who, though of the native Obrenovic dynasty, had been educated abroad and preferred the life-style of Biarritz to that of Belgrade. Yet unsophisticated societies accorded a charismatic role to their sovereigns – Ferdinand, for one, took care to cultivate an ostentatious etiquette – and this helped rulers to exploit the prerogatives of constitutional monarchy, notably rights of appointment of ministers and dissolution of parliament, in a way unthinkable for a Queen Victoria. The alternation of parties, too, was facilitated by a division between conservatives and liberals which occurred in the ranks of the educated minority in all three countries, with conservatives favouring a cautious paternalism and liberals a rhetorical nationalism. In Romania, where politics remained confined to the landlord class, this alternation became virtually formalized after 1869, with elections not so much inaugurating changes of government as ratifying those which the king had already made, by obliging his new ministers with the necessary parliamentary majority. This pattern was not as easily established in peasant Serbia and Bulgaria where the circulation of elites was from time to time threatened by more democratic forces like the Karavelov left-wing liberals in Bulgaria, or the Serbian Radicals, a genuine mass party attacking the very concept of bureaucracy in the name of local self-government and tax reductions. These had to be dealt with by sterner measures, including the suspension of the Bulgarian constitution in 1881 and the trial of the Radical Party's central committee after a peasant rising two years later. Ultimately, such tactics worked. Radical groupings had tended to split into those who stood by earlier principles and those prepared to conform to the pattern of fluctuating governments and coalitions. Whereas the governing (and royal) party had several times lost elections in Serbia and Bulgaria in the 1870s and early 1880s, by the 1890s party labels veiled faction fights easily manipulated by a resourceful monarch who could even get rid of a strong man, as Ferdinand outmanoeuvred the dictatorial Stambolov in 1894. Administrative harassment of opposition leaders and their press, handpicking of election officials and technical disqualification of opposition voters and MPs assured these results rather than bribery. It was a system suited to the interests of the great powers who preferred to work through monarchs rather than their ministers. Austria's chief contact in Serbia, for instance, was the egregious Milan Obrenovic. Having divorced his wife and abdicated in 1889, with a handsome lump sum for his gambling debts on condition he left the country, Milan blew the lot and wrote to his ex-wife threatening suicide unless she sent him 340,000 dinars (£13,600); she sent him 100,000 dinars whereupon he remarried her (temporarily), later returning to Serbia after a coup and becoming chief of staff to his son, King Alexander.

The techniques which sustained a Milan were less applicable in the Habsburg monarchy where both the German bourgeois liberals in Austria and the Magyar gentry liberals in Hungary were determined to maintain the rights won in 1867. On the other hand, the executive had certain powers of electoral influence in Austria through the *Kaisertreu* – dynastically minded – landlord curia of the parliament, and more in Hungary whose electoral set-up bore some resemblance to that of eighteenth-century England; moreover, neither German nor Magyar liberals wanted a further democratization which would have eroded their positions as dominant minorities in their respective societies. The upshot was that ministries in both countries enjoyed a fair measure of stability and could substantially pursue their own course in internal affairs, even where the emperor had misgivings, as he did over the secularizing tendencies of the liberals in Austria in the 1870s and Hungary in the 1890s. But the line was drawn on matters of the army and foreign affairs, where Franz Joseph zealously upheld his executive powers. When the Hungarian opposition leader Kalman Tisza gave up his call for greater Hungarian constitutional rights and merged his centre-left forces with the Deakist governing party in 1875 (leaving only a Kossuthite 'extreme-left' rump in opposition), his action was an implicit recognition of this balance of power. It also left Magyar politicians free to turn their fire against the non-

Magyar half of the population, whose language rights were curtailed and parliamentary representation reduced to a handful by electoral trickery.

Bismarck, who had emasculated his own liberals, urged Austrian liberals to submit to their fate, but important elements among them were unwilling to bow down to the old absolutist enemy. Their opposition to the Austrian occupation of Bosnia of 1878, essentially an imperial policy, precipitated Franz Joseph's decision to replace a German liberal government with one of Slavs and German clericals, headed by his boyhood friend Count Taaffe. Interestingly, the switch was not as easy for the monarch as it might have been in the Balkans. Franz Joseph would ideally have liked to detach moderates from the German and Slav camps to form a centrist coalition of his own devising, but the German liberals, only slightly reduced at the polls by his displeasure, passed in body into a sulky and potentially destabilizing opposition. However, this antithesis between the liberal opposition and Taaffe's coalition was not acute, for Taaffe's concessions to the Slavs fell far short of federalism and his conservatism involved no more than partial restoration of the gilds and of clerical influence in education. Party politics were also manageable in a Hungary where the opposition concentrated much of its attack on the controversial Army Bill of 1889 on the need to rename joint Austro-Hungarian institutions imperial and royal instead of imperial-royal, thus transforming Hungary's insulting hyphenated status into one of grammatical equality. All in all, the period of Taaffe's government in Austria (1879–93) and Kalman Tisza's in Hungary (1875–90) saw a consolidation of the Dualist system in the monarchy, as of the Bismarckian settlement throughout the region.

The rise of mass nationalism

Of course, the particular social circumstances enabling fairly small groups to dominate constitutional regimes, in conjunction with the monarch, could not be expected to last for ever. Yet what would be the effect of the steady advance of socio-economic change? Would it not sap romantic nationalism more than the state structures which this had hitherto assailed? Many thought so, on right and left. Tsarist agrarian policy in Poland uncharacteristically favoured the peasants in the belief that Polish nationalism was a specifically gentry phenomenon which would wither with the decay of the gentry's land-holding base. The cleverer Hungarian liberals saw industrialization as their chief Magyarizing weapon, for it would draw the most active elements of the peripheral nationalities to the dynamic Budapest region where they could be assimilated, leaving the clerical and small town professional leadership of the minority movements as generals without an army. Meanwhile, the socialist Luxemburg was arguing that the industrialization of Poland bound it to the Russian market and made separation irrelevant, while the founding programme of the Austrian Social Democratic Party in 1889 dismissed the national question in a single sentence:

The Social Democratic Party Workers' Party in Austria is an international party; it condemns the privileges of nations as it does those of birth, possession and origin and declares that the struggle against exploitation must be international as is exploitation itself.

Nor were nationalists lacking who accepted the identification of their creed with social groups threatened by democratization. 'The strength of this nation', cried the Old Czech leader Rieger in opposing a bill for universal suffrage,

rests on the middle class … and these will be deprived of political power because now the weight of the vote will go to the working class and the socialist party, which cares nothing for what will happen to our … historic individuality when given over to elements which are concerned only with filling their stomachs.

Rieger's attitude helps explain the sluggishness of the Czech national movement, which in 1879 abandoned sixteen years of fruitless abstention from the Austrian parliament in return for concessions (a Czech-language university, more official use of Czech and a Czech majority in the Bohemian diet), which went nowhere near its professed goal of restoring a Czech state under the Habsburg sceptre.

Events, however, were to confound the expectations of those who banked on the decline of nationalism. True, the splintering of national movements into a spectrum of class-based parties proceeded apace from the 1890s. Between 1896 and 1904 Bohemia saw the creation of a Czech Social Democratic Party, a Czech Agrarian Party, a Czech National Socialist Party and a Czech Christian Social Party. Socialist and peasant parties appeared in Croatia, among the Poles of Galicia, in Hungary and in Bulgaria, in each case standing to the left of traditional nationalist parties. Yet many (not all) of these new groupings eventually became as absorbed in the national struggle as their conventional nationalist rivals, and the overall tempo of nationalist movements accelerated rather than slackened in the generation before 1914. Why was this so?

Explanation presupposes a theory of nationalism. Whatever a Rieger might have chosen to believe, East European nationalism was not primarily an altruistic devotion to national destiny nor just, as its critics allege, the product of middle-class competition for clerical jobs or markets – a Czech-speaking administration here, a German chamber of commerce there. It was a matter of group dynamics. The strength of the modern nation is to have replaced older ties of kin, locality or caste as the framework of social relations within which men live out their lives. Through its community of language and culture, it determines, in fair measure, what books they read, what historic memories they imbibe, what sporting teams they follow, even, in nationally mixed areas, where they shop and through which institutions they save. Within this complex structure, different men may pursue different goals and interests, but the underlying social linkages make them susceptible to common national appeals when relations with similar group networks are at issue. Not all ethnic groups inevitably achieve this status. If, like the Welsh in Great Britain, they are isolated in a prestigious state, economically peripheral and unable to win a secure role for their language and culture in the schools and public life, then modernization may erode this culture and lead to its displacement as a mobilizing principle by civic or class values based on the larger community. But this is perhaps the exception which proves the rule. Given less heavy odds and, as in the Habsburg monarchy, basic acceptance of mother-tongue education (at least at the primary level for the masses), modernization operated to consolidate national identities. Through multiplying social links on a linguistic basis, it made national frameworks more adequate vehicles for a complex social life and obviated the need for men to break out of a cramping ethnicity into broader German, or Russian or Magyar worlds. Ethnic reading rooms, singing and gymnastic societies led on to ethnic co-operatives, credit associations and banking. By 1900 a Czech could study at university level, attend grand opera and become an entrepreneurial or financial mogul, all within the framework of Czech institutions using the Czech language; migration from a Czech-speaking countryside had made Prague, of which Franz Joseph said as late as 1868 that it had 'an entirely German appearance', the metropolis of an increasingly self-sufficient Czech world. Correspondingly, the need declined for a common Austrianism, transmitting superior culture to the empire's elite through the medium of German. Functional rather than ideological, the result of social evolution as much as of nationalist rhetoric, the 'nationalization' of the peoples of the monarchy was all the easier to underestimate and harder to reverse.

The Czechs were the supreme example of successful nation-building and set a standard for others. Political life was dominated by calls for more national institutions. The Austrian government fell in 1895 on the issue of parallel Slovene gymnasium classes in the largely German town of Celje. In the early twentieth century, the 'university question' became a burning issue in the lives of Austrian Italians, Ruthenians and Slovenes as these peoples demanded the coping-stones of their educational systems. In distant Macedonia the 'metropolitan question' dominated politics as Serbs, Greeks and Bulgars competed to build up national infra-structures in this Turkish province by capturing control of the Orthodox Church, diocese by diocese. Even Albanians began to agitate for Albanian schools, an Albanian Orthodox Church, Albanian newspapers.

It is not easy to convey the flavour of these politics to a modern reader. In one perspective, the age was still unpolitical and ill-informed, with traditional peasant insurrection still dominant over modern political processes over wide areas. 'What's the use', an old peasant told a young emissary of the Croatian Peasant Party, 'a gentleman is a gentleman and a peasant is a peasant.' But on the other hand the intensity of commitment and organization among those who did participate politically outstripped anything in our own affluent society. Politics were both more compelling, because social evils were more potent, more enjoyable because alternative pastimes were less developed, and also easier, because anyone with initiative and a modest capital could found his own political newspaper. In these circumstances, people started young. Supilo, the Croatian editor–politician, had his baptism of fire at 13, leading the shouts against the touring Crown Prince Rudolf; Radic, his compatriot, made his début by burning the Hungarian flag during a royal visit when he was 15. The politics of the class-room were a feature of the age; from the Czech 'youth' movement, repressed in a massive trial in 1893, to the celebrated Polish schoolchildren's strikes against German religious instruction in the 1900s, and the Bosnian movement which culminated in Archduke Franz Ferdinand's assassination by a Serb student in 1914. The element of symbolic protest was duplicated in adulthood in the numerous petitions to monarchs over the heads of their ministers, the boycotting or systematic obstruction of parliaments, the holding of vast public meetings and marches, the periodic issue of manifestos. Yet the obverse of this formal defiance was often tortuous negotiation and elaborate tacticizing, as Czechs were persuaded to give up obstruction in return for a Silesian Czech-language teachers' training college, Serbia switched sides from her Balkan neighbours to Turkey to gain a metropolitan in Macedonia, or Croat politicians veered from an Austrian to a Hungarian orientation to coax out a few more nationalist civil servants. Intrigue and intransigence: these were the twin sides of the coin when national ambitions clashed and constitutional channels were either unavailable or unlikely to avail.

The configuration of nationalist politics, so removed from rationalist visions of social betterment, gave rise, then and later, to the charge that it was an aberration, unrelated to people's wishes and needs. This is dubious. In some areas, notably Macedonia, it is plain that the mass of the population had little interest in the wheeler-dealing conducted in its name. In others – among Bosnian Croats, Silesian Czechs and Kashubian, Mazurian and Silesian Poles – nationalist politicians were only now creating the national consciousness on whose behalf they claimed to speak. However, there was nothing particularly artificial in this process, which followed naturally from the expanding range of the national cultures to which these regional groups were most closely aligned. By the late nineteenth century, the sense of national consciousness was unmistakable in most areas. It matters little whether the nationalism to which this gave rise is viewed functionally, as a matter of group dynamics, or as a quasi-spiritual force; the two interpretations are not incompatible. The important thing is that the national group was increasingly replacing the state or the region as the framework within which life was felt to take place. Where nationality was not bound up with a comprehensive social network it withered, despite patriotic exhortation, as it did among the 100,000 Czechs of Vienna, swamped in a German sea. Where that network existed the nation proved the most powerful of social formations. By 1911 the Czech Social Democratic Party had totally separated from the parent Austrian party, testifying to the victory of national solidarity over class, though the fact that a majority of Moravian Czechs remained in the centralist trade unions shows that the victory was not yet total. Far from eclipsing the national dimension in politics, class issues invested it with an added potency, since the underdog nations came to see their subjection as economic as well as political and cultural. As the nationalism of dominant nations moved to the right, in fear of Slav competition and resentment of Slav 'uppishness' – the Austro-German socialist leader, Adler, once tellingly commented on the Czechs' 'insufferable mania for feeling insulted' – so national alignments took on something of a left–right character. This process was far from clear-cut, for many Slav politicians adopted the social Darwinist power-political categories of their German counterparts or even, like Dmowski, anti-Semitism, but it made nationalism even less tractable. Nothing has so envenomed national relations in the modern world as the conviction of politically weaker nations that they are economically exploited.

All this analysis, however, benefits from hindsight. As they struggled against mounting head-winds from the 1890s on, the dominant elites still seem to have assumed that the old techniques could work, gingered up, here and there, with an attempt to outflank nationalism by reform. Three courses were theoretically open to them – repression, reform and, in Taaffe's phrase, 'muddling through'. The first continued to be applied in Russian and Prussian Poland and in Hungary: it failed. Between 1867 and 1910 the Poles rose in number from 63 per cent to 71 per cent of the population of Poznania, and after 1896 began to record a net gain in land transactions over the Germans. Polish co-operatives, assisted by a bank which offered better interest rates than its German rivals, strengthened inter-class co-operation among the Poles, and the Polish movement spread to previously untouched areas like Upper Silesia where Polish speakers elected Polish MPs instead of German Catholics. The struggle showed that a determined population was stronger than a nineteenth-century state which, however chauvinistic, was still not totalitarian enough to deprive minorities of the rights of press and association. The gap between assimilationist pretensions and practical realities was just as striking in Hungary, where in 1902 an investigator reported that Magyars had actually suffered a net loss of 204 communes to non-Magyars since 1867.

Yet the Hungarian parliament failed to take significant action against the non-Magyar banks and credit co-operatives or (until 1907) non-Magyar denominational schools. All these effectively undermined official Magyarization goals, flourishing in the interstices of society which Magyar capitalism and the Magyar state machine were insufficiently dynamic to penetrate. In 1906, twenty-six minority nationalist MPs were returned to the Budapest parliament, which the minorities had impotently boycotted for a generation.

In Russian Poland, too, economics defeated politics. 'Now for the first time the Poles can be certain that they will become a nation. They have become unconquerable', commented a German historian in 1899 on the economic changes that were diffusing patriotism among the rising middle classes and emancipated peasantry. The 1890s saw, alongside the socialist parties already mentioned in another context (p. 128), the emergence of Dmowski's clandestine National League, an essentially middle-class right of centre movement based on social Darwinist views of the national struggle for existence rather than gentry-style romanticism. When revolution shook the Russian empire in 1905, the ongoing Polish fact was revealed for all to see, in the general strike and insurrectionary calls of the socialists and Dmowski's demand for autonomy under the tsar. His national democrats won all thirty-four seats in the Congress Kingdom in elections to the first Russian parliament – the socialists did not stand. As a pragmatist, Dmowski was prepared to co-operate with Russia, but this sapped his popularity when the tsarist government whittled away the concessions it had made after 1905 and returned to its old ways.

Failing repression, government could essay principled reform. In 1897 the Austrian prime minister, Count Badeni, introduced decrees granting the Czech language equal status with German in Bohemia. Partly a move to get Czech support for immediate political issues, this was also a genuine attempt to heal the wounds inflicted on Czech pride by Dualism. German opposition, inflamed by demagogic journalism and charges that the decrees would deny jobs in Bohemia to Germans ignorant of Czech, spread from Bohemia to all parts of Austria and from liberal and nationalist groups to include the Christian socials, ostensibly a supranational party. Only the German socialists remained aloof from the clamour, and when the government tried to change parliamentary standing orders so as to crush obstruction, they too led the assault (literally!) on the presidium of the chamber which precipitated Badeni's fall and the eventual withdrawal of his decrees. Czech obstruction followed and essential parliamentary business was henceforth carried on largely by emergency decree. After an unsuccessful attempt by Prime Minister Koerber (1900–4) to assuage nationalism by economic measures, Prime Minister Beck grasped the nettle of universal suffrage, which was passed in 1907, with the avowed intention of displacing middle-class nationalists by politicians closer to the real interests of the masses. For reasons outlined above this was not successful and though socialist and Christian social representation increased, the Austrian parliament remained as ungovernable as before.

This semi-paralysis of the Austrian half of the monarchy greatly encouraged Magyar nationalist pretensions, already fostered by economic and cultural progress under Dualism. The Kossuthite Independence Party opposition waxed in strength, inscribing on its banner the principles of a separate Hungarian army and customs tariff. In 1905, with an assortment of aristocratic agrarian allies, the party won a majority in an election which the government had surprisingly refrained from influencing. Some significant change seemed bound to happen. On the one hand, in Croatia Serbs and Croats came together and offered their support to the independence movement against Vienna in return for genuine autonomy, while Serbia stood sympathetically in the wings, thus renewing the radical alignment of the 1860s. On the other, Franz Joseph resisted the threat to his military control by putting in power, not the victorious coalition, but a general who threatened to undermine Magyar hegemony by introducing universal suffrage. Nothing, however, came of any of these moves. The independence coalition responded tepidly to South Slav offers of help and did a deal with Franz Joseph by which it dropped its call for a Hungarian army in return for power; the suffrage proposals became the responsibility of the coalition and were effectively buried. The independence movement proved to have retained all Kossuth's 1848 chauvinism towards the nationalities while abandoning his principled fight against Vienna. Discredited, in 1909 the movement and its allies slid from power, and the supporters of Dualism were reinstated headed by Count Stephen Tisza, Kalman Tisza's son.

Was there a way forward for constructive reform in East-Central Europe before 1914? Non-governmental politicians everywhere called for federalism, as the compromise course between regimes too tenacious to be toppled and national movements too strong to be repressed. Federal schemes varied from the clearly Utopian espousal of Balkan federation by socialist conferences in Belgrade and Sofia (1910), through Dmowski's somewhat optimistic vision of a federal Russia, to detailed projects like the Transylvanian Romanian Popovici's *The United States of Great Austria* (1907) which gained attention because of its reported influence on Franz Ferdinand, the heir to the throne. Most famous of all federal plans was that adopted by the Austrian social democrats at their Brünn congress in 1899, with its devolution of cultural matters and retention of economic control at the centre. Later, the socialists Renner and Bauer tackled the problem of mixed populations by proposing that cultural federation should be personal rather than territorial; wherever they lived, individuals could be registered with their nation and liable to taxation for its cultural needs. But, however ingenious, federalist proposals shared a crucial defect: they were all only *pis allers*, means to an end for their authors. Socialists (except for the separatist Polish Socialist Party, opposed by Rosa Luxemburg) advocated them to clear the decks for the real issue, socialism; nationalists to get the best deal practicable in the circumstances; Catholics as the only way to save Catholic Austria. It is regrettable, but not surprising, that regimes paid them so little attention.

After the failure of 1897 in Austria and 1905 in Poland and Hungary to secure substantial change, things went on as before, only more so. If Tisza now cast aside the last shreds of gentry liberalism when he ringed the Hungarian parliament with troops in order to change the standing orders, and crushed universal suffrage demonstrations in blood (1912–13), Austrian governments, mainly composed of bureaucrats not politicians, preferred to 'muddle through', balancing off clamorous Poles and Ukrainians, Czechs and Germans, Slovenes and Italians in a virtuoso performance without end. Though vastly more civilized, because resting on an efficient and, within limits, humane administration, they resembled Ottoman rule in European Turkey in one respect: both were regimes without a heart, essentially relying on and shaped by the divisions of their subjects.

This may seem harsh. After all, efficient and humane administration is not to be sneezed at. While few have lamented the tsarist or Ottoman empires, many have been found to deplore the passing of the Habsburg monarchy after 1918, to point out how ultimately Magyar nationalism had no stomach for separation, how in 1906 the Czech leader Kramar called a strong Austria 'the best assurance of our nation's future'. But before such statements are taken as evidence that the stalemate in the monarchy was supportable, the nature of that stalemate must be examined. There are indications that the authorities did not exert themselves to the utmost for a settlement between the nationalities because this would make the latter, rather than the emperor and his advisers, arbiters of the state. At least once, Franz Ferdinand opposed a Czech–German compromise in Bohemia because it would have included the abolition of separate representation for landowners, whom he saw as the surest support of the dynasty. Political deadlock in the monarchy, as in the region as a whole, was not due just to the clash of nationalities but to its coexistence with an antiquated social order. This was the real predicament of the East European regimes. Rival nationalisms were counterpoised in seemingly permanent deadlock, but the society with which they were intertwined was not. Lacking a national *raison d'être* governments had not found a social one. They, not the nationalists, would be the victims of social change.

International tensions

Above all, different countries in Eastern Europe could not be considered in isolation. Semi-liberal Austria was indissolubly tied to neo-feudal Hungary, and the fate of the dual monarchy, in turn, was bound up with the state system in the region as a whole, established by a particular conjunction of social and military–diplomatic forces in the 1860s. By the early twentieth century this conjunction no longer held good. The social coalition of ex-feudalists and upper bourgeois was being challenged from below, while Bismarck's stabilizing foreign policy was being abandoned by a German elite eager to shore up its position by nationalist posturing. As a result the parliamentary democracies, Britain and France, were being drawn into conflict with the semi-autocratic Hohenzollern and Habsburg empires, making possible that conjunction of Western liberalism and small nation emancipation that East European patriots had vainly hoped for in the mid nineteenth century. The Czech philosopher–statesman Masaryk reacted to events by revising his inherited Austro-Slavism: 'Unlike Palacky', he wrote, after the war,

I had already reached and expressed the conclusion that if democratic and social movements should gain strength in Europe, we might hope to win independence. . . . It was opposition to Pan-Germanism, to whose ends Vienna and Budapest were subservient that caused me to take part in the Austro-Serb conflict, and, finally, in the World War.

In these circumstances of mounting international tension, the propaganda of Schönerer's Pan-German minority in Austria, for union with the Second Reich, or the annual congresses of Kramar's neo-Slav movement had a significance beyond their strictly limited immediate success or the protestations of loyalty that individuals might make, not necessarily insincerely, in the here and now. The European dimension loomed ever larger. Kramar sought in *La Revue de Paris* in 1899 and the *National Review* in 1902 to alert Anglo-French opinion to the Czechs' value as a barrier against German ambitions to the east. In his *Germany, Russia and the Polish Question*, published in 1908, Dmowski did the same for the Poles. Pan-Germanism's threat to the Adriatic was the chief theme of another social Darwinist, the engineer of the Serbo-Croat coalition, Frano Supilo, who, through contacts with Italian socialists, British publicists and Serbian government ministers, tried to put the Croatian question on the map, as part of a broader Yugoslav question. From 1913 a pro-Anglo-French attitude appeared, too, in the left-wing of the Hungarian Independence Party under its quixotic leader Count Michael Karolyi. The expanding power of Germandom, and Austria's subordination to it in the Austro-German Treaty of 1879: this was the burden of all these critiques. In no area was this Austro-German pressure more feared than the Balkans.

The Balkans had long been Eastern Europe's Achilles heel because the weakness of Turkish rule regularly converted internal grievances into international affairs. The Habsburg administrator of Bosnia once satirized a report he had received from one of his Belgrade agents: 'Great excitement among the population. Jovo has been robbed of two more oxen. What will Europe say to this?' In these lands of 'thieves and murderers and bandits and a few plum-trees', as Franz Ferdinand once elegantly described Serbia, Bismarck's *Realpolitik* never seemed as authoritative as elsewhere. His advice to his Austrian and Russian neighbours to delimit spheres of influence was never, in fact, really accepted by them for, while it gave Bulgaria to Russia and anti-Austrian Serbia and Montenegro to Austria, Macedonia lay awkwardly in the centre of the peninsula. Moreover, confining issues to great powers simplifies diplomacy but does not prevent misunderstandings, as Austria and Russia found in

- ——— boundaries of 1913
- **1878** dates of effective ending of Turkish rule
- territory lost by Turkey as a result of the Balkan Wars 1912-13
- Bessarabia
- Southern Bessarabia (ceded by Russia to Romania, 1856-retroceded by Romania to Russia, 1978
- South Dobrudja (ceded by Bulgaria to Romania, 1913)

CROATIA

HUNGARY

BESSARABIA

MOLDAVIA 1822

ROMANIA
united 1859

BOSNIA
Austrian occupation 1878
Austrian annexation 1908

DALMATIA

Sarajevo

Belgrade

1817

Bucharest

DOBRUDJA 1878

WALLACHIA 1822

Black Sea

S E R B I A

• Nis
1878

1878

1913

1878

Sofia

BULGARIA
1885

MONTENEGRO
effectively independent
since C16th

• Scutari

1913

• Skopje

MACEDONIA

• Adrianople

1913

Constantinople

ALBANIA

Salonika

1913

TURKEY

CORFU
English 1814-63
Greek 1863

G R E E C E

1881

Aegean Sea

• Smyrna

• Athens

1830

Mediterranean Sea

DODECANESE
Italian 1912

CRETE
Greek 1913

0   200
miles

The Balkans, 1815–1914

their differing interpretation of agreements: first in 1876–7 for the Austrian occupation of Bosnia, then in 1908 for its annexation. Even if the respective governments did agree on a conciliatory course, as by and large was the case for a generation after 1878, it was by no means certain that their subordinates would toe the line, in view of the Pan-Slav proclivities of Russian diplomats in the Balkans, including Minister Hartwig in Belgrade in 1914. Besides, the fact that a great power's prestige would be measured by the success of its protégé could be exploited by the latter to make the tail wag the dog; hence the blunt question which Pasic, the Serbian prime minister, put to St Petersburg in 1913, 'Is Russia with its friends stronger or weaker than Austria and its friends?'

But the most dubious aspect of great power *Realpolitik* in the Balkans was the contempt it implied for the Balkan peoples and their capacity for progress. The parlous circumstances of the Balkan states in the 1880s and 1890s improved in the new century. After the murder of the last Obrenovic in 1903, the new king, Peter Karadjordjevic, interfered less in constitutional life. This came to revolve around two genuinely representative parties, the Old and the Independent Radicals, much better able to push for Serbian interests in matters of international railways and access to the Adriatic. Peasant egalitarianism in Serbia and Bulgaria aided national morale in the dawning democratic age. In 1905 the University of Belgrade opened, in 1906 the University of Sofia. The ambitious Ferdinand of Bulgaria dreamed of taking Constantinople and becoming the heir to Byzantium. A Serbo-Bulgarian customs union in 1905 represented a first attempt by Serbia to escape Austrian economic tutelage. Meanwhile, Serbs and Croats were coming together in Croatia, and Serbs were completing a successful campaign for Church and school autonomy in Bosnia.

All this was lost on Austrian statesmen who habitually regarded Serbia as a backward, semi-Oriental satellite. Their inflexibility was also influenced by the rivalry of agrarian producers from Serbia and Hungary in an increasingly competitive market in which the monarchy suffered from the protectionism of its German ally and from Germany's own economic penetration of the Balkans. The upshot was an Austrian demand that the Serbo-Bulgarian customs union should be dropped and that Serbia should transfer her application for a loan and arms from France to herself. When Serbia refused, she found the monarchy's frontiers closed to her chief exports, cattle and pigs. In 1908 Austria annexed Bosnia, finally shattering Serbian hopes of inheritance, and in 1909 set on trial fifty-three members of the Serbo-Croat coalition for treasonous contacts with Serbia. The policy backfired. Serbia emerged from the 'Pig War' economically strengthened, her dependence on the Austrian market gone and her infant industry greatly advanced. In 1911 she formed a Balkan league with her neighbours, which the next year made war on Turkey, independent of the great powers and all but expelled her from Europe. After a further war, this time within the league, because of a Serbo-Bulgarian conflict over the division of Macedonia, Serbia emerged with the lion's share, her territory doubled. The conviction grew in Austrian governing circles that Serbia's pretensions must be checked, and the assassination of Archduke Franz Ferdinand by a Bosnian Serb in Sarajevo in June 1914 afforded the pretext for an ultimatum to Serbia, which in just over a week precipitated world war. Undoubtedly Austria would not have acted thus if Germany, for her own reasons, had not given her blessing.

The Bosnian background threw into exaggerated relief the issues which led the monarchy to this desperate course. The assassin, Princip, was not just a nationalist student but the son of a poor peasant struggling for existence in a province where the old Ottoman semi-serfdom had been maintained by Austria. Yet the education he and similar embittered youths received in Austrian schools was impeccably humanitarian. 'Every friend of healthy national development rejoices when youth is nationally minded, when it has ideals and dreams for these are the most beautiful prerogatives of youth', thus the government chief inspector began a report on disturbances in the Mostar gymnasium in the very month of the assassination. Finally, the Sarajevo assassination revealed both the militant and tactical faces of official nationalism, for Princip's bombs had come from a Serbian general staff officer, but Prime Minister Pasic opposed the plot when he got wind of it and tried unsuccessfully to give Austria warning. Just so was the crumbling of the old order in Eastern Europe. Only a minority may have actively worked for it but if most of the rest are sullenly indifferent, a minority is always enough.

The collapse

The First World War was expected to last a few months and continued for four years, becoming a battle of attrition in which the political, economic and moral resources of the combatants were tested to the uttermost. To the conventional military front was added an 'inner front' in which the issues of the war were fought out in every community, ultimately in every individual heart. Understandably, opinions differ as to whether the true wishes of the region's inhabitants should be measured by their attitude at the outset or the later stages of this gruelling struggle. What is clear is that initially people fell in relatively smoothly behind the flags of their respective governments, but that the flight of important politicians like Masaryk and Supilo to agitate for independence abroad gave notice, from the first months, of underlying complications. Indeed, the war was soon to make the imbroglios of the mid nineteenth century appear positively straightforward. Poles faced a choice between Dmowski's national democratic movement in the ex-Congress Kingdom, which backed Russia, and Pilsudski, the socialist leader who had built up a military following in Galicia to throw into the scales on the side of the central powers. Serbia could follow her traditional Greater Serbian policy or the united Yugoslav line developed by the Serbo-Croat coalition in the monarchy. Romanians and Italians had alliances with the central powers but were tempted to renege on them to satisfy their designs on Transylvania and the Austrian Adriatic respectively. With, in addition, a section of the Czechs looking for independence rather than Austro-Slav federalism, Bulgaria hung between loyalty to Russia and hostility to Serbia, and even the calculations of Russophile and Austrophile Ukrainians now a factor of weight, the Western entente can be forgiven for not immediately grasping the full measure of events. Their promises to Serbia and, conditionally, to the neutral Italy and Romania, involved only chipping away at the Habsburg monarchy's border provinces. There was still little realization that, if the Czech and Yugoslav radicals had their way, the monarchy would cease to exist.

Yet already in the first two years of the war the signs were that alternatives would resolve themselves in favour of maximum nationalist goals. In December 1914 the Serbian government declared itself for Yugoslav unification. Italy and Romania entered the war against their former allies, though these won Bulgaria over with the promise of Serbian Macedonia. In Poland, which was the seat of the Eastern front, caution prevailed longer till Russian defeats persuaded Dmowski to go to the West, and there for the first time, in February 1916, adopt independence rather than autonomy as his programme. For the time being the central powers might have the greater success on the battlefield – with Serbia, Romania and Congress Poland overrun – but in Britain, France and neutral America the nationalist exiles were winning the propaganda war. International celebrities like the Polish pianist Paderewski and Croatian sculptor Mestrovic lent their names to the schemes propounded by Western publicists such as R. W. Seton-Watson in his *New Europe* and Ernest Denis in *La Nation Tchèque*. No concrete promises were made, but France, Italy and Russia permitted the Czech exiles to organize military units out of Czech POWs and the allied peace terms to President Wilson in January 1917 spoke of the liberation of 'the Slavs, Roumanians and Czecho-Slovaks from foreign domination'. By contrast the central powers found peace terms extremely difficult to formulate. Hungary opposed annexation of Serbian territory because it would mean more Slavs, and the attachment of Russian Poland to the Habsburg crown because it would amount to Trialism, just as earlier she had opposed Austrian concessions to keep Italy out of the war since this would encourage Romanian claims. Dualism was revealed to be maddeningly inflexible. Germany also dithered over Russian Poland till, in November 1916, the central powers declared it a Polish puppet state economically and militarily bound to Germany. This action more or less committed the Western powers to the principle of an independent Poland.

Meanwhile, as the Western boycott tightened and living conditions worsened, the inner front grew in importance. Earlier, appearances had belied the exiles' claims that they spoke for populations champing for liberation. The American consul in Prague wrote, in January 1916, that 'life here seems absolutely normal', Russian Poles failed to respond to Pilsudski's legionaries' call to arms. But underlying tendencies were not so favourable to the authorities, even before the February and October revolutions of 1917 in Russia came to stoke up social and democratic aspirations. Government security measures, including the court-marshalling of 5000 Czechs and the internment of 20,000 more, served to remind key groups of their minority status. In 1915 Kramar was arrested and later sentenced to death for high treason. Military jurisdiction in the German language was imposed over wide areas near the front and Galicia had a German instead of a Polish governor for the first time for fifty years. War offered opportunities for the repayment of old scores. King Ferdinand of Bulgaria imprisoned Stambolisky, the outspoken republican peasant leader, and Prince Alexander, regent of Serbia, had a potential rival Apis Dimitrijevic, organizer of Franz Ferdinand's assassination, judicially murdered. For the mass of the population, though, it was war casualties and economic deprivation which counted most. By 1918 Austria–Hungary had mobilized 8.42 million men of whom 2.88 million had been killed, wounded or captured. 700,000 men fought in the colours of little Serbia whose losses through war and disease came to total 750,000 in a population of 4.7 million. Inflation multiplied the average expenditure of a working-class Austrian family fifteenfold; bread rations were successively reduced till they were less than a quarter the pre-war level in Vienna.

At least war's suffering could be alleviated by prospects of a brighter future, as when the Romanian Constituent Assembly, in Moldavian exile, passed a resolution for post-war land reform. No such solace was available, however, in the Habsburg monarchy, where Tisza stubbornly obstructed all attempts to introduce universal suffrage in Hungary. Indeed, for all the Red Cross enthusiasm of titled ladies, the war cruelly exposed the social divisions in the monarchy, with war profiteering and upper class sybaritic living reaching dangerous heights; according to Count Michael Karolyi, who opposed the war, meetings of the Hungarian parliament were timed to coincide with Austro-Hungarian offensives so that gentry officer MPs could exchange the rigours of the front for those of the debating chamber. Trade union membership shot up between 1913 and 1918 from 110,000 to nearly 250,000 in Hungary and 253,000 to 413,000 in German Austria. In January 1918 the monarchy was shaken by massive strikes. In an absorbing study, the Austrian historian Plaschke has discussed almost fifty occasions in 1918 when military units had to be used to restore order inside the monarchy, and eight instances of mutiny in the armed forces, often sparked off by POWs returning from newly Bolshevik Russia. The declaration of Czech and Yugoslav MPs in May 1917, and the Epiphany declaration of the Czechs in 1918 showed a growing tendency towards solidarity with the exiled leaders, for they demanded statehood with increasingly perfunctory reference to the Habsburg framework. Statements of the Hungarian independence opposition and the German-installed Polish state regency council in Warsaw struck similarly bold notes.

Of course, the military outcome remained crucial. It is perfectly possible that, had the central powers won the war or reached a negotiated settlement with their foes, these mutinous symptoms could have been suppressed - for a time. Zeman and Mamatey have emphasized that only after the tightening of the Austro-German military alliance in the summer of 1918 did the Western allies finally give up hope of a separate peace with the Habsburg monarchy and endorse the exiles' plans for its destruction. Yet suggesting in the allies' minds the alternatives of separate peace, or dissolution of the monarchy was a major achievement for the exiles, ultimately, indeed, a decisive one. A separate peace for Austria was just not practicable, as the failure of Emperor Charles's (Franz Joseph's successor from 1916) overtures for that end clearly showed. Small allies like Serbia and Romania which had claims on the monarchy could have been fobbed off, but hardly Italy, at least on any terms that the monarchy would have accepted. Besides, there are signs that Germany would have used coercion to prevent her ally's betrayal. The exiles had backed everything on the theory that Austria and Germany were indissolubly allied and events had proved them right.

The denouement was not far off. In summer 1918 the allies recognized the exiled Czech national council as an embryonic Czech government and approved the Rome congress of nationalities which proclaimed the Yugoslav idea. All now hung on the great German offensive of July. Its failure signalled the end of the war. Bulgaria was the first of the central powers to collapse, on 26 September. On 3 October Germany requested an armistice. It was now too late for the desperate federalist manifesto issued for Austria (Hungary still stayed out) on 16 October. In its death throes the Habsburg government endorsed the American president Woodrow Wilson's principle of national self-determination as the basis of settlement and even appointed Count Karolyi, proponent of full independence, prime minister of Hungary. Its manoeuvres went unregarded in the other centres of the monarchy where national councils declared the adhesion of their territories to new units; the republics of German Austria and Czechoslovakia, greater Romania and the state of Habsburg Serbs, Croats and Slovenes, soon (on 1 December) to be united with the kingdom of Serbia. On 11 November the regency in Warsaw transferred control over the resurrected Polish state to Marshal Pilsudski. On the same day the Emperor Charles, last ruling Habsburg, formally relinquished his powers.

Not all the tendencies jostling in the complex world of East-Central Europe before 1914 can be related to the national question, nor is the latter reducible to a crude opposition between oppressive regimes and awakening peoples. Awareness of this complexity accounts for the calls of so many contemporary observers for democratization and federalization, to provide a sophisticated framework within which different forces could find freest play. Unfortunately, political systems are stubborn growths unresponsive to rational persuasion. Shaped initially perhaps by a genuine balance of forces, they are rapidly encrusted by a shield of prejudice and vested interest penetrable all too often only by revolution or war, both blunt instruments for the solution of social problems. Once the existing system was really called in question in Eastern Europe during the First World War, only nationalism had a magnetism strong enough to draw the dislocated elements into an alternative political order - the pattern of nation states. When the chips were down, as in British general elections, people had to choose between one package and another. The choice was not, as later apologists of the Habsburg monarchy (the linchpin of the system) have tried to make out, between nationalism and internationalism. What the regimes offered ultimately was only a reaffirmation of traditional authority and traditional loyalty. 'The views of politicians, opinions about rights to be granted or states to be formed are irrelevant to our forces whose sole concern is to be ready at every opportunity to weaken the foe', laid down the Habsburg naval commander in January 1918. This sort of thing made almost all nationalism appear democratic and socially progressive. Sensing their ideological vulnerability, pre-war statesmen of the *status quo* had felt impelled to try to scotch the nationalist snake, and had only provoked it to deadly effect. The words of Count Czernin, foreign minister under Emperor Charles, are still the fittest commentary on the passing of the old order: 'We had to die. We were at liberty to choose the manner of our death, and we chose the most terrible'.

7 Independent Eastern Europe

The years from 1918–39 are unique in the modern history of Eastern Europe. For the only time since the Middle Ages the nationalities of the region enjoyed a genuine autonomy and, ostensibly, a common form of government with their Western neighbours. As democratic nation states replaced the semi-autocratic empires, the way was clear in the ideology of the victors for the energies of repressed populations to find fulfillment in harmonious alliance with the Western democracies. So strongly felt was this nexus between nationalism and democracy, between East and West in the 'New Europe' that, to its supporters like the Czech President-Liberator, Masaryk, the settlement appeared to be not so much the fruit of military victory as of an entire epoch of European progress; it was the culmination of the search for humanity begun in the Renaissance and Reformation and continued in the eighteenth century Enlightenment and the liberal national movements of the nineteenth century. Yet two brief decades after Masaryk's memoirs Winston Churchill wrote in his account of the Second World War.

there is not one of the peoples or provinces that constituted the Empire of the Habsburgs to whom gaining their independence has not brought the torture which ancient poets and theologians had reserved for the damned.

Separating the two comments was the most dramatic collapse of a major peace settlement and its attendant hopes in modern times.

Essentially the 'succession states', as the new states were called, rested on the ambiguity Masaryk had sought to scotch. They were the product of both power and principle, of a particular conjunction of interests between nationalist movements in the region and the need of the allies to destroy Germany's Habsburg partner and create buffer states on her eastern frontiers after the collapse of tsarist Russia. Their emergence represented the triumph of certain nations over others and of nationalism over rival social philosophies which had also been influential before 1914. True, nationalism had been the strongest of these pre-war tendencies but its satisfaction could not simply be equated with the triumph of Masaryk's humanist democracy, except perhaps in his own developed society where a sophisticated national consciousness had become deeply impregnated with popular democratic aspirations. Elsewhere nationalist leaders were rarely so high-minded, and political freedom was but a tentative first step to the democratization of their sluggish societies. It proved a mixed blessing for inter-war Eastern Europe that its most eloquent protagonists were idealistic westerners and Czechs. The gap between ideals and reality was to breed disillusionment and help weaken the ties with the democratic West on whose continued support the new order ultimately depended.

The peace settlement

The difficulties ahead were amply portended during the finalization of the settlement itself. The old regimes were succeeded by a medley of competing provisional administrations. Zones of friction emerged almost immediately in the outer rim of Bohemia–Moravia, in Upper Silesia, in the vast Russo-Polish borderlands, in Transylvania, Slovakia and the Banat and in Istria and the hinterland of Trieste. In the chaotic flow of events, force proved a more effective arbiter than resolutions and this tended to be with the previously subordinate nationalities. In December 1918 Czech troops, organized out of the old Habsburg army, ex-legionaries and Czech gymnastic associations, marched into German Bohemia or the Sudetenland as it came to be known; on 4 March 1919 they shot dead fifty-four demonstrating Sudeten Germans. In the same month an allied military ultimatum to the Hungarians shifting the armistice lines in Romania's favour, caused the collapse of the left-of-centre Karolyi government. Although the Hungarians organized an army strong enough to regain some of their old territories for a spell, they could not prevent a Romanian occupation of Budapest in August 1919. Only where Western allied influence was weak, as in the Polish–Russian borderlands did rival factions of Bolsheviks, Lithuanians, White Russians, Ukrainians and Poles continue to keep the future territorial pattern in the balance.

Much of the final settlement had thus been rather roughly preempted, *de facto* if not *de jure*, before the peace conference concluded its labours in June 1919. This was the inevitable

Eastern Europe between the Wars

consequence of the allies' promises to Italy and Romania and to the Czechoslovak and Yugoslav *émigrés* during the war. What remained for negotiation was a whole range of important detail on which the defeated powers still hoped for a genuine application of Wilsonian national self-determination so that the more extreme claims of the succession states could be cut down to size. It was not in human nature for these claims to be moderate. For the Czechoslovaks Benes demanded all Bohemia–Moravia–Silesia on grounds of historic right – though Masaryk had opposed such arguments before the war. He wanted a corridor across former Hungarian territory to link up with Yugoslavia, and Upper Hungary far beyond the ethnic limits of the Slovaks, to provide the new Slovakia with means of lateral communication where the Slovak-inhabited valleys debouched on to the Magyar plain. Similarly, Yugoslavia demanded Magyar Szabadka (Subotica) to push her northern frontier strategically clear of Belgrade, and Romania claimed Arad, Temesvar (Timisoara) and Szatmarnemeti (Satu Mare) to provide the railway link along her new western borders. German Danzig was to be Polish to give the Poles a Baltic port, Slav Fiume and Dalmatia should fall to Italy to make the Adriatic an Italian lake and, for the sake of a strategic frontier on the Brenner Pass, 250,000 Austro-German Tyroleans should be severed from their motherland. Opposing plebiscites, Bratianu, leader of the Romanian delegation, stated openly that 'Romania had fought to impose her national will on the Hungarian minority in Transylvania'.

In the debates on these claims among the great powers Frenchmen proved most and Americans least willing to sacrifice self-determination in favour of economically and strategically viable succession states able to fulfil an anti-German role; the British tended to a middle line except over Poland, where Lloyd-George outdid Wilson in insisting on concessions to the Germans to keep these potential trading partners out of the Bolshevik camp. Since French will proved stronger than American, the horse-trading process favoured the succession states on all but their most extreme claims. 1.25 million Germans were incorporated into Poland, 3.25 million Germans and 700,000 Magyars fell to Czechoslovakia, 1.75 million Magyars to Romania, and 500,000 Magyars to Yugoslavia. In all, Hungary lost two-thirds of its territory and three-fifths of its population. Yet several important issues were resolved only after the conference broke up, either by plebiscite as in Upper Silesia, inter-state negotiation as in the Italo-Yugoslav Adriatic dispute, force in Teschen and the Russo-Polish borderlands or, as in the case of the Austro-Hungarian frontier, a combination of all three.

No doubt such a vast reorganization could not have been accomplished without untidinesses, often made quite unavoidable by the large number of language islands in the region. Nonetheless, the range of ethnic problems created by the settlement of 1919 is daunting. It was not just a question of the extensive minorities in the new states owing allegiance to what came to the so-called 'revisionist' powers, which sought to undo the treaty terms. There were also the tensions between victorious states like Yugoslavia and Italy in the Adriatic and Czechoslovakia and Poland over the latter's claim to the mining town of Teschen. Then came the uneasy relations inside the new states between ostensible partners, like the Czechs and the Slovaks in Czechoslovakia and the Serbs and Croats in Yugoslavia. Although the Slovak Protestant minority and the Croat bourgeois parties favoured the broader link, the leaders of the parties destined for greatest popularity between the wars, Father Hlinka of the Slovak People's Party and Stjepan Radic of the Croatian Peasant Party were both interned in 1919; the former because he petitioned the peace conference for autonomy, the latter because he attempted to do so. The ethnic settlement left many hostages to fortune.

Just as 'self-determination' discounted the reactions of Slovak and Croat peasants, so it appeared irrelevant to the social turbulence of the aftermath of war. The collapse of traditional authority, near starvation after years of blockade and an economy in which everything was at a standstill except inflation, made social democracy the most powerful party in the German–Austrian Republic, in Bohemia, in Poland and in Count Karolyi's coalition government. Prisoners of war returning from Russia, often with a training as Bolshevik propagandists, brought tales of a workers' state. In November 1918 the Hungarian Communist Party was founded, with an ex-POW, Bela Kun, as leader. By dint of intensive campaigning against social democratic participation in the coalition government the Hungarian Bolsheviks gained sufficient support to spearhead a communist–social democrat government after Karolyi fell from power. Although they never exceeded 10 per cent of the social democratic membership, they were the driving force in a remarkable four month social experiment, which saw massive nationalization of industry, collectivization of the peasants, an assault on religion and the formation of a Red Army which fought successfully for a while in Slovakia and set up a Soviet regime there, inspired as much by nationalism as socialism. But the collectivist and atheist policies of Bela Kun's regime made it bitterly unpopular in the countryside, and it failed to provoke a communist coup against the social democratic leadership in Austria, thereby broadening its base. Only aid from Russia could have sustained Bela Kun against the eventual entente-backed Romanian invasion, and Russia was still locked in civil war.

However, the Russian Bolsheviks' final victory a few months later opened up another front in the Russo-Poland borderlands. Suspecting, with some reason, that the Bolsheviks would never willingly accept his vision of a great power – Poland in dominant partnership with the White Russians and Ukrainians, Poland's new strong man, Pilsudski, marched into the Russian Ukraine in spring 1920. Lenin responded to Pilsudski's fears by ordering a counterattack into the heart of Poland and setting up a political-revolutionary committee of Polish communists to take over the Polish government. The rout of the Red Army before Warsaw frustrated this plan and ensured that the Russo-Polish border was fixed well to the east of the Polish ethnic frontier, confirming Russia's status as a revisionist power – she had already forfeited Bessarabia to Romania.

Memories of these events lived on in inter-war Eastern Europe. Bela Kun's failure was reflected in at least eleven of Lenin's twenty-one theses on admission to the Communist International which became the touchstone over which the socialist parties of Europe split into communist or reformist wings. Meanwhile, the success of the communists in coming second in the Bulgarian elections of 1919 and third in the Yugoslav elections of 1920 showed how the radical tradition of the Balkans was already forging beyond national liberation. Even in Czechoslovakia the communists' lukewarm attitude to the new national state did not prevent them capturing the majority of the MPs of the old Social Democratic Party. President Masaryk promptly ordered the police to eject communists from the social democratic publishing premises and restore them to the moderates. The Democratic Party minister of the interior in Yugoslavia went one better by proscribing the Communist Party altogether. Liberal democracy, begotten by force, was willing to defend itself by the same means.

Convulsions, in the circumstances, were inevitable. The question was whether the difficulties the new regimes faced in 1919–20 were teething troubles or something more. Had eastern Europe finally achieved integration with the admired societies of the West, or was its transformation a premature and risky experiment? Only the experience of more settled times could answer fairly.

The new democracy and its problems

To contemporaries the supersession of the old ruling classes through so much of the region seemed like grounds for optimism. Masaryk was the son of an ex-serf. The Austrian socialist and clerical prime ministers, Renner and Dolfuss, were peasant sons, as was the Bulgarian agrarian prime minister, Stambolisky. Small town lawyers or doctors like the Transylvanians, Maniu and Vaida Voevod, or parish priests like the Slovene, Korosec, who had spent lifetimes battling for the rights of despised minorities, found themselves elevated to the premiership of large and populous states. These men held a variety of creeds – liberal nationalist, peasantist, socialist or clerical – but in one thing they were united; all professed belief in the people as the source of the values they cherished. Eastern European democracy was no mirage, but it took a distinctive form; it was above all populist, moulded still by the romantic image of the common folk which had first stirred languishing societies a century before. Hence it was also intensely national in tone, bolstering its democratic principles with an almost mystical faith in the sore-tried and now ultimately triumphant Serb, Romanian, Czech as the case might be.

In this broadly defined camp three elements could be made out. The old guard of the nationalist movements, represented by the Young Czech Kramar, the Polish National Democrat Dmowski, the Romanian Liberal Bratianu, and the Serb Radical Pasic, still held great power. Once the radical expression of an emergent bourgeoise or peasantry, their parties had grown over the pre-war decades into practised exponents of a maturing capitalism or an expanding state machine. Regardless of labels, the term National Democrat, formally adopted by Kramar also after the war, aptly pinpointed the decidely bourgeois, centralist and conservative tendency of their ageing leaders, who after 1919 sought only to safeguard the national gains achieved with a lifetime's toil. But in so far as the successes of 1918 appeared to vindicate these struggles, they recalled the parties' original inspiration and made it easy to overlook the extent to which this had changed.

Moreover, new elements were coming to the fore and it is a natural human tendency to assume that what is new will inherit the future. In these new forces the democratic sap still flowed vigorously and the nation state was seen as its expression, a means to popular advancement rather than an abstract ideal. Masaryk's star rose above Kramar's in Czechoslovakia and the relation of the pre-war socialist, Pilsudski, to Dmowski tended to be seen in the same light in Poland. In Romania and Yugoslavia the former repressed Habsburg communities retained a lively sensitivity to democratic rights which found expression in the Transylvanian National Party and the Yugoslav Democratic Party, the latter grouping together Pasic's Independent Radical opponents in Serbia and the former Serbo-Croat coalition. Meanwhile the more conservative bourgeois parties in Bulgaria appeared discredited by the defeat of their pro-German cause in the war. Even in Albania the Harvard-educated Fan Noli stood for a classic Western democracy.

Alongside radical democrats the new situation brought to prominence peasantist parties which before 1914 had either not existed or had been denied influence by a limited franchise. These movements held heady ideas about the unique virtues of Eastern Europe's distinctive peasant societies; often their ideology had a traditional Christian tinge in contrast to secular democracy, particularly in parties which were not formally peasantist but which came to make their basic appeal to peasants, like the Austrian Christian Social Party and the People's Parties of Slovenia and Slovakia. Yet their argument that society should be ruled in the interests of the peasant majority and the fact that some of their leaders were intellectuals, drawn to the cause out of humane commitment to the masses, like middle-class socialists in the West, brought them closer to the mainstream of liberal democratic thought than at first appeared. Even the Austrian Christian Social Party, Franz Ferdinand's old ally, bowed to the democratic tide when Monsignor Seipel persuaded it that nothing in Catholic teaching opposed the recognition of a republic.

So, at least, contemporary optimists could interpret the situation. To all appearances, liberal democracy had a clear and comprehensive programme. Politically, it stood for the introduction of the full paraphernalia of parliamentary democracy; socially, it entailed far-reaching land reform, the expropriation and repartition of large estates among the peasantry; economically, its goal was a measure of industrialization to bring Eastern Europe more closely into line with the Western model; and finally, in the diplomatic sphere, liberal democrats hoped to seal their triumph by a network of alliances among themselves and with the entente.

The first two items were settled relatively quickly. Land reform legislation was a first priority, though detailed enactment, as in Yugoslavia, might be delayed. In the meantime, however, peasants effectively farmed the land intended for them, while the state provided the nominal landlords with the rent. These arrangements were sufficient to their purpose of quietening unrest on the land. Only in Hungary as the old gentry and magnate groups regained their hold did the initial promises go largely unkept, and to a lesser extent in Poland; in Romania 40 per cent of arable land was redistributed, in Yugoslavia a quarter.

Political democracy was affirmed in constitutions promulgated in 1920 in Czechoslovakia, 1921 in Poland and Yugoslavia and 1923 in Rumania. All these constitutions came into existence without the participation of ethnic minorities and even sections of the allegedly state-building nationalities, like the Croatian Peasant Party and the Transylvanian Romanians, who abstained in protest against centralism. Yet this centralism does not seem quite to merit the censure of the historians. It was based on the French model established under the Jacobins with the cry of 'La Patrie en danger', allied to Mazzini's critique of federalism as a timid dis-avowal of democracy's transforming power. Certainly the leaders of the traditional Croatian parties freely acquiesced in Croatia's rapid union with Serbia out of fear of Italian designs, and undoubted democrats like the Croatian Serb Pribicevic embraced centralism enthusiastically. Disturbing signs, however, were the refusal to make German a second state language in Czechoslovakia and the prerogatives preserved to royalty in Yugoslavia and Romania. By contrast, the Polish presidency was given few powers for fear of Pilsudski's dominant personality.

In 1920 the Czechoslovak foreign minister, Benes, claimed that the Czechs had had a measure of political freedom before 1914; what they had fought for was economic freedom. These words had an ironic echo. Agricultural and industrial production everywhere stood at a fraction of pre-war levels, livestock had been decimated and railway stock severely depleted, currencies were depreciating at record speeds, international trade was nugatory. To these consequences of the war were added those of the peace, the virtual destruction of the great Viennese capital market, the severing of previous economic units and yoking together of formerly disparate zones. Poland had inherited three railway systems with separate gauges and 160 different kinds of engine; only 7–8 per cent of her pre-war trade had been between her three territories.

Nonetheless, the politicians of the succession states were not dismayed, certainly not by the plight of 'parasitic' Vienna, which Czechoslovakia starved of coal. Economic nationalism was at a premium. Prestige led the emergent states to set their new post-inflation currencies at higher rates than pure economics would have warranted, which caused some hardship in Czechoslovakia, more in Romania and disaster in Poland. Clauses in the peace treaties permitting Austria, Hungary and Czechoslovakia to establish mutually preferential tariffs for five years were not taken up, but there was vigorous, if patchy implementation of treaty powers to liquidate German and Austrian economic interests in the succession states – 'nostrification'. The agrarian reforms played a similar role in that the expropriated estates were very often Austro-German or Magyar properties. Having righted history's wrongs, the new states, and their defeated rivals, proceeded to claw their way back to economic viability through import quotas, exchange control and state-subsidized dumping of exports, often developing products mainly imported previously, as Austria did with sugar and wheat. Romania under the liberals became the exemplar of 'through ourselves'. It was the state's function, wrote Duca in *The Liberal State* in 1924, to assist Romanian society in making good its backwardness *vis-à-vis* Western liberal societies. Even the complex oil industry was to be Romanianized in its share capital and directors' boards.

Given extensive protection and the natural pick-up of economic activity after the end of wartime stagnation, it is not surprising that industrial recovery did take place in the first post-war decade. Industrial production rose from around one third of the pre-war level in 1919, almost to equal it by 1926, and exceeded it in every East European country but Poland by 1929 – by a margin varying from 72 per cent in Czechoslovakia to 12 per cent in Hungary. Yet this progress had sharp limitations. The rate of increase of production was well below early twenteith century levels, and this was paralleled by consistently higher interest rates, lower profits and lower savings than in the pre-war years. Eastern European statesmen had assumed that the world economy would continue to expand at its old pace and that the protectionism in which they themselves so enthusiastically engaged would soon yield to a climate of freer trade. In fact, economic liberalism faltered just when political liberalism appeared to have triumphed. The great nineteenth-century breakthroughs in industrial technique had run their course; those of the twentieth century filtered only slowly from the New World – not that industrial rationalization would have availed much anyway. Before the Second World War, the United States had 205 motorcars per 1000 inhabitants, Britain 45, Czechoslovakia 8 and Poland 0.7: yet the length of Polish railways only increased from 15,800 to 18,300 kilometres in this period, half the West European density.

Far from becoming independent economic units in their own right the states of the region merely exchanged the tutelage of Austro-German capital for that of Western Europe and America. This was the real significance of nostrification in certain key industries, even for advanced Czechoslovakia. Thus of the Big Three firms which dominated Czechoslovak heavy industry between the wars, one passed from the Viennese to the London Rothschilds, another from Austrian control to French, and the third and weakest eventually fell under preponderant German influence. The dependence of Eastern Europe upon foreign capital and loans increased in the 1920s. 60 per cent of Polish capital was foreign in 1928, including 40 per cent in industry; the figures for Hungary were 50 per cent and 25 per cent. In the Balkans 50–70 per cent of the economy was foreign financed, and government securities almost entirely. Perhaps the most interesting feature of loans policy was the way it mirrored political concerns. Germany, Austria and Hungary were all baled out in return for promises to eschew agitation for 'revision' of the 1919 territorial settlement. Predictable though this condition was, it conflicted with liberal economic principles which posited the emancipation of economic processes from political control and the triumph of liberalism through the sheer efficiency of free economic systems. Independent Eastern Europe's precarious economic recovery in the 1920s did not follow this route but depended at every point on support from the political forces which had created it.

Thus real security for the new order could come only from a relaxation of international tension. In theory this was the task of the League of Nations as envisaged at Versailles. In practice, doubts about the 'Geneva spirit's' power to dispel aggression rehabilitated the pre-war regional alliances which the League's covenant had been intended to displace. Czechoslovakia, Romania and Yugoslavia banded together in the Little Entente in 1920–1 and later individually concluded treaties with France between 1924 and 1927. Yet the Little Entente was not extended to include the largest of the succession states, Poland, because it was primarily directed against Hungarian revisionism which did not affect Poland; mutual Czecho-Polish dislike also played a part, stoked by Teschen and the conviction each held that the frontiers of the other were in the long run untenable. When East European states themselves doubted each other's viability it is not surprising that, in the famous Locarno Treaties of 1925, Britain was only prepared to guarantee Germany's western but not her eastern frontier. Locarno, the high-point of *détente* in the 1920s which led to Germany's entry into the League of Nations, therefore confirmed the provisionality of the East European settlement and the continuing split between the policies of Britain and France. Since diplomacy had not closed the door Germans could hope that, with the return to normality, their economic power would open it still wider. 'For the Succession States of the former Austro-Hungarian Monarchy', wrote the German minister in Bucharest in 1928, 'the impulse towards the German language, economy and culture bears the character of a geographic-historical necessity.' The same concept of historic necessity appeared in Benes's remarks to the French ambassador a year earlier following the entry of two Sudeten German ministers into the Czech government. Observing that despite this development the Sudeten Germans must be considered enemies of the Czech state in any serious crisis, Benes commented that, 'a constant and unvarying line of policy' towards them was impossible in a parliamentary democracy but that, 'the conditions of our national development and the course of our internal life' would probably force the Czechs to impose alternately hard and soft policies on their minorities. These two statements show how little either side assumed the verdict of 1919 had become definitive almost a decade later.

However conditional the economic and diplomatic stability of the 1920s, it did provide a framework in which East European countries could put their democratic professions to the test. Two countries may be expected from this judgement, Hungary because its leaders repudiated democracy from the start, Albania because its few democrats faced well-nigh insurmountable odds. In the former country the collapse of Bela Kun's regime was followed by the restoration of upper-class government as before 1914. The discrediting of the left, the absence of a real peasant party and the weakness of democratic traditions in the middle class made it relatively easy for the skilful Count Bethlen to build up a majority government party, coalescing the conservative pro-Habsburg legitimists and the gentry-style free electors who favoured a Hungarian King. Peasantist elements were fobbed off with a sham land reform which transferred 1.5 million acres of poorish land to some 700,000 recipients, who became hopelessly impoverished dwarf-holders. The socialists also came to an agreement with Bethlen to abstain from agitation among farm labourers or public employees in return for freedom of trade union organization and the socialist press. In 1922 Bethlen heightened the impression of *déjà vu* by restoring the limited franchise and open voting in the countryside. What could not be so easily restored was Magyar dominion over the 10 million non-Magyars of 'historic Hungary,' but the urge to achieve this, too, became the leitmotiv of all Hungarian policy and a convenient distraction from domestic reform.

Albania was a small, mountainous country of 10,500 square miles and a million inhabitants, divided between tribal Ghegs in the north and semi-feudally organized southern Tosks. Not till 1908 had it acquired an agreed alphabet of its own. In 1924 the six-month government of the democrat, Fan Noli, fell after promising various reforms, including land reform, which it then failed to implement. It was succeeded by the most competent of the clan chieftains, Ahmed Zogu, who in 1928 assumed the title of 'Zog I, king of the Albanians' and pursued a shrewd policy of persecuting brigands and courting Italy, the only power willing, for her own purposes, to provide subsidies.

In all other countries of the region democracy was attempted but had generally encountered substantial difficulties by 1929. The sheer complexity of the new states was an obvious factor. The national homogeneity and simple two-party systems of pre-war Romania and Serbia vanished in the new multi-national states of 120,000 and 90,000 square miles respectively, in which Romanians were 70 per cent and Serbs only 43 per cent of the total population. This new situation frightened inherited ruling circles. In 1920 King Ferdinand arbitrarily dismissed the opening government of peasantists and Transylvanian nationalists because of its decentralist tendencies and the Croatian Peasant Party suffered administrative harrassment in the early years of the Yugoslav state. Thereafter, in conjunction with Bratianu, the liberal strong man, Ferdinand resumed the pre-war royal practice of manipulating elections; the liberals won 260 seats in 1922, sixteen when they chose to retire temporarily in 1926 and 298 when they resumed office in 1927. In comparison the Yugoslav estimate, that the party organizing the elections could expect to benefit by some twenty-five seats, makes the system in that country appear positively sporting. Here, too, however, King Alexander played a dubious role, delaying the appointment of a Democrat government in 1924 although it was obvious the Democrat leader had a parliamentary majority because of Croatian support, then dismissing this government as soon as possible and entrusting elections to the Radicals.

One result of these tactics was to push sincere democrats into united opposition so as to recreate the possibility of a two-party system. This occurred in Romania when the Peasant Party and the National Party of Transylvania united in 1926 to form the National Peasant Party as a credible alternative to the liberals; it became a possibility in Yugoslavia after former Habsburg Serbs formed the Independent Democratic Party and allied with the Croatian peasantists. But the Democrats of old Serbia declined to strengthen this opposition and stalemate ensued; it was broken when the peasantist leader and two other Croat MPs were assassinated by a Montenegrin deputy in full parliamentary session. King Alexander responded in January 1929 by abolishing all parties and declaring a royal dictatorship. In Romania the National Peasant Party did sweep to power with 324 seats to the liberals' thirteen in a free election in 1928, but their ministry was a disappointment because of its failure to act effectively on rural credit and agricultural co-operatives for their peasant constituents. They fell from power shortly after their leader, Maniu, resigned because he objected to King Carol installing his mistress in the royal palace.

Poland also inherited disparate regions and diverse political traditions. The kaleidoscope of parties thrown up by proportional representation – and only roughly classifiable into four blocks of right, left, centre and the national minorities – was offered to a population unused to the compromises and responsibilities of government. In 1922 the president was assassinated by a nationalist extremist because he had been elected with the votes of the national minorities. By May 1926 fourteen ministries and successive economic crises had taken their toll and the attempt to form a new centre-right government, though justified by parliamentary arithmetic, provoked a coup led by Pilsudski and backed by the left. But Pilsudski had by this time divested himself of his socialist commitment and moved towards a regime of semi-dictatorship, accelerated by the imprisonment of some eighty MPs of the centre-left opposition in 1930.

Technically speaking, parliamentary democracy requires the representation of interests and the construction of majorities. The experience of Romania, Yugoslavia and Poland in the 1920s suggests that, when diverse territories with different historical and social patterns are thrown together, as so often in the post-imperial states of the modern world, the number of interests in the system becomes too great, the process of negotiating a majority too complex and the opportunities for breakdown too frequent for successful functioning. Thus technical and sociological factors interact to incline the modern commentator to pessimism about the prospects of democracy in such societies. The argument is persuasive but perhaps not quite complete. The technical requirements of parliamentary government in Yugoslavia and Romania in the 1920s did eventually throw up combinations which plausibly represented the best hopes for those countries. Although these combinations should not be overestimated, as Maniu's relative failure shows, the reluctance of ultra-conservative factors to accept their legitimacy contributed just as much to their unfruitfulness as any unsuitability of democracy as such. Ideological or purely personal factors, in other words, can be as important in the fate of a democracy as objective technical and social constraints.

The experience of inter-war Bulgaria and Austria tends to confirm this view. These were both small and socially straightforward societies with fairly egalitarian and well-organized peasantries sharply distinct from an urban population. The issue of Anschluss to Germany in Austria and the Macedonian question in Bulgaria were the only further complications. The resultant party system in Austria was extremely simple, just the social democrats predominant in the towns, the Christian Social Party in the countryside and a smaller, middle-class Pan-German Party. Bulgarian politics, because based on personalities, were superficially involved, but boiled down eventually to the Agrarian Union, a bourgeois democratic block, and the communists and socialists.

The political convulsions in these two societies, therefore, seem to have been more the product of ideological heat than sociological necessity. Stambolisky, the Bulgarian agrarian leader, elected prime minister with a relative plurality in 1919, nurtured dreams of peasant hegemony. His challenge to the status of the urban professional classes, through increased taxation, educational changes and compulsory labour service for the under 40s, no doubt stirred the social balance even in egalitarian Bulgaria, but he need not have come undone if he had not recklessly intimidated his opponents and carried through a semi-authoritarian election. In 1923 he was assassinated in a coup organized by bourgeois circles and nationalistic army officers, to be succeeded by a bourgeois block, the dubiously named Democratic Concord. Striking personalities also dominated Austrian politics in the 1920s, the totally dissimilar Christian social leader, Monsignor Seipel, and the social democrat, Otto Bauer. The first was an ascetic Catholic monk who had written a thesis on the social ethics of the Church Fathers, and had never read Marx. The second was a Viennese Jew and inveterate Marxist dialectician, the leader of the Austro-Marxist school which claimed a central position between the Bolshevik revolutionaries and the social democratic reformists of the West. Neither man helped bridge the undoubted gulf between the pious Alpine peasantry and 'Red' Vienna or dispel the dangers implicit in the existence of Pan-German and socialist paramilitary organizations. Bauer's rather otiose enumeration of the conditions on which his party would defend itself by force at the Linz Congress of 1926 was followed by the shooting of fifty-seven demonstrating workers outside the palace of justice in 1927, which Chancellor Seipel unbendingly justified. Seipel thereafter moved towards the Pan-Germans and visions of 'true' democracy where factious parties would be replaced by organic estates and a strengthened presidency would counteract the damage done by crude counting of heads. He died in 1932 a bitter man, apparently murmuring, 'One must shoot, shoot, shoot' of the enemies of the Church; such a spirit had already soured Austrian democracy.

Why, then, did Czechoslovakia maintain an unquestioned democracy through this period? Czechoslovakian society was as complex as Yugoslav or Polish and on no higher a cultural plane than Austrian. Its cohesion was not just due to its social development but to its ideological conditioning by the national sentiment which united Czech people and was in turn associated with democratic institutions for which nineteenth-century Czechs had fought. The

Agrarian Party, the organ of prosperous farmers and their contacts in the towns, played the mediating role lacking in Poland between the national democrats on the right and the social democrats on the left, becoming the nucleus of the Petka or permanent governing coalition of the five major parties. The stability afforded by this system encouraged participation by the minorities and made this participation appear less frightening to the Czechs. In the late 1920s Sudeten German agrarians, Christian socials and social democrats all entered the Czechoslovak government and their parties captured fifty-one of the sixty-five German seats in the elections of 1929.

The distinction drawn in the last few pages between objective hindrances to democracy and the problems caused by subjective perceptions is no doubt over-subtle. As has been argued earlier (see Chapter 5, p. 131), the baneful plethora of mutually hostile historical and intellectual traditions which weighed upon the region was itself a product of socio-economic backwardness. The prejudices, fears and suspiciousness of so many East European politicians did not proceed just from a personal 'lack of moral fibre'. Nonetheless, the isolation of the subjective factor serves to remind us that developing regions, alongside concrete reforms, need, above all, time in which to digest their complex heritage. Stability is the fruit of custom, familiarity and trust, which develop only gradually even in favourable circumstances. In so far as our survey emphasizes this point, it emphasizes also the importance of the will of the great powers, for as long as they chose to uphold the settlement they had forged, it had a future.

The alternatives to liberal democracy

It was precisely time which was to be denied. In 1929 depression brought on by falling grain prices hit the New York stock exchange and was passed on to America's European debtors as loan capital was withdrawn. In the crisis years that followed agricultural income decreased by between 50 per cent and 60 per cent in Poland, Romania and Bulgaria and by 36 per cent in Hungary. Industrial output fell badly, the more sharply the more developed the economy, by 11 per cent in Romania and 40 per cent in Austria and Czechoslovakia. Eastern Europe's export income sank to two-fifths of the pre-crisis level and inability to fund foreign debt rose accordingly. Within months of the failure of the prestigious Austrian

Creditanstalt in 1931, all countries in the region had introduced foreign exchange control which quickly became a basis for regulating imports, backed by a battery of variable exchange rates, quota restrictions and export subsidies. Trade between the Danubian countries in 1935 was one-sixth what it had been in 1913.

The slump transformed the international climate, helping Hitler to power in Germany and sending anti-democratic shock waves throughout neighbouring states. In 1933 the Austrian Christian socials outlawed their social democrat rivals and proclaimed a Fatherland Front; in 1935 60 per cent of the industrially depressed Sudeten German electorate voted for the neo-nazi Sudeten German Party. King Boris took personal control in Bulgaria in 1935. At the same time the Soviet Union emerged from isolation to assume an active role in European affairs. Eastern Europe in the 1930s became a battleground of rival ideologies.

Liberal democracy was beaten, or on the defensive, everywhere except Czechoslovakia, but it was not yet dead, particularly when aligned with peasantist movements as in the Romanian National Peasant Party, the centre-left Polish opposition and the Croatian Peasant Party–Independent Democrat alliance. The link was logical for public-spirited urban bourgeois in societies where peasants were a majority and could be viewed patriotically as the bulwark of the nation, patiently suffering ills that needed to be put right. Unfortunately the land reforms had not done this because land was insufficent to supply each peasant with a viable plot. Though five hectares (12.3 acres) was the agreed minimum for family support in the 1930s, 85 per cent of all holdings were below this figure in Hungary, 75 per cent in Romania, 71 per cent in Czechoslovakia, 68 per cent in Yugoslavia and 62 per cent in Bulgaria. Surplus labour on the land therefore was vast, perhaps one-third of the whole, yet because of extensive farming methods wheat yields remained between 2.5 and 3 times below Danish levels.

While economists embroiled themselves in debates on the respective merits of large-scale farming and peasant proprietorship, the urban-based authorities maintained a policy of patronizing neglect. Yugoslavia, 80 per cent of whose population were peasants, devoted 20 per cent of her investment to agriculture. One-third of Bosnian children attended school in 1939; infant mortality in the Romanian countryside ran at 20 per cent; Bulgaria had 450,000 wooden ploughs to 250,000 iron ones in 1936. In that year Dutch farmers were using 311 kilogrammes of fertilizer per hectare, Yugoslav and Romanian farmers 0.2 kilogrammes. The 'price-scissors' effect during the slump, which depressed agricultural prices far lower than industrial ones, only increased the already massive problem of peasant indebtedness. Inter-war Eastern Europe's problems stemmed ultimately from the plight of its peasant majority.

Peasantist leaders could approach these problems in different ways. The hard-headed Stambolisky had envisaged a network of railways serving electrified villages, each with its hall of popular culture and silo beside the track. The dreamier Croat, Ante Radic, once commented that his party did not need a programme because the peasant lived it out in his daily life; 'let's be ourselves, each keep his own, and united defend our Croatian home', as he once said. Yet economists as far apart as the British Doreen Warriner and the Romanian peasantist Madgearu argued cogently that the idea of a self-sufficient peasant world with its unique values was not really viable. The economic and cultural health of the East European peasantry depended on raising the low economic level of the society as a whole, so as to provide outlets to drain off the rapidly increasing population from the land and to afford the resources in credit, technology and education necessary for better productivity and marketing. Paradoxically, Radic's approach also facilitated an urban alignment for his party because its patriotic motifs appealed to the middle class's national romanticism, and its very lack of concreteness constrained the movement to turn to them for intellectual support. The convergence of peasantist and urban thought had, however, the disadvantage that peasants lost interest in their own party (this happened in Romania in the 1930s) and that peasantism could merge with conventional nationalism. Thus in 1939, the CPP did a deal for Croatian autonomy with the Belgrade government, abandoning its allies in the Serbian democratic opposition.

Nevertheless, peasant movements made a distinctive contribution to Eastern European life between the wars, notably in their elaborate co-operative organization. Agricultural co-operation was particularly successful in Bulgaria and Slovenia, but the CPP too was responsible for some important ventures in the later 1930s. The Economic Concord, founded in 1935, grouped 227,000 members in 4570 committees by 1940, and bought them cheap implements and seeds, built them warehouses, negotiated collective labour agreements for them and helped raise profits by eliminating middlemen. A parallel organization, Peasant Concord, concentrated on cultural life, holding literary classes, organizing dance troupes, even exhibiting peasant paintings in Zagreb. Indeed, it would be a mistake to see the 'peasant problem' in Eastern Europe as one of hopelessly antiquated subsistence farmers ground down by unfeeling oligarchies or ruthless dictatorships. The problem was subtler, and more difficult. Under Boris's personal rule in Bulgaria in 1937 an American anthropologist found in his village of residence, admittedly only five miles from Sofia, three co-operatives, a school board, a Church board, a branch of the Red Cross, a 'people's university' offering lectures, a Union for the Protection of Children, an Association of the Decorated for Valour and an Association for Orthodox Christianization of Bulgarian youth. Doreen Warriner noted that the desperately poor peasants of southern Poland had a high level of cultural interest and community organization. Peasant Eastern Europe was not a world apart which could, as some have supposed, survive the slump more comfortably than its urban neighbours; rather it was a hopelessly under-capitalized, over-populated bottom rung of the European economy.

The failure of the peasant movements to achieve a breakthrough raised the prospects of more militant movements, to left and right. Throughout the inter-war years communists, working through trade unions and 'front' parties (for they came to be formally banned everywhere except in Czechoslovakia) outdid social democrats in the agrarian societies and lagged behind them in the more industrial ones. While the tolerated social democrats of Yugoslavia, Hungary, Romania and Bulgaria vegetated as small, urban movements with a fixed clientele in certain intellectual and trade union circles and a regular posse of up to a dozen MPs, communist fortunes fluctuated according to the level of repression and internal strife. Every now and then a surprising potential was revealed, as for example in the front Labour Party's victory in the Sofia municipal elections in 1932.

However, as often as not communists were their own worst enemy. The success of the Bolsheviks gave the Communist International they founded almost unchallengeable authority over the various national parties. This caused problems when its line came to reflect internal Bolshevik squabbles more than non-Russian realities. Plainly, communists needed allies, and discontented peasants and national minorities as well as social democrats at once suggested themselves. But communist nationality policy was dominated by Russia's dislike of the succession states created at a peace conference she had not attended, so that any success gained among Magyars in Slovakia or Ukrainians and White Russians in Poland was more than offset by popular hostility to communists' separatist slogans.

East European communists were also expected to fraternize with the peasant parties and somehow manipulate these immensely stronger mass organizations. When the left turned out to have backed the wrong horse in Pilsudski in the 1926 coup, however, the line was changed and, instead of supporting Maniu, the Romanian communists were encouraged to initiate action on their own, which led to a pathetic little communist insurrection in 1928. By this time the rise of Stalin and his anti-peasant collectivization drive led to a repudiationof all co-operation with other movements till in 1935 the line changed once more, to accommodate a popular front against facism with all democratic forces, in the first instance social democrats.

These self-defeating manoeuvres apart, Stalinization did achieve something: a cadre of hardened professional revolutionaries with a programme of supra-industrialization and collective farms which offered a solution, if a ruthless one, to the problem of backwardness. Milovan Djilas, the Yugoslav dissident, has said that communism's force for his generation was the prospect it offered of an escape from the region's soul-destroying poverty, through a cause in which rebellious peasant students like himself and guilty scions of the bourgeoisie could prove themselves to themselves and to their peer group. But fanaticism fed on itself; the entire Polish party leadership perished in Stalin's purges. Those who combined fanaticism with circumspection might survive, however, like the former Croatian mechanic, Josip Broz, who, as Tito, became general secretary of the Yugoslav Party in 1937.

Disillusioned with the peasantist centre, repelled by the socialist left, the masses could turn to the right-wing radicalism or fascism that had triumphed in Italy and Germany. Yet the experience of Poland and Croatia, where fascism remained confined to the fringe of the nationalist bourgeoisie – right-wing national democrats or Ustasha – suggests that they were reluctant to do so as long as the peasant parties retained any credibility. Fascism germinated best in a political vacuum, and in Hungary, and Romania after Maniu's failure, this condition obtained. The Hungarian Szalasi's

Arrow Cross and the Romanian Codreanu's Iron Guard showed many classic fascist features: national megalomania and anti-Semitism, glorification of the redeeming powers of violence and blood, contempt for 'Jewish' liberal democracy, and a demagogic if not necessarily insincere social reformism in the interests of the small man. Founded in 1927, the Iron Guard won five seats in 1932 and sixty-six in 1937. The Arrow Cross emerged out of a medley of right-radical Hungarian parties in the late 1930s to poll a quarter of the votes in the elections of May 1939 and take, among others, the two seats of Csepel island, the heart of proletarian Budapest.

Yet these movements lacked the potential of their Western counterparts, ironically because of the very weakness of the left. Fascism in Italy and Germany gained ground because it appealed not just to the prejudices and grievances of the small man, but to the anti-socialism of the possessing classes. In both Romania and Hungary these classes remained firmly in control and proved as tough, if not tougher than the fascists. King Carol responded to the 1937 election by introducing a royalist dictatorship and having Codreanu shot, 'while trying to escape'. The Arrow Cross showed no capacity to bid for power until Hitler put them there in 1944. Indeed, German preference for working with the authoritarian regimes rather than the fascists was another important reason for the latter's lack of success.

By 1938 Kings Carol of Romania, Boris of Bulgaria, Zog of Albania and Prince Regent Paul of Yugoslavia all presided over authoritarian regimes; Poland was similarly ruled by a cohort of the dead Pilsudski's aides, Austria by the Fatherland Front of the clerical Schussnigg. These right-wing governments predictably followed a German orientation, except for Poland's which prided itself on its policy of the free hand. Economic interest reinforced the German course, for Nazi Germany had used the trade clearing arrangements arising out of the slump to buy up South East Europe's agrarian surplus provided her industrial goods were bought in exchange. From the first agreements with Bulgaria, Hungary and Yugoslavia in 1933–4 to those with Romania (strengthened by her oil) in 1938–9 Germany's share of the total trade of South East Europe rose from a sixth to a half.

One country, Czechoslovakia, stood out from this trend; diversification of her trade reduced her exports to Germany from 19 per cent to 13 per cent between 1927 and 1937. But the independence of Czechoslovakia meant little without that of the region as a whole. The Czech economist Basch lamented the West's failure to intervene with vital purchases in the region when temporary economic recovery made it less dependent on Germany in 1936–7. Yet the very liberalism Britain stood for made such bulk government intervention in the economic process implausible.

The fact of the matter was that the slump had speeded the resumption of German power in a traditional sphere of influence. In the democratic camp the initiative had passed from France to Britain, always more sceptical of the 1919 settlement. Hitler's unopposed reoccupation of the Rhineland in 1936 deprived the French of the means of bringing quick military aid to her Eastern allies. Despite Benes's endeavours, the Little Entente began to break up and the annexation of Austria to Germany became accepted as inevitable. Once this had occurred in March 1938, and Germany surrounded Czechoslovakia on three sides, the death of that state too became certain unless the Western powers showed more resolution than before. In the event, Czechoslovakia fell in two moves, first the amputation of the Sudentenland, Teschen and southern Slovakia by Germany, Poland and Hungary respectively in October 1938, then the occupation of the remaining Czech lands by Germany in March 1939. This event shocked Britain into an offer of guarantee to Poland which she had been unwilling to make in twenty years. Hence when Hitler attacked Poland in September 1939 the outcome was the Second World War.

Independent Eastern Europe had not quite reached its majority. Yet it should be remembered that its collapse was engineered by the most ruthless regime known to history and followed the worst depression in modern times. How far, if at all, did it bring this regime and this depression on itself by the circumstances of its birth?

The slump was certainly, in part, the product of the war and the peace settlement but it also had roots in an economic crisis of over-production which might well have curtailed early twentieth-century growth rates in some way, even had the old empires survived. As to the political issue, the Nazi movement arose out of nationalism, as did independent Eastern Europe, but there the resemblance ends. Nazism horrifies by the enormity of its wickedness; the bad side of East European nationalism was more a matter of selfishness, pettiness and parochialism. Certainly the national question was not solved by the destruction of the multi-national empires. As a recent historian of German–Czech relations has well said, the collapse of the old empires merely transposed the problem to the international sphere. But while many particular features of this East European nationalism may be regretted it would be rash to condemn the whole phenomenon *tout court*. For it is necessary to recall what the nationalists felt they were defending: the freedom and security of communities reunited after centuries in a home of their own. Before 1914 only a minority of East European people could so regard themselves; after 1919 by any count it was a majority. The reintegration of Poland was no mean achievement; though they grumbled, the Slovaks did not think of exchanging their new status for the old Hungary; only a handful of Croats in inter-war Yugoslavia were irremediably separatist. If ethnic protest seemed almost as shrill as ever, it was because modernization had amplified some grievances and picked up others which would once have gone unheard.

What must be admitted is that the Masarykian integration of nationalism with a broader concept of humanity had not taken place, any more than it had with Herder or Mazzini, earlier exponents of the same creed. The trouble lay in the nature of nationalism itself. To be ruled by men one considers alien is a very elementary humiliation out of which it is difficult to construct a sophisticated political philosophy. Yet humiliation it remains and of such an elemental kind that it tends to produce obsession in the victim, so that on gaining his freedom his strongest instinct is to shape all statecraft around the nation for which he has fought. He finds it difficult to see that national self-determination is but a stage, if an essential one, along the path to human emancipation. In this perspective, nationalism is short-sighted rather than fundamentally misguided. Like all steps in human evolution it is a step into the dark, and thus fraught with risk. It would be unfair to condemn the creation of independent Eastern Europe because in this case the risk was Adolf Hitler.

8 From Hitler to Stalin

The sequence of events triggered off by Hitler's invasion of Poland led directly to the advance of the Soviet Union into central Europe and the communization of the 'lands between'. Not surprisingly, the future-pointing confrontation between communist and non-communist, between Russia and the smaller powers has dominated ever since the investigations of historians and political scientists alike. But as so often in history, contemporaries had different perceptions. For them the war brought to a climax the conflicts of the past; it was the culminating point in the great struggle of Slav and Teuton, in whose eddies swirled the minor currents of a century of auxiliary nationalisms fair and foul. Ultimately, communism was installed in Eastern Europe by Soviet power. But the ability of East European communists to fit themselves into the anti-German scenario, to present their movement as the fulfilment of everything that was decent in the national tradition and the antithesis of everything that was not, greatly facilitated their dramatic success.

The Second World War

Between 1939 and 1941, in wary alliance with Stalin, Nazi Germany built up her power in Eastern Europe to an unprecedented peak. The rump Czech lands had been swallowed whole as a Reich protectorate in March 1939, with Slovakia cast adrift as a nominally independent state under German tutelage. Poland was divided up between Germany and Russia in September. Though not territorially interested in the Balkans, Hitler approved his Italian partner's invasion of Greece in 1940 as a means of launching a peripheral strategy against Britain and her far-flung empire, for the moment invulnerable in its island heart. Could Russia be persuaded to turn her attention from Eastern Europe to India and the Persian Gulf? It was the strategy which Napoleon at the height of his continental power had urged on Tsar Alexander, and like Napoleon, Hitler responded to the Russian demurrals by an attack on Russia herself, having first secured his right flank by the subjugation of Yugoslavia and Greece. 'Operation Barbarossa' was launched in June 1941.

As Versailles crumbled, ancient enmities burst forth and nations looked hungrily to the new master to toss them long-coveted territories. Muslims and Serbs fell on each other in the west Balkans; the Croatian fascist leader Pavelic hurried to Zagreb; the Iron Guard ruled temporarily in Bucharest. From these ugly materials of greed and fear, Hitler constructed his 'New Order', almost exactly inverting the fortunes of 1919. The revisionist states, Hungary and Bulgaria, retained their independence and extended their frontiers in return for close alignment of their economic and foreign policies with German interests; Hungary, but not Bulgaria, joined the war against Russia; Romania, though a victor at Versailles, was allowed into this trio of fellow-travellers at the cost of disgorging most of her territorial gains to her neighbours and undertaking the most active military role in the anti-Soviet campaign. Below these three in the second rank came the Slovaks and Croats, dissatisfied minor partners in 1919 who received the trappings of statehood under closely supervised native fascists; of these regimes Monsignor Tiso's clerico-fascist Slovak People's Party had more popular support than Pavelic's Ustashas. At the bottom rung in the New Order were the victors of 1919, the Poles, Serbs and Czechs, their states dismembered and the rumps administered by puppet collaborators or, in the case of the Poles, directly by Germans.

Yet the goals of German power in Eastern Europe could not be identified simply with the undoing of Versailles. The wartime structure had a provisional air, which hid unclear designs for the future. Ambiguity was indeed the Nazi New Order's most striking characteristic. On the one hand, it employed many career-officials who operated with all the bureaucratic regard for which the old Prussia and Habsburg regimes had been famous. The fact that an ex-Habsburg general, Glaise-Horstenau, commanded the Reich's forces in Croatia could only increase the sense of *déjà vu*. The immediate purpose of these men, which was to ensure docility and a maximum economic contribution of the new dependencies and allies to the German war effort, was not incompatible with a measure of prosperity for the territories concerned. Real wages seem to have risen slightly in Bohemia–Moravia before 1942, and in Slovakia, Hungary and Romania industrial mini-booms certainly set in. Yet underlying all relations with puppets and allies alike was the threat of the mailed fist, the peremptory summons to a meeting with a bullying Hitler, the direct military occupation such as Hungary and Slovakia eventually underwent. The SS was powerful throughout the region and held megalomanic views about the future, in which the 'final solution' of the Jewish question was to be only the first instalment. Czechs and Poles were to be divided up for assimilation to Germandom or euphemistic 'special treatment'. Pseudo-science mingled with vulgar prejudice as German doctors declared the Czech intelligentsia to be largely slavicized Germans, Pavelic pronounced the Croats not to be Slavs but Goths and a Nazi circular defined Slav racial traits as, 'for instance, a markedly disorderly and careless family life'; embarrassingly, preliminary secret surveys revealed Czechs to be racially superior to Sudeten Germans. Undaunted, Hitler spoke of a century's campaign to eliminate the Czechs and urged Pavelic to fifty years of 'intolerance' to the Serbs. While able-bodied workers could toil in German factories, their intellectual leadership was to be decapitated by the closure of all institutions of higher learning, as happened in Czech and Polish lands throughout the war. The taking of hostages, the setting of vicious retribution ratios (100 Serbs to die for one German, for example), selective executions designed to intimidate rather than punish: all this was licit where compliance wavered.

The dualism in German policy between traditional elements and Nazi fanaticism, repeated in country after country, placed harrassed native leaders before a terrible dilemma. Was it cowardice and betrayal to hope that the traditional face represented the truer Germany and could be honourably appeased? For small elements there was no problem; Nazi brutality and Nazi benevolence were two sides of the same coin, the new fascist way to which these kindred spirits instinctively responded. Such were Colonel Moravec in Bohemia, Ljotic in Serbia and the Slovak Rodobrana, not to speak of the established fascist movements of Hungary and Romania. But these groups were too weak to be put in power, and everywhere except Croatia (where the Peasant Party refused to co-operate) the Germans preferred rightist regimes which they could threaten with the prospect of a fascist take-over. Generally these regimes followed the tactics of appeasement, anticipating German wishes and implementing them in part in the hope of avoiding worse. The presence of German minorities (the *Volksdeutsche*) in their midst; sometimes, (as in the Hungarian general staff) their own ethnic origins; above all a sense of historic fatalism before German power, smoothed the psychology of collaboration. 'What we held for a solution to last for ages proved to be merely a short episode in our national history', said the Czech president, Hacha, over the radio. 'The unity of the Reich has been restored.' Historians have argued, as did German defendants at Nuremburg, that the collaborators were unnecessarily craven. Did not King Boris of Bulgaria and Regent Horthy of Hungary – albeit belatedly – successfully defy Germany over the deportation of the Jews? Lest we should be too scornful let us recall the toll of the collaborators themselves – the suicide of the guilt-striken Hungarian prime minister, Teleki, the execution by the Germans of his Czech counterpart Elias – as well as the real force of Hacha's cry to his critics that they did not have to see 'the tears of mothers and wives' addressing their 'desperate pleas' to him to intervene for their dear ones, doomed to die for their resistance work.

However, by 1941 the breaking of such as Hacha and the broadening of the war to the turbulent Balkans and the Soviet Union strengthened outright resistance to Hitler's sway. Topography, ideology and national traditions shaped a wide variety of resistance patterns. Patriotically inspired non-communist movements were largely confined to the territories which had suffered most at German hands, Poland, the Czech lands and Serbia, though there was also a dramatic rising in Slovakia towards the end of the war. The Czechs concentrated on intelligence and minor espionage but were all but decimated in 1941–2. Lacking even a puppet regime the better equipped Polish 'government delegacy' also saw a responsibility to maintain an underground administrative and educational structure; by 1944 this had enrolled over 100,000 high school students while the 'Home Army' at its peak numbered 380,000 men. The Serbian Chetniks in the mountains traced their traditions from nationalist guerilla bands in Turkish Macedonia at the turn of the century. None of these movements envisaged open warfare with the occupation forces until the hoped-for allied advance transpired. The decisive role of the Western powers and the Slav exiles in the First World War cast its spell over their strategy just as the inter-war settlements, albeit updated by an infusion of social reform, remained their goal. The Chetniks, however, along with their archaizing beards and peasant dress, embraced a bed-rock traditionalism which sought to secure even more strongly the great Serb character of the Yugoslav state.

Meanwhile, the activities of the resistance bolstered the campaign of the exiled governments for the restoration of their countries within the old 1919 frontiers. Acknowledging the breakdown of Versailles in the 1930s they harked back to the nineteenth century federal or confederal schemes of the region's nationalities directed against the great powers on either flank. Thus Benes, the Czech president in exile, signed an agreement with the Poles in November 1940 for closer association after the war which would become the 'basis of a new order in Central Europe and a guarantee of its stability'. The Greek–Yugoslav agreement of 1942 for post-war Balkan union resurrected the cry, 'The Balkans for the Balkan peoples'. Hungary's democratic leader of 1918–19, Count Michael Karolyi, revived Kossuth's programme of Danubian federation; Sudeten German anti-fascists dreamt of a popular coup against Hitler and a vindicated greater Germany on the lines of the German left in 1848. Books flowed from the presses on the Danubian concept, on customs unions, preferential quotas for East European agricultural surpluses and the like; and the influential American journal *Foreign Affairs* published an article by Dr Otto von Habsburg.

However the communist resistance in Eastern Europe was fighting for none of this. Admittedly its role, though brave, was limited outside the Balkans. There, however, in the Yugoslav partisans, the communists had produced the resistance movement *par excellence* of the war. Tito's call to arms followed immediately on Hitler's invasion of the Soviet Union. While the Chetniks remained passive against the occupier for fear of reprisals against the civilian population and as Serb nationalists became embroiled with Muslim and Albanian minorities, the communist-led partisans stood out consistently for a militant line and the 'brotherhood and unity' of the Yugoslav peoples. As massacres by Nazis and rival Yugoslavs mounted, the partisan resort to the woods seemed both the safest way out for the able-bodied young and the one most compatible with Balkan martial traditions, ideological issues aside. The outmatched Chetniks were driven back to tacit alliance with the German and Italian occupiers against their Marxist rivals. By the time Tito declared a provisional government in autumn 1943, he had 275,000 people under arms.

For all Tito's achievement the future settlement still appeared to hinge on the agreement of the anti-Hitler great powers. Stalin rebuked him for the terms of the provisional government proclamation which pursued revolutionary goals beyond the national liberation policies on which the war-time coalition was ostensibly based. However, after the German surrender at Stalingrad early in 1943 there could be no doubt that the balance of power in the coalition was shifting more in Russia's favour. In November of that year a Soviet journal spelt out one of the ominous implications:

The security system of the small states of Eastern Europe must be based on the alliance of each one of them with the Soviet Union without all these artificial and lifeless unions which are dubbed federations.

Of non-communist Eastern European politicians only Edvard Benes faced the rise of Soviet power with equanimity. Discarding his Czecho-Polish and other schemes he signed a Czechoslovak–Soviet treaty in Moscow in December 1943. But even this apparent flexibility was firmly rooted in Benes's previous experience. Shock at the West's betrayal at Munich, traditional Czech Russophilia and the conviction that the normalization of post-revolutionary Russia, which he had long predicted, was now irreversible all inclined Benes to an alliance which he saw as the completion of Versailles rather than its overthrow. While the treaty bound Russia not to interfere in Czechoslovak internal affairs, the Czechs themselves would extend their political democracy after the war into a social one much on the lines of the Labour Party's plans for Britain.

Other East European countries, fighting alongside Hitler against the Soviets or, like Poland, traditionally Russophobe, could not afford to be so sanguine. Their response to Russian strength was to draw closer to the Western powers, denouncing their alliances with Germany (as did Romania and Bulgaria in August 1944 and Hungary in October) or like the Chetniks awaiting the presumed Dalmatian landing of Anglo-American troops. The likely Soviet answer to these manoeuvres had been foreshadowed in Benes's negotiations in Moscow. There the Czech president had had to negotiate on equal terms with the Czech communist leader for the formation of a communist-led National Front which would proceed to reorganize liberated Czechoslovakia through 'people's committees' bearing an unmistakable likeness to the Soviets of 1917. While Benes's co-operation gained him some control over a genuinely multi-party National Front the same was not true of his 'bourgeois' counterparts in neighbouring states, who viewed with dismay the communist-dominated Lublin government installed by Soviet troops in eastern Poland, the seizure of power by the Fatherland Front in Soviet-occupied Bulgaria and the increasing pressure of the National Democratic Front in Soviet-occupied Romania. More and more insistent became the call from anti-communist politicians for Anglo-American intervention to redress the balance.

Yet the West had already defined its position, effectively, if not explicitly, in 1943 and the first half of 1944. In the former year Churchill had switched British support for the Chetniks to Tito's partisans; reminded that these were communist-led, he had asked the reminder whether he personally intended to live in Yugoslavia after the war; the chief thing was that the partisans were fighting the Germans. As to the non-communist Poles, Churchill concluded by July of 1944 that he could support them only if they yielded their non-Polish territories to the Soviet Union and accepted the fusion of their London-exiled government with the Soviet-backed Lublin body. This was the sort of governmental arrangement Benes had agreed to in Moscow, but the distrust aroused by the frontier issue, among others, made it infinitely less palatable to the Poles. In the absence of a clear American line, Churchill was actually heading for a 'spheres of influence' agreement with the Russians, which he eventually signed in Moscow in October. His motives for such an agreement were no doubt twofold: recognition that the Soviets could not be denied a preponderance on the territories against their borders, and determination to secure a similar position for Britain in an area which did directly concern her, Greece. But in other respects Churchill's *Realpolitik* appears less hard-headed. There is no evidence that it entailed a clear thinking through of what a sphere of influence meant to Russians, in terms of post-war military administration, diplomatic safeguards or more permanent political controls. Nor is it clear how Churchill interpreted or intended to back up the 50 per cent claim for Britain in Yugoslavia and Hungary which the agreement laid down. With the idea of a Balkan campaign abandoned, the Western allies approached our area toilsomely across a battered Germany. Nevertheless, it would have been possible, as Churchill urged, for American troops to have liberated Prague in advance of the Red Army, but Eisenhower decided not to for military reasons and to please the Russians – who therefore gained entire physical control of the 'lands between'.

Eisenhower's decision should not, however, surprise. In May 1945 the issue still did not appear to most observers to be the people versus communism, as it was later depicted. The exiled politicians lacked the moral authority of their First World War predecessors, except for Benes, and he had signed a treaty with Russia. The Yugoslav royalists were hopelessly compromised by Serbo-Croat feuding; the London Poles were basically a coalition of the parties which had brought Polish democracy to its knees in 1926. Of Germany's former allies, the Popular Front governments, in Bulgaria and Hungary at least, were more representative of the people than those they had overthrown. Much appeared to depend on the evolution of these Popular Fronts and this, in turn, on the future of the wartime alliance.

The communist take-over

In the event, within three years of the cease-fire every state in the region had passed under exclusive communist rule. Within three more the assault, which had first been launched against the comparatively recent and fragile growth of liberal capitalism, was being extended to age-old institutions of religious belief and peasant proprietorship, against a background of show trials reproducing the worst features of the Stalinism of the 1930s. The very weight of these dramatic events has tended to crush balance in the commentators. In the immediate aftermath of communization Western writers interpreted it as a cynical subversion of democracy by Moscow and its local agents, a manifestation of the Soviet lust for world dominion. From the late 1960s, in tandem with the Vietnam War, the New Left school of revisionist historiography in America saw the same events as a legitimate response of the Soviets to American imperialism's schemes of military and economic encirclement. In each case the stereotyped formulae relate more to the great powers than to the peoples actually in dispute. Mere pawns in a struggle of good and evil, their fate becomes all the more mysterious. The aim of this account is to dispel the mystery and soften the antitheses, without suggesting glibly thereby: 'tout comprendre c'est tout pardonner'. The prerequisite of this is to restore the peoples of Eastern Europe to the centre of the stage, in the political, economic and psychological context in which they

Poland, 1809–1918

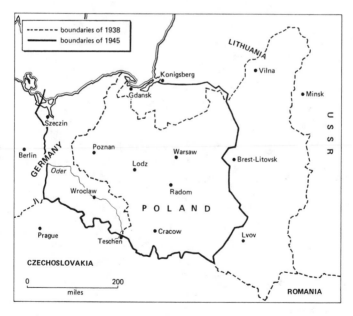

Poland since 1945

Eastern Europe in 1942

found themselves in the aftermath of an appalling war.

In 1945 and 1946 Eastern Europe presented a desolation even greater than in 1919. Poland had lost 6 million dead. Yugoslavia 1.7 million, Romania over 500,000. More than half all Polish and Yugoslav livestock had been destroyed. The transport situation was chaotic, symbolized most aptly by the fact that all bridges over the Danube at Budapest, with which Szechenyi had begun his economic modernization of Hungary, had been destroyed. The total cost of German looting has been estimated at $20 billion to $25 billion and Poland's loss from all sources at $18.2 billion. In Romania, industrial production actually fell from 1945–6 to less than half pre-war levels, assisted by ruthless Russian counter-looting in the guise of reparations. Inflation raged in Hungary and Romania till brought to an end by a currency reform which wiped out savings. To all this was added the misery of a succession of droughts, so that Moldavia experienced famine in the winter of 1946–7 for the first time for a century.

In both economics and politics the German hegemony had left structural changes which ruled out a return to pre-war patterns. Industrial concentration, trade union regimentation and the transfer of vast assets into German hands which now defaulted to the state all made an *étatiste* approach to economic management more plausible. The whole Polish state had shifted 150 miles to the west with compensation in East Germany for territories lost to the Soviet Union. Poland thus became a nationally homogenous state for the first time, since like others in the region she had also lost her large Jewish population. The Soviets in addition had taken Bessarabia and northern Bukovina from Romania and Carpatho-Ruthenia from Czechoslovakia. 8 million Germans were in process of expulsion from new Polish territory and almost 3 million, with many atrocities, from Czechoslovakia. Among indigenous populations important sections of pre-war opinion were banned by Popular Front fiat from the political stage: the organizations of the Hungarian gentry, the Slovak People's Party, the Czech and Polish national democrats, the Czech agrarians. Where they had not saved themselves by flight, men like the president of independent Slovakia, Monsignor Tiso, the Chetnik leader Mihajlovic and the prime minister of wartime Romania, Antonescu, met death by firing squads, or on the gallows. Indeed, a subtle brutalization, a carelessness for legal forms and human life, even as the victory propaganda trumpeted humanist slogans, was perhaps the most telling end-product of the wartime experience. The Yugoslav Djilas's war memoirs brilliantly show how inevitably the resolve of the partisans not to use torture, not to execute prisoners, not to requisition unwilling villagers broke down in the face of provocation from the other side. Even more sapping of the spirit was the life of ostensibly civilian societies like the Bohemian protectorate, dominated by patterns of torture and intimidation, denunciation and dissembling. For many the raping and looting of the Red Army liberators set the seal on an experience which, for all the individual and occasionally collective heroism, fundamentally exposed the sordid and seamy sides of human nature under stress.

The communists were peculiarly suited to be spokesmen of these stark times. The immensity of the reconstruction task gave fresh meaning to their message of a society built anew. Psychologically, too, their Stalinist heritage attuned them to the curious mix of messianism, cynicism and brutalization which characterized overwrought times; for Stalin had drawn out the 'Jesuitical' potentialities of Marxism. Since the ultimate triumph of the cause was certain and the mouthings of liberal democracy were merely a smoke screen for bourgeois ideology, why should communists not dissemble in the pursuit of their goals? If Marx's feat had been to place idealism on a pragmatic rather than a Utopian foundation by exposing the material base of the power structure, the intoxication of Stalinism was to combine an inner idealism with an unprecedentedly ruthless grasp of the workings of power. The harsh life experience of men like the Hungarian Rakosi who had spent fifteen years in the gentry's jails, or the Bulgarian Kostov, a hunchback since leaping from a prison window to escape his torturers, suited them to receive the message. The very demands of the movement, while keeping pre-war membership small and fluctuating, also attracted a disproportionate number of able and dedicated leaders: the prestigious Bulgar Comintern chiefs, Dimitrov and Kolarov, the middle-class intellectual Rakosi, fluent in seven languages, the head of the 1933 Romanian railwaymen's strike, Gheorghiu-Dej, the rugged Polish locksmith Gomulka. It was such men who now appeared, with the Red Army at their backs, to proclaim their programme of patriotism and social reform within the framework of the Popular Front.

How much conviction and how much opportunism underlay the rise in Romanian communist membership from 1000 to hundreds of thousands within a few weeks of Antonescu's overthrow or in

Hungarian communist membership from 3000 to 150,000 in the first five months of 1945? Seen in context the two motives may not have been as easily distinguishable as normal circumstances might lead to suppose. Certainly the communists had a ready appeal to urban workers, poor peasants and youth. They led the German expulsion campaigns and the land reforms. Their concept of the Popular Front coalition as a permanent form of government - people's democracy – absolved them from the charge of totalitarianism and endeared them to other parties in the front whose organization was negligible by comparison. Indeed, they could count on numerous fellow travellers in the ranks of these parties, notably left-wing peasantists and social democrats who saw the communists' hot line to Moscow as a valuable guarantee that much needed reforms would go through without obstruction. The social democrats in particular agonized between a pro-communist left-wing radicalized by the war and a right which emphasized social democracy's anti-communist past. How far the fellow travellers were attracted primarily by the gradualist overtones of the communists' 'specific national road to socialism' or how far they would have supported them in sterner measures is not always clear; no less than the Czech socialist leader, Fierlinger, and army commander, Svoboda, seem to have been under communist orders to lie low as early as 1945. What is clear is that the existence of the fellow travellers gave the communists alone the party cohesion and organization necessary to seize power in 1945.

Yet, except in Yugoslavia, the communists did not seize power. No doubt this reflected genuine support for a Popular Front line which shared out the responsibilities of reconstruction and promised increasing popularity. But a line it was, which would certainly have been changed had Stalin's view of the international situation required it. As it was, the Yalta Declaration on Liberated Europe in February 1945 called for 'the earliest possible establishment through free elections of government responsible to the will of the people'. America felt this was violated by the Soviet-backed imposition of a National Democratic Front government in Bucharest following a somewhat polemical broadcast by Prime Minister Radescu - he had called two communist leaders 'horrible hyenas'. In response to Western pressure Stalin agreed to the broadening of the Romanian and Polish governments with members of the traditional parties. Free elections took place in October 1945 in Hungary and May 1946 in Czechoslovakia. In the latter the communists dominated the Czechoslovak National Front with 38 per cent of the votes, but came a poor second to the Hungarian Smallholders with only 17 per cent.

These events did not necessarily mean that Stalin did not intend the full communization at least of Poland and Romania, which had a tradition of hostility to Russia and had just had to cede her territory. However, they did suggest that the state of international relations might influence the pace and manner of this process, and no doubt the fate of states further afield as well. Certainly articles in the Western press in early 1946 by Oszkar Jaszi and President Benes showed every confidence in Hungary's and Czechosolvakia's prospects of retaining a genuine internal autonomy on condition that their foreign policy avoided any threat to Societ security. It was an optimism vitiated by the rapid deterioriation of the international climate.

The controversy surrounding this deterioration has already been mentioned. Was it the product of mutual misunderstanding, or of bad faith on one or both sides? Can it be precisely dated? The New Left school tends to emphasize variously the economic ambitions of American capitalism or the encirclement of Russia by American atomic and military power. The anti-communism of 1947 that inspired the Truman doctrine of support for 'free governments' and the Marshall Aid Plan already, it argues, ran through America's use of the atom bomb and the stopping of aid to Russia in 1945. Hence Russian intransigence in Eastern Europe in 1946 was consequence not cause of the Cold War. It is hard not to agree with Kennan, a serving American diplomat in Moscow from 1944, that Russian distrust of the West went back a good deal earlier than this, and that the Soviet demeanour never suggested much expectation of a continuing peacetime alliance. In a sense differences in political culture as much as divergent interests exacerbated relations. The Russians, not surprisingly, found the stream of complaints from the West about their procedure in Poland and Romania hypercritical if not menacing, when they made no criticism of the British suppression of the communists in Athens in their own sphere of influence. Western representatives, on the other hand, were taken aback by the cynicism and ruthlessness of Soviet operations. Out of this revulsion came the famous Kennan 'long telegram' in spring 1946 which convinced the White House that the Russian communists were a race apart who could not be conciliated, only contained. Thus events in Eastern Europe shaped the international climate quite as much as the reverse.

Whatever the cause, 1946 was a year of mounting discord. In Bulgaria, Romania and increasingly in Hungary the communists applied what Rakosi later called 'salami tactics', dividing non-communists into 'progressives' and 'reactionaries' and picking off the latter group by group on charges of anti-Sovietism, pro-fascist antecedents or imperilling the economy or the unity of the Popular Front. With communists everywhere in control of the crucial interior and propaganda ministries, with the Soviets at hand and the Western powers contenting themselves with protest or occasional economic pressure, the resistance of the demoralized non-communists became increasingly ineffectual and the popular fronts a mere facade for communist power. No special moral turpitude need be invoked to explain the communists' blatantly 'unfair' methods. Political perceptions could still in all honesty be different. After all, the 'democrats' in the Western sense had not opposed the execution of Tiso and Antonescu who had been guilty of no concrete crimes. The men who were now being purged, Maniu and the liberal Tatarescu in Romania, the agrarian Petkov in Bulgaria were all prominent politicians in the pre-war states which were roundly condemned on all sides; there was no guarantee that their leadership would have produced successful Western-style democracy. Just the same could be argued of the Smallholders who remained at the head of the Hungarian Popular Front coalition by virtue of their 1945 electoral victory. In the absence of pre-war conservative parties they had plainly become the home of all right-wing elements in the country; how otherwise explain a smallholder party which won a majority in the municipal elections in Budapest! Its slogan in the parliamentary elections – 'Law, Order, Security' – bespoke its conservative tendencies, as did the reluctance of many at its 1945 conference even to abolish the monarchy which technically had vegetated on under Regent Horthy since 1920. Nagy, the smallholder leader, himself of middling peasant stock – his mother had been a passionate Kossuthite nationalist – recorded in his memoirs his preference for the old regime officials over the poor peasants whom the communist yoked in to administer the land reform. It is not difficult to see that a skilled communist polemicist would have felt no qualms about justifying the assumption of sole power in Hungary, which took place after Nagy's departure abroad in May 1947.

By 1948 genuine coalition government still existed only in

Czechoslovakia. Czechoslovakia, however, was a different matter. There communists and non-communists could only agree that it had been a functioning democracy between the wars and had every prospect of remaining one, that there was no tradition of anti-Russianism and that the preponderance in the National Front was weighted to the left. To this extent the communization of Czechoslovakia could not be envisaged in terms of an inner collapse of the non-Communist forces such as could be argued (somewhat tendentiously) to have occured elsewhere. It could only be interpreted as the direct product of the Cold War and the distorting influence of the Soviet Union. That such a communization was intended by Stalin is suggested by the fact that the Czechoslovak Communist Party was the only non-governing party (besides the French and Italians) to attend the opening meeting of the Cominform (Communist Information Bureau), held in autumn 1947 to concert responses to the American challenge.

Yet party papers used by a dissident Czechoslovak historian reveal that there was no communist plot to seize power. The coup of February 1948 was actually provoked by an ill-judged mass resignation of non-communist ministers aimed at constraining President Benes to appoint a new, substantially non-communist government. In fact, it gave the communists the opportunity to mobilize their impressive trade union support in the streets and subject the sick president to days of mass demonstrations till he gave way, accepted the resignations and called Gottwald, the communist leader, to form a cabinet of communists and fellow-travellers. Though the crisis was catalysed by the threat of Soviet intervention – the Soviet deputy prime minister arrived at its height, ostensibly to attend a minor conference – the actual events revealed the same pattern as elsewhere: the ruthless efficiency of the communist minority and the weakness of the non-communist majority. In the Czech case the non-communists in the National Front had been made complacent by straw polls indicating their vote would rise in the anticipated general election. They placed too much reliance on President Benes without making their plans wholly clear to him, and on matters of clericalism, Slovak autonomy and state control of the economy they failed to overcome pre-war rifts. Indeed, social democratic support was never co-ordinated for the fateful ministerial resignations.

It is clear that only the interrelation of local circumstances and international events can fully explain the communization of Eastern

Europe after the Second World War. The search for new directions imposed by the tasks of reconstruction, the energy and ambition of local communists and disunity and miscalculations of their opponents, the fatalism and opportunism induced by the experiences of war all combined to facilitate the path towards communism that geo-political realities foreboded. Recently, the Kolkos have suggested that, whatever the role of constraint in Eastern Europe's orientation in these years, it nonetheless corresponded to the objective needs of the region's development. Eastern Europe, 'where political democracy, literacy, land reform, social welfare and indigenous capitalist enterprise have never existed', could only modernize through nationalized economies which necessarily aligned them with the Soviet Union against American capitalism. This oversimplification of East European history cannot be sustained, if only because it overlooks the fact that American investments in the region were slight, that by 1945 nationalization was no longer an exclusively communist policy and that purely economic considerations urged alignment with Western capital rather than with an impoverished and light-fingered Soviet Union – as Polish and Czech communists recognized when they accepted the Marshall Aid Plan before Stalin called them to heel.

To argue this is not to argue that there was a natural beneficent course of East European development which was violated after 1945. Whether successful Western-style democracy could have evolved after the war is, anyway, an academic question for most of the region, as no alternative course of action would have been likely to avert what came about; the examples of Greece and Turkey moderate optimism. Again, however, Czechoslovakia is the exception. It is tempting to ask whether, had they played their hand better, the non-communists there could have forced the communists on to a downward slope, as the Finns forced their communists, not without sharp practice, in the same period. The parallel is all the more interesting because Finland was obviously relevant to Soviet security and had actually fought Russia alongside Germany in the Second World War. But the Finns had a record of successful resistance to communist take-overs. Additionally, Finnish neutrality as formulated after the war lacked the pretensions Benes gave Czechoslovakia of being a bridge-builder between East and West, with the implications of independent initiative. Besides, Finland had no close communist neighbours to influence whereas Czechoslovakia had several.

The implication of the comparison is that the fate of Czechoslovakia's liberal democracy was bound up with that of its small power neighbours. It is an implication which should have suggested itself to Benes, who had been a leading participant in the Treaty of Versailles. The end of liberal democracy came in a way which underlined that treaty's chief weaknesses, framed as it was by the western powers at a moment when both German and Russian influence was in eclipse. Events after 1945, as before 1939, confirmed that the West would not fight for Eastern Europe and that the East European states could not co-operate against a mighty neighbour. Benes's complacency at the prior fate of his Polish and Hungarian neighbours was a final indication of liberal nationalism's failure to transcend a narrowly perceived self-interest. It was in fact the desire to find a broader solidarity, both between nations and classes, that led so many Czechs into the communist camp. The formula of the 'specific road to socialism' beckoned invitingly to those who wished to step out further into the social future without wholly abandoning the direction set by their forefathers.

Stalinization

They were not to get very far. Whatever Stalin had intended – and he was capable of deep-laid calculation – the worsening of the Cold War after the Prague coup and the insubordination of Yugoslavia impelled a process of uniformization which quickly reduced the East European states to slavish models of the Soviet Union.

By virtue of her unique partisan struggle communist Yugoslavia had proudly assumed the role of favourite son of the Soviet Union; Belgrade was the seat of the Cominform. No doubt it was this pride which riled Stalin, for it made the Yugoslavs unco-operative on matters where he expected unquestioning obedience, like the Soviet right to infiltrate satellite armies and secret services, the conclusion of one-sided commercial agreements and the ascription of liberation to the valorous might of the Red Army. Yugoslavia also showed pretensions to Balkan leadership. In March 1948 Moscow called on the Yugoslavs to amend their ways. To its astonishment the Yugoslavs answered back. After mounting epistolary recrimination the Cominform opened the dispute to the world by expelling Yugoslavia and calling on the Yugoslavs to revolt. Trade contacts between Yugoslavia and the communist block were first reduced and then embargoed, a massive campaign of propaganda and border incidents was launched but Stalin did not attack and Tito's 'gang of spies, provocateurs and murderers' survived with only minor defections.

To one of Stalin's nature, Tito's successful defiance inevitably called for a ruthless purge to rid other satellite leaderships of all who had displayed or might display similar independence. Between 1949 and 1952 the former ministers of the interior of Albania and Hungary, the vice-premier and economic chief of Bulgaria and the general secretary and foreign minister of Czechoslovakia were arrested, tried and executed, while the former general secretary of Poland was detained under imminent expectation of the same fate. Titoism was laid at the door of them all, while other crimes varied from Trotskyism, imperialist espionage and service to the Gestapo to Zionism, anti-Sovietism and Slovak bourgeois nationalism. A pattern can be discerned in these lamentable proceedings. Xoxe, the Albanian, was indeed a protégé of Tito's and favoured closer Albano-Yugoslav ties. Kostov, the Bulgarian, had queried one-sided economic deals with Russia. Gomulka, the Pole, had opposed collectivization and Clementis, the Czechoslovak foreign minister, the Nazi-Soviet Pact of 1939. No such obvious motive appears in the case of the Hungarian Rajk except that he was a 'home communist' who had spent the war years in Hungary not Moscow. He was also a Spanish Civil War veteran whose experience made him suspect to the inbred circle of Soviet communism. The charges against General Secretary Slansky of plotting to restore Czechoslovak capitalism under guise of the separate Czechoslovak socialist road suggested a warning to the entire Czech party, whose programme this had been, not to presume too much, like the Yugoslavs, from its strong popular base.

The memoirs of a lesser victim, the Czechoslovak deputy minister, Loebl, help to illuminate the inner workings of the show trials. Loebl's chief crime was to have stood out against exploitative economic deals with Russia. He was never physically tortured – this occurred only when speedy confessions were required and generally yielded results within two days – but after more than a year of interrogation for sixteen hours a day in a standing position and jumping to attention every ten minutes through the night to repeat his prison number, he eventually confessed all that was required, indeed, himself composed for his non-academic interrogators the questions and answers which he then learnt for his own trial. Only

Kostov, incidentally, retracted his confessions in open court. But despite Loebl's and other accounts, many aspects of the show trails remain obscure. Those of Xoxe, Kostov and Rajk were completed within months of arrest; however, Loebl was detained in November 1949, Slansky in 1951 and the trial itself was not held till December 1952; Gomulka was never tried at all. Perhaps more care was taken in later trials to avoid the patent errors and implausibilities in those of Kostov and Rajk. Perhaps, too, the Polish leadership was protecting Gomulka. Indeed, the Romanians like the Poles avoided death sentences in their trials, maybe because they persuaded the Soviets their popular base was too narrow for blood-letting. Their purge was actually directed against ethnically non-Romanian 'Muscovites' by a 'home communist', Gheorghiu-Dej. Traditional cultural and linguistic ties may well have influenced the degree of Soviet intervention; Loebl's interrogators were supervised by Soviet agents known as 'the Teachers'. For all the intriguing variations it is hard to imagine that Stalin or his police chief, Beria, did not have oversight over the whole. As the Bulgarian leadership wired him after their late comrade's execution: 'Only your deeply penetrating eye could see in time the criminal spy gang of Kostov.'

Amid this welter of sensation and intrigue the Sovietization of the 'people's democracies' went under way. More or less identical constitutions of 1948 or 1949 (1952 in Romania) reflected the transformation. Behind the nominally sovereign national assemblies, which met only a few days each year, the council of ministers and the Politburo of the Communist Party exercised real power. People's councils, dominated by their executive committees, took over local government; judges and lay assessors, in theory elected but in practice appointed, assumed control of the judiciary. The division of governmental powers, intended to restrain despotism, was abolished because the people had nothing to fear from themselves. The public prosecutor's task as spokesman for the prosecution was extended to that of 'defender of socialist legality' and could be exercised independent of the courts, thereby nullifying sweeping constitutional provision for personal rights. Only the Communist Party, 'vanguard of the working people', could nominate candidates to the National Assembly by the single list system; sometimes this function was allotted to the national fronts, lifeless vestiges of the post-1945 coalitions which existed under various names in all countries of the region.

Along with the Stalinist political system came the Stalinist command economy. Between 1946 and 1948 the East European states had adopted what would now be termed mixed economies, with an extensive nationalized sector covering the key branches of industry and finance and the larger firms in other branches. 50 per cent of the Czechoslovak national income derived from the socialized sector in 1948. On such a basis short-term plans of national recovery had been formulated using indicative (or recommended) targets for a limited number of important products – 142 in the Czech case. The five year Soviet-style plans, which were now successively introduced, laid down binding targets for several thousand commodities in economies from which all traces of private business were eliminated. These massively ambitious targets, as in Stalin's first Five Year Plan of 1929, deliberately emphasized heavy industry at the expense of consumer goods. The sacrifice of contemporary living standards was to engineer an industrial future. Between 20 per cent and 25 per cent of national income would be reinvested anually, far above the 4 per cent of pre-war years or the 10 per cent since posited by Professor Rostow for industrial breakthrough. The doubling and trebling of hydro-electric power would spearhead totally new industries and a decisive shift in the balance between the value of agricultural and industrial products, even in backward Albania. Attention would be directed to spectacular projects symbolic of the new era: Sztalinvaros, the new Hungarian steel town, Dimitrovo, formerly Pernik, centre of the first ever Bulgarian machine goods industry, the Danube–Black Sea Canal in Romania, the flowering of a great metallurgical industry in the wilds of Bosnia. But the other side of the picture was that some of the projects worked with prison labour, piecework was being stepped up to unprecedented levels, labour mobility restricted through the introduction of labour cards, and trade unions emasculated under the system of one man rule in the factories.

Stalin had realized in the late 1920s that rapid industrialization entailed regimentation of agriculture to ensure food supplies for the expanding cities. The better to control peasants whose resources were effectively being squeezed to finance industrialization, he introduced the programme of collectivization in which incalculable numbers died. No aspect of Stalinism was less welcome to Stalin's East European comrades. 'Any Hungarian government which aimed to give up the principle of private property would be digging its own grave and the nation's. We aim to fortify the new peasants', said the Hungarian prime minister in 1947. But the Soviet attack on Yugoslavia included criticism of the Yugoslav's failure to collectivize. With some forebodings, all East European regimes, including Yugoslavia, set about driving peasants into the state system with an appropriate use of carrot and stick, the carrot being the offer of milder forms of collective ownership, the stick the punitive taxes and delivery demands for private peasants. Still, by 1952 only Bulgaria claimed to have more than half its arable land in the state sector, as compared to a quarter in Yugoslavia and Hungary, and less than a sixth in Romania.

No doubt it was the symbolic force of the peasant idea in Eastern Europe which gave the communist leaders pause, as well as the practical difficulties collectivization entailed. Here was a notion which went so close to the heart of national identity and self-image that its violation must have seemed a flagrant challenge to the national cultural tradition in whose name the communists still claimed to speak. Culture, and, linked to it, education, were extremely important to the communists. Within a few years of their assumption of power, secondary school attendance had doubled, and attendance in higher education more than doubled almost throughout the socialist block, while correspondence courses and adult education, libraries, museums and archives received a new priority. Youth especially, neglected in traditional culture, became the object of attention; and through the youth movements which grouped the majority of young people in each country, grew the new facilities for sport and recreation and the emphasis on female emancipation. Concomitantly, the regimes moved against the clerical guardians of social and cultural norms. The Hungarian Catholic primate, Mindszenty, lost his freedom for resisting, among other things, the abolition of church schools. The archbishop of Zagreb was imprisoned for alleged wartime collaboration with the Ustasha. Hundreds more bishops and priests fell foul of the authorities because they resisted a process designed to consign them and their cause to 'the rubbish-bin of history'.

For the communists had their own message to hammer home in their new institutions. It was Lenin's vision of a culture national in form but socialist in content, to which Stalinism had added the rider that socialist culture must harmonize with the traditions of the Soviet Union and the Great Russian people. Within this framework communists could plausibly equate the East European tradition of resistance to foreigners with their own anti-imperialist world view. This principle once established, the 'cultural worker' faced the essentially technical task of allotting individuals or forces in the nation's past to the 'progressive' or 'reactionary' traditions, according to whether they pointed towards or led away from the consummation of People's Democracy: thumbs up for Palacky and down for Masaryk, up for Kossuth and down for Deak, up for Strossmayer but down for Jelacic as the case might be. Leading party members, a Revai in Hungary, a Kardelj in Yugoslavia, a Nejedly in Czechoslovakia, even the Bulgarian party leader Chervenkov busied themselves with historical or literary evaluation, not just for its ideological utility but its inherent attraction. The claims of Marxism to provide a total socio-historical philosophy have always fascinated intellectuals; and what more can a revolutionary achieve than to remould the very cultural categories of his age?

Of course, the constraints of Stalinist cultural policy could be irritating. The misdeeds of German, Turkish and Western exploiters could be freely castigated, those of Russians, even tsarist ones, less so. There was something bizarre about exponents of socialist realism trying sycophantically to demonstrate that the Romance language of the Romanians was structurally quite Slavonic. Nonetheless, the force of the Stalinists' intellectual vision must be appreciated. They looked forward to a future, set in train by their policies, in which the region would be free from its age-old curse of technological backwardness, and its inhabitants liberated from the gratuitous humiliations of poverty, ignorance and avoidable disease. They looked back to a past whose struggles for religious, political and national rights, as illumined by Marxist science, stood revealed as only facets of a greater struggle now nearing its climax between exploiter and exploited, reaction and progress. Of course, idealism was not unalloyed. The Polish writer Milosz has brilliantly documented the almost Orwellian cynicism of many high party officials, mesmerized by the ruthlessness of Stalinism to see it as universal and inescapable destiny. The victory of progress could not come without sacrifice and suffering; 'history', Engels had said 'is about the most cruel of all goddesses'. No doubt a majority in Eastern Europe did not yet share this vision. They were the possessing classes, blinded by self-interest, or *petit bourgeois*, cocooned in petty individualism and simplistic nationalism, or peasants whose rational faculties had been stunted by priestcraft and unending toil. Most dangerous were those nearest the communists, radical democrats, peasantists and social democrats who did not yet recognize that their reformist hopes and combinations had been condemned in the collapse of inter-war Eastern Europe, in the horrors of war and occupation and in the surrender of Benes to the people in 1948. Dangerous, too, were those communists who failed to see that the class struggle had to sharpen the nearer the socialist goal was approached.

It is not difficult to see the power of the Stalinist appeal for able and determined men. Indeed, it had to be powerful to lead so many who vaunted the liberating force of rationality to subject their own reason to the will of a cruel and capricious dictator.

9 Communist Eastern Europe

Stalin died on 6 March 1953. World communism since his death has seen the emergence of the Soviet Union as an industrial super-power, the acquisition of extensive new territories and the socio-economic transformation of Eastern Europe; but it has also been dominated by the search for mechanisms of political control more supportable than the terror and cult of personality he bequeathed. Polycentric ideas have challenged the exclusive sway of Moscow in the movement as a whole, while notions of national communism, socialism with a human face, cultural revolution, Eurocommunism and the like have undermined Stalinist orthodoxies inside particular parties. The shocks of adjustment have been severe. By a certain irony, the movement whose concentration on socio-economic reconstruction was to transform politics into the simple administ-ration of things has proved exceptionally rich in political drama. Eastern Europe alone since 1953 has experienced the Soviet invasions of Hungary in 1956 and Czechoslovakia in 1968, the riots in Poland in 1956, 1970 and 1976 and the strikes of 1980, the secession of Albania from the Soviet block and the partial secession of Romania. The result has been to focus observers' attention on the political crises rather than the social transformation. De-Stalinization has appeared as an essentially politico-moral issue, involving, for Western writers, the problem of 'liberalization' or the dismantling of totalitarianism in the teeth of bureaucratic and Soviet opposition, and for East European communists, the problem of strengthening 'socialist legality' without opening the way to the 'enemies of socialism'. Yet the chequered course of de-Stalinization can only be understood in relation to the fortunes of Stalin's most enduring legacy, the command economy. The history of communist Eastern Europe strikingly vindicates the Marxist postulate of the interrelation of economics and politics.

Economic and political development

The command economy was developed in Russia from the late 1920s as a means of speeding industrialization in a relatively backward society. Through it, central planning agencies controlled the entire economic process, first by calculating 'material balances' matching the supply and demand for key economic factors like steel, energy, capital and labour, then by plotting on this basis the exact bulk of given articles which individual enterprises were to produce. The emphasis was on producer rather than consumer goods – for instance, iron and steel – and on bulk rather than quality or profitability of output. Indeed, profitability could hardly figure as a factor in production because, in the absence of a free market, prices were fixed arbitrarily by the government, to suit policy priorities. Any waste that this system might entail was amply allowed for by massive diversion of investment to the industrial sphere. It was a crude system but not without its rationale when the first need was to create an industrial infrastructure at almost any cost. Even the notorious heavy industry fetish had a sound economic justification. Textiles, the classic consumer product of the first industrial revolution, have declined from one-half to one-fifth of industrial production in the West in this century, and Western Europe, too, was to see a great expansion of the producer goods industries in the post-war period.

However, in Stalin's last years the system had been applied with characteristic brutality. Capital accumulation, calculated in Western terms, probably amounted to two-fifths of national income as opposed to one-fifth in the West; by contrast, a vital consumer item like housing acquired one-eight of investment, or half the Western figure – less than a square metre per head of new floor space was built for Romania's additional 2 million urban dwellers. Even official figures showed a 6 per cent drop in the Hungarian standard of living in these years. The sheer privation of a workforce subjected to mounting norms to achieve unrealistic targets actually led to physical revolt in East Berlin in June 1953.

Even had Stalin lived economic logic might well have imposed a relaxation of pressure. But the 'thaw' which followed his death, as rival groups battled for the succession in Moscow, permitted party intellectuals to investigate and to an extent publicize the suffering that had been caused.

It was the communist poet Kucska's disturbing account of

conditions in the collectivized countryside in autumn 1953, together with the reappearance of show trial victims, which sparked off the questioning movement in party ranks in Hungary. Broad sections of the communist intelligentsia, guilt-striken that they had been persuaded to smother *petit bourgeois* misgivings at the Stalinist violation of human rights, now looked to Imre Nagy, the one veteran communist who had criticized forced collectivization, reckless industrialization and party repression. However, Nagy's 'New Course' as prime minister, launched with Russian approval in 1953, foundered on the continued obstruction of party chief Rakosi and the fall of Nagy's patrons in Moscow. In Poland, debating clubs and the periodical *Po Prostu* provided a forum for similar ideals to those of Nagy, whose Polish counterpart Gomulka remained in official disfavour. But Krushchev's denunciation of Stalin at the twentieth Soviet congress in spring 1956 helped precipitate renewed protest movements by party liberalizers in both countries, which in October spilled over into mass demonstrations of disaffected workers and students, bringing Gomulka and restoring Nagy to power. In Hungary events took a violent turn. The lynching of police officials and the siding of army units with the people provoked two bloody Soviet interventions in which about 25,000 Hungarians died and the reform movement was extinguished, not before Nagy had accepted a multi-party system and announced the withdrawal of Hungary from the Soviet block's military alliance, the Warsaw pact.

Although it lasted only thirteen days, the Hungarian Revolution had a profoundly dramatic impact. As the state radio reported on 28 October, when the reform current seemed to have won the upperhand.

We are opening a new chapter in the history of Hungarian radio at this hour. For long years past the radio was an instrument of lies ... it lied during the night and in the daytime, it lied on all wavelengths. Not even in the hour of our country's rebirth did it cease its campaign of lies. ... In future you will hear new voices on the old wavelengths. We think of ourselves as the mouthpiece of the Hungarian revolution as a whole and wish to let the Hungarian nation's voice be heard throughout our homeland and the world.

Ideologically, that voice bore a relatively simple message, a compound of conventional nationalism, 'national communism' and working-class disillusionment, which produced a general strike for the first few weeks of the Russian occupation. If some Trotskyists have subsequently seen this episode somewhat rosily as an attempt at workers' control, it was Nagy's national communism which aroused most comment at the time. In a famous apologia written before his return to power Nagy had argued passionately – mainly inspired by the emerging non-aligned movement in the third world and by Yugoslavia's reconciliation with the Kremlin in 1955 – that Hungary's security lay in an independent, even a neutralist foreign policy. Yet his comments on domestic policy, his abuse of 'sectarian, left-wing deviationists' and his defence of the New Course in terms of Lenin's 'New Economic Policy', were couched in the clichés of Stalinist polemic and revealed no willingness to relax the Communist Party's monopoly of power or to devise new categories of economic analysis. Most commentators have concluded that national communism was just a gut reaction to Stalinist and Soviet excesses rather than a comprehensive social philosophy, and find this view confirmed by the fact that Gomulka's regime, which the Russians had chosen not to obstruct, subsequently cleaved ever closer to Marxist-Leninist orthodoxy and the Soviet alliance. Perhaps they exaggerate. Gomulka's course was influenced by the special circumstance that, more than any other East European communist leader, he genuinely believed that Polish national interests required strong ties with Russian against German *revanchisme*; Nagy's stereotyped style disguised a resourceful critique of Stalinist economics. But the events of 1956 downgraded these subtleties and showed that national communism was a very blunt instrument for change. Essentially a highly personalized amalgam of Marxist ideas and patriotic instincts, it proved an unstable basis for a broader movement and gravitated under pressure either to its nationalist or its communist poles.

In the decade following 1956 many of the abuses against which Nagy had protested were alleviated in much of Eastern Europe. More attention was paid to living standards, burdens on collective farmers were reduced, the role of the secret police became less obtrusive and cultural policies less crass. Yet in these years pressure mounted for a reformist critique which would penetrate to the heart of continuing social malaise as well as identifying its symptoms. Rejigging the mechanism of the command economy could mollify Hungarian workers with a 21 per cent increase in real income in 1957, but it could not obscure the fact that this mechanism was becoming less and less suited to the region's needs.

Economies biased to put sheer output ahead of quality, expense or saleability necessarily incurred much waste. Although material balance totals could be calculated for a year as a whole, it was statistically impossible to derive all the product interrelationships for all points during the year; hence the constant shortages and bottle-necks characteristic of command economies, leading to hoarding of raw materials and misreporting of capacity by enterprises, and the setting of exaggerated targets by planners in order to tease these out. Planned economies revealed themselves to be quite as arbitrary, if not more so, than capitalist ones. In the absence of market prices the authorities found it very difficult to gauge real efficiency in the economy; producer goods, which were very costly in real terms, could be encouraged at the expense of more efficient products because artificial prices and huge subsidies made them more profitable for the enterprise concerned. Nor did it help that enterprise managers were often appointed more for political reliability than business expertise and that Eastern Europe abounded in so-called political factories erected as a sop to regional pride or to pay off political debts, rather than with regard to real economic viability. Even the spectacular rises in output which made criticism seem alarmist were in part the product of double-counting, pricing and other statistical factors which led a Russian economist to admit in the mid 1950s that the Soviet economy had probably only risen 63 per cent as fast since 1929 as the offical figures suggested.

Growth was achieved under these terms through inflated investment levels, entailing not just the depression of consumption but the depletion of depreciation and amortization funds. Thus Eastern Europe had a far higher proportion of obsolete and obsolescent industrial equipment than the West, which exacerbated the problem of low-grade output and placed a question mark over the long-term continuation of growth. For two reasons this problem was more serious for Eastern Europe than for the Soviet Union; first, because its small states lacked the vast Soviet internal market and second, because they mainly stood at a higher level of development, and would more quickly reach the stage where further economic progress could only come from technological improvements rather than the simple displacement of peasants into the urban labour force. In each case, Eastern Europe more than Russia needed closer economic ties with the West, which would entail a move towards competitive world market prices and greater product specialization, instead of the extensive pattern of development characteristic of the command economy. As it was, a bizarre result of the current system was that Eastern European states could only make up their deficits in Western trade by competing to offload onto each other large quantities of their inferior and almost identical engineering goods.

In the late 1950s even the Soviet Union began to experience a decline in the rate of growth and a rise in the capital-output ratio. Discussion of economic reform began to appear in economic journals, cast in the arcane language of Marxist debate. 'Rehabilitation of the law of value' meant more attention to real costs in price policy; 'the problem of the equivalence of prices' disclosed tension between, for instance, advanced Czechoslovakia and backward Romania as to whether the latter should be offered special help to achieve industrialization or should accept a more agrarian and raw producer role within a socialist division of labour. In Poland and East Germany, which had both experienced working-class unrest in the mid 1950s, economic reform looked briefly like becoming a matter of public debate. Swiftly, the East German reformist tendency was proscribed, while Gomulka's reluctance to put his weight behind the Polish economists' proposals was one of the first signs of his essential conservatism. It was in Romania that the theoretical debate first gave rise to serious political controversy when Krushchev decided for specialization inside Comecon (a watered down East European parallel to the EEC founded in 1949) and was defied by the Romanian communist leaders. Between 1961 and 1964 the Romanians' stance broadened from defence of their heavy industry ambitions to a more general autonomous position within the Soviet block, exemplified by Romania's refusal to take the Soviets' side in their quarrel with China. The Romanian initiative was a classic case of carefully controlled national communism, for the Romanian leader, Gheorghiu-Dej, allowed no relaxation of the Communist Party grip inside the country, while making it more palatable by his independent line towards Romania's traditional Russian foe. However, his maintenance of the Stalinist heavy industrialization policy also had an economic rationale, in that Romania as the least developed East European state (always excepting Albania) had not yet experienced the drawbacks of this policy in their acute form.

Most other countries in the region did introduce economic reform in the mid 1960s as, in very attenuated form, did the Soviet Union. All acknowledged three principles, with differing degrees of emphasis and boldness: a measure of decentralization to enter-prises, which henceforth could vary their production within broad limits to suit consumer needs; the introduction of the profit motive as a regulator, with more realistic prices and bonuses for successful managers and workers; and a change in industrial financing, transferring part of the state role in investment to enterprise self-funding and to banks acting on economic rather than ideological criteria. Implementation, however, bristled with difficulties, made worse by the obstruction of conservatives in key positions. The purpose of the reform was to reduce the state central planning role, but the complex task of carrying it out actually increased this role in the short-term. Prices were to be gradually liberalized, but there was endless scope for argument about exceptions for key raw materials and consumer necessities. Yet as long as prices remained arbitrary it was hardly fair to judge enterprises by profitability, if the prices of their products were fixed low. Indeed, in some ways the reforms merely introduced more criteria which harassed managers had to take into account. Often the administ-rative reorganization entailed bureaucratic upheaval without really bringing enterprises closer to consumer needs, for enterprises tended to be grouped in cartels which held a virtual monopoly of their particular market. Of course, underlying the caution of the reform was the daring of the principle involved. In theory at least it involved removing the economic sphere from direct party control and making technological and management expertise rather than ideology the determining factor in its operation. For Marxists trained to believe that political structures arise from the economic base, this was plainly a bold and risky experiment.

Events in Czechoslovakia in the 1960s fully bore this out. Advanced Czechoslovakia suffered acutely from the straitjacket of the command economy. A small country of 14 million inhabitants suited to an intensive rather than extensive pattern of development, she was manufacturing nearly three quarters of the world product assortment in engineering (which, by American standards, would have required 500,000 researchers in engineering alone) and consuming twice as much energy and two and a half times as much steel as the United States to achieve the same given result. By 1963 she had a capital-output ratio of 9.5 and had actually recorded a decline in industrial growth. Czech economists, led by the liberal communist Oto Sik, feared that their country was losing out altogether in the latest phase of industrialization being spearheaded in the West, in which inputs of science and technology were more important than those of capital and labour. Sik's reform programme aimed to eliminate waste and restore Czechoslovak competitiveness. Significantly, this economic thinking, drawing on Western experience and directed at restoring something of Czechoslovakia's trade with the West, was paralleled by a movement in political philosophy which echoed much of the discussion of interest groups, pluralism and Marxist humanism then also current in the West. Writers like Mlynar and Lakatos argued that it was time to abandon the Stalinist vision of a monolithic society; non-antagonistic conflicts of interest did, indeed, exist under socialism which should be permitted expression within a revitalized National Front, in which the Communist Party should play an inspiratory and co-ordinating but not an authoritarian role. Meanwhile, party philosophers like Kosik increasingly interpreted the Marxist message in terms of the liberation of individual man rather than the struggle of classes. What was happening was a recrudescence of traditional Czechoslovak themes in protest at the bankrupt neo-Stalinism of the unimaginative party chief, Novotny, whose centralism even succeeded in driving the far from radical Slovak communists into the reformist camp.

Probably it was this strong party opposition to Novotny which persuaded the Soviet leadership not to oppose his ousting in favour of the Slovak Alexander Dubcek at the end of 1967; the Czech situation was judged to be more akin to that in Poland in 1956 than that in Hungary. In the event Dubcek presided over a remarkable explosion of reform activity known as the Prague Spring. Encouraged by the virtual cessation of censorship and police surveillance, Czechoslovak society set about creating the socialist pluralism for which the Communist Party called in its April Action Programme. The media, the trade unions, the youth movement and other official bodies were reorganized and rejuvenated; Slovaks, national minorities and the churches made rapid strides; agrarian co-operatives and workers' control came on the agenda; and even 'non-party intellectuals', the victims of the Stalinist purges and the old Social Democratic Party began to organize. Caught between this tide of public enthusiasm and the suspicion of party conservatives, the Dubcek leadership eventually allowed itself to be carried along by the former, despite clear Soviet backing for the conservatives and the ominous manoeuvres of the Warsaw military pact. Since he had no intention of leading Czechoslovakia out of the pact or of permitting a multi-party system as Nagy had done, Dubcek was convinced that his country would escape Hungary's fate. Direct negotiations between the Czechoslovak leaders and their Warsaw pact partners at the end of July appeared to confirm this view. The invasion of an unresisting Czechoslovakia by troops from five pact countries on 21 August therefore came as a great shock to Czechoslovakia and the world.

In hindsight the invasion is easier to understand. Opinion in the Soviet Union throughout the Prague Spring had been divided between hawks, concerned for its effects on dissent elsewhere, and doves, primarily interested in good relations with the United States and the international communist movement. The final decision to intervene in August probably resulted less from fear of Western designs to exploit the Czechoslovak crisis, or of the collapse of Czechoslovak party authority, than from a shift in the balance between these two camps, occasioned by Dubcek's failure to head off a looming purge of Czechoslovak party conservatives. In addition, Moscow had underestimated Dubcek's popular support and imagined that, as with Kadar in Hungary in 1956, it would be easy to establish a government of communist hard-liners. When this proved impossible, Dubcek and his colleagues had to be reinstated despite their arrest following the invasion. But under Soviet occupation and relentless pressure, the Prague Spring withered, and after Dubcek's enforced resignation in April 1969 another Slovak, Husak, led the country back to the rigid orthodoxy of 'normalization'.

East Germany, Poland, Hungary and Bulgaria participated in the Soviet-led invasion of Czechoslovakia; Romania and Yugoslavia did not. Romanian dissidence was limited to a stubborn independence in the international sphere, manifested in her policies towards China and Israel and her fitful contribution to Comecon and the Warsaw pact; internally, she remained under Ceausescu (from 1965), as under Gheorghiu-Dej, a strictly regimented society. Thus after the failure of the Prague Spring only Yugoslavia continued to offer a pattern of development substantially different from the Soviet model.

The Yugoslavs' distinctiveness dated not from their break with Stalin in 1948 but the period 1950–2, in which they boldly repudiated the Stalinist command economy. In these years they reintroduced private farming on the land and formulated a policy of workers' control in industry which grew by degrees into the celebrated doctrine of social self-management. By this, all state enterprises, broken down into their constituent units, are controlled by elected councils, to which alone belongs the right to appoint managerial personnel, to approve annual production plans and to allocate wages and benefits. Thus decentralization in the economy corresponds to decentralization in the six republics and two autonomous regions of multi-national Yugoslavia, and the defects of the Soviets are firmly ascribed to the twin-headed ogre of bureaucratic centralism.

However, till the 1960s, continued state controls on wages and investment made Yugoslavia's self-management more theory than reality. It was pressures for economic liberalization, allied to ethnic aspirations of the non-Serbs, which brought about the economic reform of 1965 and the dismissal of the obstructive and centralist Serbian police chief, Rankovic, the next year. Henceforth Yugoslavia operated a 'socialist market' with a more consumer-orientated economy, greater decentralization of investment, freer prices and higher receptivity to foreign capital than any of her neighbours. She has stuck to her guns despite considerable economic and political difficulties. Reduction of controls saw Yugoslavia rapidly acquire high rates of inflation (30 per cent) and unemployment (10–15 per cent) despite the outflow of nearly a million 'guest-workers' into Central Europe, as well as mounting foreign debts and a widening gap between the richest and poorest region. National feeling also rose sharply as the federal and republican assemblies were allowed more play. Nationality ratios in public office became the norm, as also did the requirement of republican unanimity for the passage of important federal business. To this time dates the complex collective leadership in party and state which has taken over the functions of the charismatic Tito. Tito himself seems to have felt that 'anarcho-liberalism' was becoming a greater menace than 'bureaucratism' and *étatisme*. In the early 1970s he intervened to force the resignation of the nationalistically tinged Croatian communist leadership and the liberal-minded Serbs. The constitution of 1974 underscored his commitment to self-management as a specific form of socialism rather than a euphemism for liberalistic trends. The self-management organs and the League of Communists between them were to elect the majority of members of parliamentary and other representative assemblies, emphasizing the claim that Yugoslavia was a truly democratic pluralist society unlike the Soviet and Western parliamentary regimes where the dominant party holds a monopoly of power. The constitution also established 'social compact' procedures, by which self-management and political organs at all levels can co-operate to meet the complex needs of a modern economy.

Sceptics have long argued that social self-management is either an elaborate charade in which all the real decisions are taken by the managers, or else a prescription for anarchy. They point to the Belgrade public's loss of their milk supply in late 1979 as a result of the relevant self-managing suppliers' decisions to seek more lucrative customers in capitalist Greece; they look with interest to see how far the local communities on the Adriatic will succeed in pressing their claims against the vast petro-chemical complex currently being installed there. Nevertheless, self-management works, if somewhat creakily. A not unsympathetic historian has concluded by envisaging 'another moderately oppressive, semi-efficient, semi-authoritarian state run by an oligarchy of contending elites . . . in which many people are free and participating and many are not. Like most states'. The rather elaborate social philosophy which has grown out around social self-management disguises the fact that it has been, in a sense, an attempt to make a virtue of necessity, in a society uniquely ill-suited to centralism. Arousing wonder, admiration and scepticism in turns, the course of Yugoslav self-management does not yet permit the conclusion that it is a stable and universalizable model for peaceful evolution from Stalinism.

Contemporary communist society

But since the suppression of the Prague Spring a feature of East European life has been a decline of ideological concern of any kind. Nagy and Dubcek, Tito and Kardelj, were committed communists, deeply concerned to rescue their Marxist faith from the associations of Stalinism. Younger politicians coming to the fore in the 1970s knew no such driving force. As the direct memory of Stalinism fades, so the impulse to revisionism also withers. This is the thesis of Leszek Kolakowski, once leader of the liberal Marxist school in Poland in the early 1960s, now an *émigré* in Britain who has shed his Marxist creed. Just as the ideals of 1848 lived longest among nineteenth-century East European emigrants, so 'socialism with a human face' is discussed most eagerly among the 80,000 Czechs who fled their land in 1968. In Eastern Europe itself rulers and ruled have become less concerned with ideas and more with bread and butter issues.

In part this is a natural response of weary populations to years of alternating hope and disillusion. Even more it reflects a conscious decision of communist leaders to try the carrot of affluence in place of, or at least as well as, the stick of ideology. Such a calculation underlay the Hungarian leader Kadar's declaration as early as 1961: 'He who is not against us is for us.' It explains the 40 per cent rise of real wages in Poland in the early 1970s after virtual stagnation of living standards helped topple Gomulka in 1970. It is the unspoken theme of 'normalization' in the post-Dubcek Czechoslovakia. Crucial to the relative success of this tactic in recent years is that it has corresponded to a certain reality. After a generation of austerity Eastern Europe is beginning to see prosperity on the horizon.

It remains moot whether this development vindicates the command economy or has been unnecessarily obstructed by it. However, by the 1960s a basic infrastructure for industrial growth had been created which permitted Eastern Europe to shed some of its obsession for crude steel and develop its engineering strength. By 1974 machine construction and metal processing industries were accounting for a quarter to a third of industrial output in the countries of the Eastern block, a figure quite close to performance in the West. The 1970s saw a further shift in East European industrialization to chemicals, petro-chemicals and electronic products, which demanded high technology and increased the tendency already noticeable in the 1960s for the Eastern block to seek to increase its trade with the West. By the close of the decade, twenty-five years of more or less continuous growth could be summed up in the official figures, impressive for all the likely distortions: a rise in industrial output of nineteenfold for Romania, sixteenfold for Bulgaria, twelvefold for Yugoslavia, elevenfold for Poland, and six to sevenfold for Hungary and Czechoslovakia. Moreover, the place of Eastern Europe in the world economy had changed. The bulk of its exports were now fabricated or semi-fabricated goods. It had even begun to demonstrate its modernity by cutting down its railway network!

The great change which had come about could be summarized

	GNP per capita 1978 (in dollars)	population mid-1979 (millions)
Albania	740	2.6
Bulgaria	3210	8.8
Czechoslovakia	4730	15.1
Hungary	3480	10.7
Poland	3650	35
Romania	1650	21.8
Yugoslavia	2100	21.9

Source: The World Bank Atlas

The figures for GNP per head and foreign debts are estimates, and should be treated with caution.

Communist Eastern Europe

in a single phrase: once preponderantly agrarian, Eastern Europe had become preponderantly urban. Writing in 1951, the Trotskyist Glückstein had calculated that it would be necessary to quintuple pre-war investment ratios merely to absorb surplus rural population into industry over the next two generations. Yet all this and far more had occurred. It was not so much that the capitals had swollen – Bucharest and Budapest to 2 million apiece, Warsaw to 1.5 million, Prague 1.25 million, Sofia and Belgrade to 1 million – for these had always been large. It was the provincial centres, like the 14 Romanian and 21 Polish cities with over 150,000 inhabitants, which best demonstrated galloping urbanization. Well over half all Bulgarians and Poles and half all Romanians now lived in towns. Moreover, the remaining rural dwellers were increasingly less likely to be employed in agriculture. Between 1965 and 1975, agricultural workers as a proportion of the labouring force fell from fifty-seven to thirty-seven in Romania, forty-five to twenty-six in Bulgaria and twenty to fourteen in Czechoslovakia. The worker-peasant who lived on the family farm, commuted to the town and supplemented his income by part-time agriculture became a common feature of the two societies which retained private agriculture – Yugoslavia and Poland. It is currently estimated that half of all Yugoslav farms house permanent urban employees, who together make up a third of the industrial work force. Bulgaria, which put least emphasis on super-industrialization, was also the country which went furthest in organizing agriculture on industrial lines, amalgamating its collective farms in the 1970s into some 150 huge 'agro-technical complexes'. Hungary also made notable experiments in encouraging auxiliary activities on collective farms, which already accounted for 30 per cent of their total output in 1970. In that year she declared herself the first country in Eastern Europe where the average standard of living in the countryside had caught up with that of workers in the towns.

With the emergence of more modern settlement patterns has come assimilation to Western demographic norms. Birth rates and death rates have both halved since the war, infant mortality in the Balkans is a fifth of its pre-war level and people can expect to live from a dozen to twenty years longer. This healthier, more homogenous population has come to participate in the vagaries of the consumer society. Personal incomes have risen sharply, despite the tendency of communist planning to keep wage increases below the expansion of national income; real wages seem to have gone up on average three to four times since 1950. It is in the last decade that consumerism has made most progress. In that time television and washing machines have become all but universal, with a certain lag in Romania, fridges have become normal in urban homes if not in the countryside, and telephones and cars have ceased to be rarities. One in eleven owns a car in Czechoslovakia, a figure equalled only in Yugoslavia and by workers elsewhere; in Hungary it is one family in four, with Romania again well in arrears. East Europeans have followed their Western counterparts in taking less bread and potatoes and more sugar, meat and spirits. Dress styles of course had not been unchanging in the older society. Joel Halpern in 1953 traced at least four successive variations among the peasants of the Serbian Sumadija over the previous century, to which the ill-fitting, drab-coloured modern garments which had triumphed everywhere by the 1960s seemed a tawdry heir. Now these in turn have yielded to altogether smarter and more colourful styling. Housing, however, remains a bugbear, largely because governments have been reluctant to commit sufficient funds. Only Hungary has kept its promise to achieve an equal ratio between households and household units. Unmarried people have difficulty in obtaining flats, and accommodation problems account for much of the rapid labour turnover among young people. Anti-government feeling is fuelled as much as anything by suspicions that party members can jump long waiting lists for desirable homes, and in general exert undue influence in economies where much depends on the black market and on specially equipped 'hard-currency' stores. Consumerism has brought some relief, and many new headaches, to rulers and ruled alike. But with the passing of an old agrarian-dominated society has gone also much of the substance and symbolism of the various national cultures. They have by no means receded as far as in the West. Professional folk dance ensembles hog the stages of Eastern Europe; 'national music' blares as often as 'pop' from transistor radios. However, national integration is now even more a matter of the state educational system than under the old bourgeois regimes. While illiteracy has been reduced to pockets in the Balkans, the most striking development has come in the secondary and higher fields, previously reserved for the relative few. The number of university students in the area quintupled to 250,000 between 1937–8 and 1965–6. By the mid 1970s, there were almost as many in Yugoslavia alone, with 175,000 in Romania and 150,000 in

Poland. About double these numbers, taken together, attended polytechnics, teachers' training colleges and medical, agrarian and economic academies. The bulk of these students have entered the technological field, and the system has been flexible; thus Romania was able to double her agricultural and forestry personnel quickly when the need was felt in the early 1960s.

The creation of a mass intelligentsia no doubt also helps explain the large sales of the, to Western minds, extremely stodgy East European newspapers. The Hungarian party daily *Nepszabadsag* published 745,000 copies in 1971, proportionately equivalent to the sale of the *Sun* or *Daily Mirror* in Britain. The dull press contrasted oddly with the continuing high standards of the East European theatrical tradition which, however, remained static. On average two in every three Poles and Hungarians attended the theatre once a year in 1960, a much higher proportion than in Britain, but it was slightly down fifteen years later. During this period, for the first time attendance at museums exceeded that at the theatre. Book production *per capita* substantially exceeded that of Western countries, and a third to a quarter of Polish manual workers claimed to read them regularly. The films of Jancso in Hungary and Wajda in Poland acquired an international reputation, although cinema audiences were on the decline. But sport was the most vital element in the entertainment field. Football was universally popular, and took up most of the daily sports papers several countries boasted. Land-locked Hungary was several times world water-polo champion, Czechoslovakia excelled at ice-hockey, Yugoslavia at basketball, Poland at athletics, Bulgaria at women's field events; Romania produced Ilie Nastase and Nadia Comaneci. Polish sports clubs in 1975 had over a million members. Even self-isolated Albania competed in the European Champions' Cup. Sport could, however, lead to the selfish pursuit of individual or club glory, the luring of talented palyers and rise of monopolist tendencies. 'Steps have to be taken', warned a Hungarian government pronouncement, 'against the ever-prevailing material minded-ness and more attention has to be devoted to educating sports people to socialist patriotism and internationalism; the national interest should prevail and be normative in the life of sports clubs.'

Decidedly un-Western though this exhortation is, the very fact that it had to be made suggests how, in many ways, Eastern Europe was coming to resemble the West, more than it had for centuries. An increasingly homogenous, literate, urban-orientated consumer society of television watchers and sports followers was emerging, whose chief ambitions were a family car and a foreign holiday. Sixteen times more Hungarians and thirty-four times more Poles went abroad in the mid 1970s than in 1960, about a half and a quarter of the total population respectively. Mainly it was to other socialist countries, but there was also a far greater chance of visiting the West, just as *émigrés* were much freer to return on vacation. Factory bonus schemes sometimes included vouchers for foreign travel. Polish citizens could open bank accounts in foreign currency; the Polish Peirex state chain store, the Czech Tugex shops and the Hungarian Intertourist shops sold high quality goods for Western currency. Nor were growing resemblances to the West just a matter of superficial consumption. Contrary to some Western views, which saw Eastern Europe as a battleground between persecuting atheists and pious masses, attitudes to religion, except in Poland, veered towards Western patterns, sentimental, moral and national–historical predilections on the one hand being countered by intellectual scepticism and a sense of social irrelevance on the other. It was the internationally organized Catholic Church which aroused greatest controversy, not just in Poland but also in Croatia in Yugoslavia though the Vatican reached agreements with both countries in the 1970s. Other creeds gave little trouble. Billy Graham preached to 15,000 Hungarians on a hillside outside Budapest; the Bulgarian and Romanian Orthodox Churches received a modest niche in the new national consensus by virtue of their historic role. In Yugoslavia in the early 1970s a de luxe translation of the Koran became something of a status symbol on the bookshelves of first generation intelligentsia along, incidentally with Churchill's *History of the Second World War* and Galsworthy's *Forsyte Saga*, stunningly successful as a television series through much of the region. As in the West the decline of traditional religious and social restraints led to concern over hooliganism and youth. 'Permissiveness' was not on public show, except to an extent in Yugoslav magazines, but it has become a fact of private life. Nearly one in three marriages in Hungary now ends in divorce, as against one in ten in Romania, one in nine in Poland and one in eight in Yugoslavia. To deal with such problems, regimes increasingly turned to sociology and related disciplines which had been frowned on as strangers to dialectical materialism in the Stalin years. From the 1960s all East European countries have established organs to poll public opinion. It is symptomatic that having decided to espouse sociology they should have opted for its most quint-essentially empirical Western form.

Of course, these trends have not gone without criticism in some quarters in Eastern Europe. An article in *New Albania* in February 1979 indicates some of the many heresies against which that citadel of orthodoxy feels called to fight:

Albanian cinematography is developing completely divorced from sentimentalism, pornography, sadism and all other physiological and moral abnormalities; divorced from pycho-analytical sophistications and the Freudian delvings into the human subconscious, from naturalism and the pursuit of sensational subjects, divorced from idealism and human individualism which often leads to the blackest pessimism or to the alienation of heroes; the Albanian film is not lured by commercialism in selecting themes or subject . . . .

Needless to say, socialist realism proves to be the necessary and sufficient condition for the flowering of the Albanian cinema.

At almost the other end of the pole, Kadar's Hungary best represents the sort of society that seems possible within the limits set by the Soviet invasion of Czechoslovakia in 1968. Formally, the Kadar regime rejects the concept of pluralism with its Western overtones, but it recognizes the need for meaningful representation of different interest groups in the nation. The task of the Communist Party is not to replace other organizations, but to define 'essential principles' and to provide 'general orientation'. Marxism must not be treated as a dogma, but must reflect changing reality; neverthe-less, social scientists should confine themselves to describing and analysing social phenomena rather than – as the disgraced Hegedüs tried to do – usurping the party's guiding role by essaying prescriptive or normative theories. In other words, they should help the party carry out its policies more effectively rather than tell it what the policies should be. Within this framework, limited freedom of expression and action is possible, resting more on self-censorship than on direct physical control and greater for institutions than for individuals. The trade unions and associations of agricultural co-operatives have become powerful bodies, able on certain issues to impose their wishes on the government. Thus the restrictions placed on economic reform in 1973–4 owed something to union fears of inflation, though other factors also obtained. Parliament is marginally bolder than before; since 1966 safe multi-candidatures have been permitted but have not reached the same scale as in

Yugoslav elections, where five anti-government candidates were returned in 1969. As in a number of other East European countries, incentives have been offered to raise the number of artisans and private retailers whose services are badly needed, particularly in the smaller towns. Strikes are not explicitly prohibited, and have occurred on a minor scale. To concede in general terms that there is some truth in both ultra-left and conservative critiques of the present course is permissible; to advocate one of these critiques oneself is to invite prosecution. There seems no intrinsic reason why these conditions could not obtain in other countries of Eastern Europe. In practice, Poland has had, till recently, less economic but somewhat more political freedom, and Romania, Bulgaria and Czechoslovakia less of both, for reasons lying beyond the scope of this general survey.

Stabilization?

The 1970s have, then, seen something of a stabilization of the East European communist block. With the decline in ideological strife has come a decline in the saliency of the region in international affairs. Indignation at the Soviets is now focused on events in other continents; none look to the states of the Warsaw pact for models of alternative socialism, fewer than formerly look to Yugoslavia. Russia's world position has strengthened. The non-aligned movement, which Yugoslavia did so much to create, is no longer the force it was. Both she and Romania ended the 1970s arguably closer to the Soviet Union than a decade before, if no doubt more from calculation than affection. The impact of the invasion of Afghanistan or the free trade-union movement in Poland cannot yet be assessed.

As Eastern Europe has lost its role as the ideological front line in the East–West conflict, so East Europeans have seemed more prepared to accept the geo-political implications of their position. Even a certain sense of regional identity can be discerned *vis-à-vis* the West which has consistently withheld a helping hand in the past and is currently pressing Eastern Europe hard commercially through the protectionism of the EEC. By contrast the relationship with Russia is now probably economically beneficial. Comecon member states are assured of Soviet energy supplies, which all of them but Poland and Romania badly need, and of access to the Russian markets for their industrial goods. On average two-thirds of their trade is with other members and one-third or more with Russia alone. The 4000 kilometre network of the Friendship pipeline supplies Poland, East Germany, Czechoslovakia and Hungary with Soviet oil; the 1700 kilometre Orenburg pipeline performs an equivalent service for gas and a high tension electrical power grid is being developed based on a nuclear power station on the Polish border in the west Ukraine.

Commercial arrangements between Russia and her neighbours are bilateral, often on a semi-barter basis and with wide potential price variations which have aroused bitterness. But it is not clear that, since the mid 1950s the overall pattern of these transactions has been exploitative of the smaller states. The terms of Russian loans, though shorter than those of the West, have been far more generous than those Eastern Europe had to accept in the 1920s. Indeed, a relatively advanced Eastern block member like Hungary would like closer, not looser inter-block ties, with Comecon operating on a multi-lateral trading basis and using a convertible rouble.

It is against this background that the absence of movements like the Prague Spring should be judged. The ideology of 1968 is widely seen as utopian, if not presumptuous and naive. Just before his death in 1979 the Yugoslav theoretician, Kardelj, spoke scathingly of the 'so-called Czechoslovak crisis in the course of which the playing up of an empiricist and liberalist cliché blocked the search for a genuine democracy, and at the same time a socialist way out'. Intervention by a third force was 'understandable enough'. A recent book by two East European Marxist dissidents – now resident in the West – has argued interestingly that the reform communism of the 1960s failed because of the unwillingness of its managerial and technocratic sponsors to endorse a really far-reaching economic reform, which would have raised the question of the dormant power and aspirations of the working class. Their interests, the authors argue, aligned and align them ultimately with the bureaucratic establishment, leaving only the braver spirits of the intelligentsia – and potentially the workers – in opposition to the system. This thesis extends the well-known argument of Milovan Djilas from the 1950s that East European communism has produced its own kind of class society; but whereas Djilas's 'New Class' contained just the party bureaucrats, in the new version it incorporates the managerial element as well. Events in the 1970s lend some support to these theories. The importance of the intelligentsia when not supported either by dissident party elements above or by the masses below is illustrated by the waning fortunes of the Czechoslovak 'Chartists'. Conversely, it has been workers who have played the only significant dissident role in Eastern Europe in the 1970s, in the two successful but bloody protests against rising food prices in Poland, the remarkable recent strike in that country, and to a lesser extent the coal-miners strike in Romania in 1977.

It is the Polish crises which reveal the fragile basis of the region's recent security. Despite the greater sophistication of government (Gierek had consulted polls before cutting food subsidies in 1976) it still appeared that rioting might be the easiest way for public opinion to be heard in a one-party regime. Even more disconcerting for the regime in the longer term was the disciplined non-violent action of 1980, in which the demand for free trade unions posed an explicit challenge to the exclusive authority of the Communist Party. Moreover, the working class promises to be an increasingly volatile element in future East European society. Until recently it has been recruited largely from peasant migrants, whose arrival in the towns marked a rise in social status. As social structures conform more closely to the Western pattern, the avenues for advancement will be narrowed. The economic progress necessary to satisfy rising aspirations will have to be met through improved technology rather than expansion of the labour force. Reliance on the West, as the chief source of this technology, will increase still further Eastern Europe's massive Western debt, estimated at $20 billion in 1975 and probably treble that today.

These vast debts, servicing which took up half of Poland's hard currency earnings and 42 per cent of Romania's, reflected the difficulties of adjustment to world market conditions from the 1960s, compounded by the down turn in the world economy since 1973. The region had to pay more for its oil – though Russia increased her prices to it much less than the Arabs – at the same time that it met declining receptivity to its overtures in the West. But even these terms may not be available for long, as Comecon's hopes of self-sufficiency in energy by 1990 fade and Russia, in order to continue her profitable oil exports to the West, will have to cut down her supplies to Eastern Europe and pressurize her partners to buy some of their oil from OPEC at world market prices. As it is already, the technological gap is not being bridged and a sudden slow down in the regional rate of growth seems inevitable. Any future bout of economic reform will probably have to face more openly than the movement of the 1960s that effective competitiveness cannot be achieved without a measure of the two evils supposedly banished since 1948 - unemployment and inflation. Hungary has already officially admitted to an inflation of 9 per cent in 1979; Poland recorded a 2.8 per cent drop in national income. As the general manager of the great Hungarian engineering enterprise, Raba, commented after introducing an unprecedented redundancy programme at its Gyor plant; 'the constitution guarantees every citizen the right to a job, but it does not stipulate that it should be here in my factories'.

Whatever strains result will be taken by societies still in the throes of modernization. No doubt students should be included alongside workers as a potentially volatile category. A recent study has painted a grim picture of the poverty, inadequate facilities, unreformed courses and high failure rate which lies behind the vast inflation of student numbers in Yugoslavia. Whether here there is tinder for protest movements criticizing current regimes from the left for their flirtation with consumerism, such as briefly developed in Yugoslavia and Hungary in the late 1960s and early 1970s, remains to be seen. Increasingly complex dissident alliances may be expected, as the diverse backing for the Workers' Defence Committee (KOR) in Poland after 1976 has shown. When it is recalled that subsidies in 1976 took up one-eighth of the Polish national income, yet the attempt to reduce that on meat led to the sacking of a party headquarters and overturning of a locomotive, then the potential for social disturbance in the event of a severe depression will become apparent.

Thus, as Eastern Europe enters the 1980s, its fortunes remain as unpredictable as at any time in its stormy history. Great progress has been made under the communist order in the industrial, social and educational fields. But with the initial breakthrough now achieved virtually everywhere, the region moves into a different and equally problematic stage, that of satisfying the aspirations of increasingly sophisticated populations subject to all the stresses of modern life, the anonymity of large-scale organizations, the conflict between social amenity and economic growth, the rise of the crime rate among the young, the declining power of sustaining ideologies, whether Marxist or traditional, the loosening of the moorings to a known past which have shaped European societies in all previous phases of their existence. These new tasks are faced in an uncertain international climate, as the economic growth and *détente* of the 1960s stand increasingly under threat. As in the past, so again tensions within the region may oscillate with tensions in a wider sphere. The way ahead is obscure. All that can presently be said is that the security of the Eastern European regimes still rests, not on a positively accepted general order, but on the authority of one of the neighbouring super powers which have always claimed the right to preside over the destinies of 'the lands between'.

10 Epilogue

The communist take-over has trenched a deep divide in the continuity of East European history, even more in that of East European historiography. For probably more foreign researchers are working on aspects of the communist period than on the entire earlier span of the region's experience. Predictably, this imbalance has distorted attempts to relate the communist and pre-communist phrases of the region's life into a common interpretative framework.

Indeed, both Western and communist students of the most recent period often all but reverse the positions of their colleagues working on earlier themes. Western academics, as this book has had occasion to observe, are assiduous in pointing out the self-interested motives which could underly the rhetoric of past idealisms: the Enlightenment of the eighteenth century, the liberalism and nationalism of the nineteenth century. Marxist historians, on the other hand, are prepared to condone much human frailty in what they deem ultimately the progressive cause. In the modern period all this changes. It is Western writers who laud the struggles of anti-regime elements, showing their movements the same undifferentiated benevolence their ancestors accorded nineteenth century Magyars and Poles; and it is communists who push forward sociological and historical issues, pointing to the revival of bourgeois and nationalist motifs in contemporary dissidence, the role of ambitious technocrats and the uncertain relationship of the intelligentsia and the workers.

However tendentious the communist case is in particular instances, it has a certain general plausibility. The preoccupation of Western academics with ideological issues in Eastern Europe – national sovereignty and political liberty – contrasts not only with their approach to the East European past but also their understanding of the Western present, which gives pride of place to issues of welfare and class. Should Eastern Europe be viewed in a totally different light? May it not be as helpful to see the Czech leader Novotny, for example, as the rather narrow-minded working-class party bureaucrat he was as to label him a 'Stalinist'? The Prague Spring *was* in its origin a movement of intellectuals and reformist technocrats, in other words, a middle-class movement which sought to increase pay differentials and enhance the role of managers and a free intelligentsia; its leaders' frequent appeals to the working class suggest that it was not altogether confident of the working-class backing it did eventually receive. Much the same may be said of the Croatian movement of 1970–1. When the Polish Catholic episcopate, emboldened by greater official tolerance of dissent, inveighs against divorce, abortion and the permissive society, it is clear that communists may sometimes be more liberal than the liberalizers.

To adopt this perspective is not to endorse a hard-line communist view of the East European situation. On the contrary, the implication of such an approach is that a generation of communist rule has done little to deflect East Europeans' loyalties away from earlier habits of thought to a common commitment to proletarian internationalism. Communists remain a sectarian minority, the bearers of a perfectly respectable political creed - a form of centralist welfarism - which, however, has been elevated to its dominant position through an accident of history rather than as the natural expression of some purportedly new society. The continuities with the past remain.

This fact of continuity has been seized upon by communists and non-communists alike as a means of sidestepping the ambiguities lurking in their respective partisan interpretations. For communists, the socialist republics of today are presented not so much as stages on the road to the brotherhood of man as the fulfilment of national aspirations across the centuries. Romania, with its negligible socialist traditions, has led the way in this regard. People's Poland, making a virtue of necessity, reiterates the message that its boundaries correspond almost exactly with those of the earliest Polish state, so that the centuries of intervening German occupation in the western territories till 1945 appear merely as a temporary usurpation. The Kossuth cult in Hungary has taken on even vaster proportions; the Hungarian Jacobins of 1793–5 have been researched down to the last hand bill; Szechenyi's reputation has been rescued from his conservative inter-war admirers. Far more than in an ostensibly tradition-bound country like Britain, historical symbolism plays a role in communist politics. One of the steps on the road to the Prague Spring was the rehabilitation of the Slovak patriot Stur, on the occasion of his one hundred and fiftieth anniversary. At the height of the Croatian movement in 1970 the communist mayor and the party chief in Zagreb hung flags in the cathedral to celebrate the tercentenary of the execution of two Croatian nobles by the Habsburgs, men who bore as much relation to Croatia then and now as Bonnie Prince Charlie to the Scots.

For their part, Western writers have emphasized those aspects of the nationalist heritage which do not fit neatly into received communist interpretations. Yugoslavia's claim to have solved the Macedonian question is denied by Bulgaria; Romania openly resents the loss of Bessarabia to Russia and Albania the inclusion of a third of all Albanians in the Yugoslav state. A former Hungarian member of the Romanian central committee and a leading littérateur in Hungary have recently attacked the treatment of the 2 million strong Magyar minority in Transylvania. The 1968 disturbances in Poland were sparked off by a prohibition of Mickiewicz's nineteenth-century anti-Russian drama; and some of the opposition groups springing up in Poland appear to stand in the tradition of the inter-war nationalist leader, Dmowski. Nor is anti-Semitism dead in that country. The increasing concern of Milovan Djilas, Eastern Europe's most famous dissident, for his Serbian and Montenegrin roots is but the most vivid instance of the way in which sensitivity to personal history is frequently linked throughout the region to a rejection of the communists' claims to political and moral leadership.

Thus the case can be made that an inextinguishable nationalism remains, as it has been for a century and a half, the leading theme of the Eastern European story. It is a seductive but perhaps over-glib generalization, a convenient *deus ex machina* for the weary historian reaching the end of his narration. For nationalism is a universal category in the modern world which happened to assume particular prominence in Eastern Europe because its evolution was fraught by special difficulties. The question is not, therefore, whether or not nationalism exists in a modern society, but what particular form it assumes within this protean category.

The thesis of this book has been that Eastern European nationalism arose as a response to the backwardness of the region in comparison to the West, as a means of resolving the socio-economic and pychological problems arising therefrom. Seen in this light, communist Eastern Europe represents a very important stage in the region's long struggle to bridge the gap with the West. For the first time the life-style of the majority of East Europeans has come to approximate that of their Western counterparts. Urbanization, industry, secondary education, the mass media, organized sport and leisure and finally the consumer society with its materialist values have become the common lot of the European continent. Modernization now supplies its own dynamic. Nationalism has forfeited some of its mobilizing power or appears in close conjunction with the material preoccupations of the age, whether it is a matter of Croats reluctant to subsidize more backward republics, Albanian Yugoslavs alienated by regional poverty, Romanians and Slovaks fearful that more powerful neighbours will hinder their industrialization or Czechs resentful of their relative economic decline within the Soviet block. Croatian surveys carried out in the late 1960s, a time of some ethnic fervour, suggest that the working class, an expanding class in Eastern Europe, is less susceptible to nationalist appeals than other sections of the population.

Yet it would be idle to assume that Eastern Europe is finally set on some convergence course with the West or that its volcanic nationalist legacy will soon be dormant. Nationalism sleeps when a sense of socio-economic well-being is associated with the free exercise of national sovereignty. It is not impossible, though unlikely, that a sufficient number of people in Eastern Europe will come to see their situation in these terms, just as many Hungarians accepted Dualism after 1867. At the time of writing, however, too many are too close to their troubled past to entertain such complacency. They still see the native communist regimes as existing on the sufferance of their Soviet suzerains or in precarious defiance of Soviet will. The arduous struggles of Eastern Europe for progress and emancipation have yielded an ambiguous and perhaps provisional result. Eastern Europe retains its own distinctive and enigmatic destiny. In a fascinating document written after his expulsion from the Yugoslav Communist Party, which occured on the eve of an official visit he was to have paid to Scandinavia, Milovan Djilas vividly expresses the feelings of a sensitive East European, torn between his attraction for the placid, prosperous democracy that modern Scandinavia symbolizes and his proud affirmation of the differentness of his own embattled land. While paying eloquent tribute to the factors which have made Scandinavia what it is, the continuity of tradition, the respect for human personality and its dignity, the preference for science and freedom over ideology and fanaticism, he interjects:

I don't like you Nordic countries, with all your wealth, your social harmony, your distant black mountains and your white plains. I want my country! – its bitterness and its poisons, its joys and its splendours. I want to plunge into its dank, foul cellars and into its misery and dirt, its lies and betrayals, so that I may ascend into its sunny and drunken assault on the stars, on unattainable bliss.

The language is Djilas's own, fervent and highly coloured, but the sentiments his document expresses go to the heart of the modern East European experience.

Appendix 1
Chronology of chief events mentioned in the text

The Danubian lands: Austria, Hungary, Czechoslovakia

1526	The Habsburgs acquire the Crowns of Hungary and Bohemia
1620	Battle of the White Mountain; end of Bohemian automony
1699	Treaty of Karlowitz; Turks withdraw from Hungary

1740-80 Reign of Maria Theresa

1740-9	War of Austrian Succession (1740-8); first reform period (1748-9)
1756-63	Seven Years War; second reform period starts (1760)

1780-90 Reign of Joseph II

1781	Toleration Edict; serfs no longer 'bound to the soil'
1789	Tax law
1788-91	Austro-Turkish War

1792-1835 Reign of Francis I

1793-1815	Napoleonic wars; Vienna captured, 1805, 1809; Metternich chancellor, 1809
1818	Czech Museum founded; Czech Renaissance develops
1825	Beginning of Hungarian reform movement

1835-48 Reign of Ferdinand

1842	Leseverein (reading union); beginnings of liberalism
1848	Revolution; abolition of feudalism; Hungarian April laws; Prague Slav Congress

December 1848-1916 Reign of Franz Joseph

1849	Hungarian Declaration of Independence; Vilagos

1850	Abolition of Austro-Hungarian customs union
1859–61	Austria loses Franco-Austrian War; Reichsrat meets
1866–7	Austria loses Austro-Prussian War; Austro-Hungarian compromise
1879	Fall of Austro-German liberal cabinet; clerical–Slav coalition
1882	Czech University of Prague
1897	Badeni decrees; crisis of constitutionalism in Austria
1903–9	Constitutional crisis in Hungary
1914–18	First World War; end of Habsburg monarchy (1918)
1919	Paris peace conference; succession states; Bolshevik revolution in Hungary
1938	Nazi Germany annexes Austria and Sudetenland
1939–45	Second World War; Reich protectorate of Bohemia–Moravia
1948	Communist coup in Prague
1956	Hungarian Revolution
1968	Prague Spring; Warsaw pact countries invade Czechoslovakia

The Balkans: Romania, Yugoslavia, Bulgaria, Albania

C6–C7	Arrival of south Slavs
1389	Battle of Kosovo; Turks cripple medieval Serbian state
1690	Chief Serb migration from Turkish rule to Hungary
1711–1822	Greek Phanariot regime in the Romanian principalities
1774	Treaty of Kutchuk-Kainardji; Russian protectorate over Ottoman Orthodox
1804–17	First Serbian insurrection begins; Serbia gains autonomy
1821–9	Vladimirescu's revolt; Treaty of Adrianople
1835	First modern Bulgarian school
1848	Revolution in Wallachia
1853–6	Crimean War
1859	Unification of Romania
1860s	First Balkan alliance system
1875–8	Near Eastern crisis; Bosnian revolt; Bulgarian revolt; Serbo-Turkish War; Russo-Turkish War
1878	Treaty of Berlin; Serbia and Romania independent;

	Bulgaria autonomous; Austrian occupation of Bosnia–Hercegovina
1881	Austro-Serb secret treaty
1895	Serbian state bankruptcy
1903	Assassination of King Alexander Obrenovic; return of Karadjordjevic dynasty
1905–6	University of Belgrade; University of Sofia
1905–11	Austro-Serb 'Pig War'
1908	Austria annexes Bosnia
1912–13	Balkan wars; Albania independent (1913)
1914	Archduke Franz Ferdinand assassinated at Sarajevo
1918	Formation of Yugoslavia and greater Romania
1923	Assassination of Stambolisky
1929	King Alexander assumes personal rule in Yugoslavia
1938	King Carol assumes personal rule in Romania
1941–5	Hitler dismembers Yugoslavia; partisan struggle
1948	Yugoslavia expelled from Cominform
1961–4	Romania distances herself from the Soviet Union
1965	Yugoslav economic reform
1980	Death of Tito

The Northern Plain: Poland

1764–95	Reign of Stanislas Augustus; Polish Enlightenment
1772	First Partition of Poland
1775–88	Permanent Council under Russian aegis
1788–92	Four Year Diet; constitution of 1791
1793	Second Partition of Poland
1794	Kosciuszko insurrection
1795	Third Partition of Poland
1807–13	Napoleonic duchy of Warsaw
1815	Creation of Congress Kingdom
1822	Mickiewcz's first published poems; Polish romanticism
1830–1	First Polish revolt
1846	Galician rising
1861	Emancipation of peasants in the Russian empire
1863	Second Polish revolt
1863–1905	Decline of romanticism; formation of political parties
1863	Second Polish revolt
1863–1905	Decline of romanticism; formation of political parties

1886	Beginning of anti-Polish policy in Prussia
1905	Revolution in Russia and congress Poland; limited constitutionalism
1918	Restoration of Polish independence
1926	Pilsudski's *coup d'état*
1939	Hitler invades Poland; Russo-German division of Poland
1945	Polish state reconstituted 200 kilometres to the west
1956	Polish October; Gomulka comes to power
1970	Worker riots; fall of Gomulka
1976	Worker riots
1980	Workers strike; fall of Gierek; free trade unions – 'Solidarity'

Glossary

amortization funds   Funds set aside to pay off the cost of a loan for investment purposes.

boyars   Romanian nobles.

cameralism   In economics, the Central European variant of the mercantilist doctrines of the seventeenth and eighteenth centuries, which prescribed state action for the increase of prosperity.

capital-output ratio   The rate by which a given increase in investment increases the volume of output.

Chartists   Signatories of the Charter of Czechoslovak dissidents, launched in 1977.

Chetniks   Guerilla fighters: in particular, the Serbian nationalist resistance movement in the Second World War.

chiftluk sahibije   Turkish – a category of Ottoman landowners, expanding from the seventeenth century, who, unlike the spahis, treated their estates as private property over which they exercised semi-feudal powers, constraining the peasants to share-cropping and forced labour.

collectivization   A type of socialized agriculture introduced by Stalin into the Soviet Union from 1929, in which peasants farm the bulk of the land collectively, while retaining small plots for private use.

Cossacks   From the sixteenth to the eighteenth century, inhabitants of the unsettled Ukrainian border lands between Poland, the Ottoman empire and Muscovy, living in fortified villages free from any lord.

Daco-Romanian aspirations   The concept of a Greater Romania encompassing all Romanian speakers, so-called from the Roman province of Dacia (founded *c*. 106 AD), from which Romanians trace their national origins.

exarchate   In Orthodox Christianity, an ecclesiastical province enjoying autonomy under a patriarchate.

Haiduks   Christian brigands on Slav territory in the Balkans under Ottoman rule.

Hanswurst   Hans Wurst, a stock figure in eighteenth-century comedy, gave his name to this genre.

indicative targets (in economy)   Targets recommended as guidelines to production, as opposed to the obligatory targets set in the Stalinist command economy.

janissaries   Ottoman professional soldiers recruited originally through levies of Christian boys.

Jansenism   An anti-Jesuit tendency in seventeenth- and eighteenth-century Catholicism which espoused a semi-Calvinist approach to grace and predestination.

Kaisertreu   German – loyal to the emperor or dynastically minded.

labour contract system   A system common in Romania after the servile emancipation of 1864, whereby peasants supplemented their meagre plots by renting land from large landowners, contracting to meet the rent by labour service on the latter's estates: effectively a form of neo-serfdom.

latifundia   Great landed estates.

Laws of Nature/Natural Law   Natural Law theory, as expounded by the eighteenth-century Enlightenment, posited a system of right and justice inherent in nature, and therefore common to all mankind, on which political legislation should be based.

liberum veto   Latin – free veto: the right of any member of the Polish Sejm or parliament by his dissent to bring an end to a parliamentary session and nullify its legislation.

multilateral trade   The system whereby country A's trade surplus with country B can be used to finance A's deficit with country C.

neo-Slav movement   A series of congresses of Slav public figures held between 1905 and 1912 in an attempt to emulate the Pan-Slav congresses of 1848 and 1867.

New Economic Policy   Launched by Lenin in 1921 and making concessions to peasants and private enterprise.

organic estates   In one strand of right-wing thought, the natural groupings in society (e.g. peasants, artisans etc.), which should therefore be the basis of political representation. In this view modern parliamentarism merely represented atomized individuals and should be replaced by an updated version of medieval estates.

Pan-Slavism   The doctrine of the essential unity and auspicious destiny of the Slavs.

parlementaires   Members of the thirteen · *parlements* of pre-revolutionary France, empowered to register (or refuse to register) royal edicts, a right they used to set themselves up as champions of popular liberties.

Pashalik   An Ottoman administrative division.

Phanariots   Upper-class Greeks in the Ottoman empire, to whom wide administrative powers over the empire's Christian subjects were devolved: so-called from the Phanar district of Constantinople, the quarter for wealthy Greeks.

physiocrats   An eighteenth-century economic school which opposed the mercantilists' stress of trade and industry, seeing land as the chief source of wealth.

(full) plot   A unit for the assessment of obligations to state and lord, a half peasant providing half the obligations of a full peasant and so on. The size of a full holding varied according to locality and the quality of the land, commonly being between thirty and sixty acres.

polycentrism   The doctrine that there can be diversity or 'different roads' in international communism.

Porte   From the Italian word, *porta* (gate) – the Ottoman government. Probably so-called after the ancient place of audience at the entrance to the ruler's tent among the originally nomadic Turks.

Pragmatic Sanction   A common medieval and early modern term for important acts of state by a sovereign, hence fundamental law.

robota   Feudal labour service – from a Slav word meaning work. *Robot* in German-language sources.

Rodobrana   A fascist-inclined paramilitary grouping of the Hlinka Slovak People's Party in wartime Slovakia.

Rechtstaat   German – state based on law.

social Darwinism   A socio-political doctrine which applies Darwin's ideas of the 'struggle for existence' and 'survival of the fittest' to relations between social groups and nations.

spahis   Horsemen making up the cavalry of the Ottoman armies and holding, in return, non-hereditary land grants or timars over which they had revenue rights, but not feudal rights in the Western sense.

Tsintsars   An urban mercantile element in the Balkans, of Vlach origin, i.e. descended from the pre-Slavic inhabitants of the Balkans.

Uniate Church   Inaugurated by the union of Brest-Litovsk in Poland in 1596, it retained its Orthodox liturgy and parochial married clergy, but entered into communion with Rome.

Ustasha   Croatian fascists.

vilayet   An Ottoman province.

zadrugas   Balkan joint households – extended families living and cultivating together.

Bibliography

This bibliography has been framed with the needs of teaching rather than scholarship in mind. Consequently, it is based on English-language material, with a sprinkling of works in French. A knowledge of German opens many a further door. Selection has been shaped by the emphases of the text and, as far as possible, is limited to books which are either eminently readable or offer unique insights or information. Obviously, for reasons of space many books which have one or all of these qualities have had to be omitted. As a further practical aid, articles have been included whenever these broach a broad field or offer a short cut to views expressed in better-known but lengthier works.

No other book sets itself quite the same task as this one. A. W. Palmer's *The Lands between: A History of East-Central Europe since the Congress of Vienna* (London 1970) offers a somewhat traditional narrative for the period after 1815. I. T. Berend and G. Ranki in *East Central Europe in the Nineteenth and Twentieth Centuries* (Budapest 1977) cover the years 1848–1945 with a heavy socio-economic emphasis. There is a fine set of relevant documents in S. Fischer-Galati's *Man, State and Society in East European History* (New York 1970).

Admirable surveys exist for a number of individual countries: E. Pamlenyi (ed.) *A History of Hungary* (London 1975); C. M. Macartney, *Hungary: A History* (Edinburgh 1962); A. Gieysztor *et al., History of Poland* (Warsaw 1968); P. S. Wandycz, *The Lands of Partitioned Poland, 1795–1918* (Washington 1974); and M. B. Petrovich, *A History of Modern Serbia, 1804–1918*, 2 vols. (New York 1976). Likewise the Habsburg monarchy is covered in C. A. Macartney, *The Habsburg Empire* (London 1969); V. L. Tapie, *The Rise and Fall of the Habsburg Monarchy* (Paris 1969); English trans., London 1971); and R. A. Kann, *A History of the Habsburg Empire, 1526–1918* (University of California Press 1974). Of these famous scholars Tapie has best combined analysis and narrative flow; C. A. Macartney's rather detailed text is available in more convenient, condensed form as *The House of Austria: A Later Phase, 1790–1918* (Edinburgh 1978). All these writers refer extensively, in bibliographies or notes, to the historical literature in German and East European languages omitted here.

Of considerable importance are the historical journals published by several East European countries in major languages. Articles appear in English, French, German and occasionally, Russian. Such are *Acta Poloniae Historica* (Warsaw), *Acta Historica* (Budapest), *Revue Romaine d'Histoire* (Bucharest), *Historica* (Prague), the *Bulgarian Historical Review* (Sofia) and *Balkan Studies* (Thessaloniki). The leading Western journals in English covering the area are the *Austrian History Yearbook* (University of Texas, Houston), the *Slavic Review* - formerly the *American Slavic and East European Review* (Illinois), the *Slavonic and East European Review* (London), and the *East European Quarterly* (Boulder, Colorado).

Historical bibliography in English is limited. Mention may be made of R. J. Kerner's comprehensive but now old *Slavic Europe: A Selected Bibliography in Western European Languages* (Cambridge, Mass. 1918); N. Davies, *Poland Past and Present: A. Select Bibliography of Works in English* (Newtonville, Mass. 1977); and F. R. Bridge, *The Habsburg Monarchy, 1804–1918: A Critical Bibliography* (London 1967) which lists British literature on the monarchy.

Chapter 1: The feudal inheritance

The background may be studied in books mentioned in the general section and in P. F. Sugar, *South Eastern Europe under Ottoman Rule, 1354–1804*, (University of Washington 1977). In addition, fascinating insights into the geographical conditions of the region's life are offered in W. H. McNeill, *Europe's Steppe Frontier, 1500–1800* (Chicago 1964). Z. S. Pach discusses the 'second serfdom' in *Agrarian Development in Western Europe and Hungary from the Fifteenth to the Seventeenth Centuries* (Budapest 1963), and R. Rosdolsky considers the nature of East European serfdom in his articles, 'The distribution of the agrarian product in feudalism', *Journal of Economic History*, vol. 11, no. 3 (1951), pp. 247-65 and 'On the nature of peasant serfdom in Central and Eastern Europe', *Journal of Central and East European Affairs*, vol. 12, no. 2 (1952-3), pp. 128-39. See also H. Inalcik, *The Ottoman Empire: The*

Classical Age, 1300–1600 (English trans., London 1973), and T. Stoianovitch, 'The conquering Balkan Orthodox merchant, 1600–1800', *Journal of Economic History,* vol. 20, no. 2 (1960), pp. 236–313.

Chapter 2: Enlightenment

The most convenient introduction to Enlightenment in Eastern Europe is T. C. W. Blanning, *Joseph II and Enlightened Despotism* (Longman, London 1970), which also contains helpful documents. The Romanian Enlightenment is well covered in V. Georgescu's *Political Ideas and the Enlightenment in the Romanian Principalities 1750–1831* (Boulder, Colorado 1971) and the Polish Enlightenment is brilliantly covered in J. Fabre, *S. A. Poniatowski et L'Europe des Lumières* (Paris 1952); see also the *East European Quarterly,* vol. 9, no. 4 1975–6) for a symposium on the Enlightenment in the Balkans. There is no equivalent for the Habsburg monarchy to the splendid syntheses of J. Rutkowski, *Histoire Economique de la Pologne avant les Partages* (Paris 1927) and W. Kula, 'L'histoire économique de la Pologne du 18e siècle', *Acta Poloniae Historica,* vol. 4 (1961), pp. 133–46, but much can be gained from A. Klima, 'Industrial development in Bohemia, 1648–1781', *Past and Present,* vol. 11 (1957), pp. 87–99, A. Klima 'Mercantilism in the Habsburg Monarchy with special reference to the Bohemian lands', *Historica,* vol 11 (1965), pp. 95–120, W. E. Wright, *Serf, Seigneur and Sovereign: Agrarian Reform in Eighteenth Century Bohemia* (Minnesota 1966) and H. Freudenberger, 'Industrialisation in Bohemia and Moravia in the eighteenth century', *Journal of Central and East European Affairs,* vol. 19, no. 4 (1959), pp. 347–56.

Of many relevant biographies the most readable are E. Crankshaw, *Maria Theresa* (London 1969) and S. K. Padover, *The Revolutionary Emperor: Joseph II of Austria,* 2nd edn. (London 1967). A. J. P. Taylor's view of Joseph is in his *The Habsburg Monarchy, 1809–1918* (London 1948; Peregrine, London 1967) a characteristically provocative and brilliant work; E. Wangerman expresses his view in his stimulating *From Joseph II to the Jacobin Trials* (Oxford 1959). Wangermann developed his views also in a broader context in *The Austrian Achievement 1780–1800* (London 1973). P. B. Bernard's various works throw valuable information into the scales, particularly his *Jesuits and Jacobins: Enlightenment and Enlightened Despotism in Austria* (University of Illinois 1971). For events in Hungary, B. Kiraly, *Hungary in the Late Eighteenth Century* (Columbia University Press, New York 1969), may be referred to.

Chapter 3: Liberalism and nationalism

Metternich's many biographers mainly deal with his diplomatic activity. I prefer C. de Grünwald's *Metternich* (English translation, London 1953) and G. A. de Bertier de Sauvigny's fascinating *Metternich and his Times* (London 1962) compiled largely from Metternich's own words. R. W. Seton-Watson's article 'Metternich and internal Austrian policy', *Slavonic Review* Vols. 17–18 (1939) is still the best of a bad job on this topic. Socio-economic information on the monarchy is mainly in German, except for J. Blum, *Noble Landowners and Agriculture in Austria, 1815–48* (Baltimore 1948) and B. Ivanyi, 'From feudalism to capitalism: the economic background to Szechenyi's reform of Hungary', *Journal of Central and East European Affairs*, vol. 20, no. 3 (1960–1), pp. 268–88. The researches of the Bulgarian scholar, N. Todorov, in 'La genèse du capitalisme dans les provinces Bulgares de l'Empire Ottomane au cours de la première moitié du dix-neuvième siècle', *Études Historiques*, vol. 1 (1960), and *La Ville Balkanique sous les Ottomanes* (London 1977); relevant articles in English offer rare insights into Balkan economic history in this period.

The development of liberalism (and much else) in Poland is masterfully covered by R. F. Leslie, *Polish Politics and the Revolution of November 1830* (Athelone Press, London 1956); Leslie has also written a convenient article, 'Politics and economics in Congress Poland, 1815–64', *Past and Present*, no. 8 (1955), pp. 43–63. The movement elsewhere may be followed in the first chapter of R. J. Rath, *The Viennese Revolution of 1848* (University of Texas Press 1957), and in G. Barany, *Count Stephen Szechenyi and the awakening of Hungarian nationalism, 1791–1841* (Princeton University Press 1968). Barany's views are more briefly available in 'The Szechenyi problem', *Journal of Central European Affairs*, vol. 20, no. 3 (1960–62) pp. 251–69, this whole number is devoted to Szechenyi. H. Kohn's *Panslavism* (Vintage Books, New York 1953) analyses romantic nationalism; M. Hroch's attempt at a social analysis is in his chapter, 'The social composition of the Czech patriots in Bohemia, 1827–48' in P. Brock and H. G.

Skilling, *The Czech Renaissance of the Nineteenth Century* (Toronto 1970). Accounts of nationalism in all the individual countries of Eastern Europe are available in the *Austrian History Yearbook, vol. 3 (1967)* vol 3 (1967) and in P. Sugar and I. Lederer (eds.), *Nationalism in Eastern Europe* (Washington 1969). For an astringent critique of nationalism see E. Kedourie's *Nationalism*, 3rd edn. (Hutchinson, London 1966).

Chapter 4: Storm and settlement, 1848–70

Of the many books on 1848, P. Robertson, *Revolutions of 1848* (Princeton University Press 1952) is still the most readable, though F. Fejto (ed.) *The Opening of an Era, 1848* (London 1948) offers more analysis. Developments in the different theatres can be studied in R. J. Rath, *The Viennese Revolution of 1848* (University of Texas Press 1957) – a helpful Rath article entitled 'Public opinion during the Viennese revolution of 1848' is also available in the *Journal of Central European Affairs*, vol. 8, no. 2 (1948–9), pp. 160–80; I. Deak, *The Lawful Revolution: Louis Kossuth and the Hungarians 1848–9* (New York 1979); and S. Pech, *The Czech Revolution of 1848* (University of North Carolina Press 1969); F. Eyck, *The Frankfurt Parliament, 1848–9* (London 1968) and J. C. Campbell, *French Influence and the Rise of Rumanian Nationalism* (New York 1971). Marx and Engels made their comments in K. Marx, *Revolution and Counter-Revolution, or Germany in 1848* (Glasgow 1896), which has been interestingly reassessed by N. W. Swoboda's article, 'The changing views of Marx and Engels about the nationalities in the Austrian Monarchy, 1845–55' in the *Austrian History Yearbook*, vols. 9–10 (1973–4), pp. 3–28. Sir Lewis Namier's famous anti-German polemic was the theme of *1848: The Revolution of the Intellectuals* (London 1944).

The strategy of international revolution can be followed by Campbell's work above and Louis Kossuth's *Memories of My Exile* (English translation, London 1880). R. F. Leslie's *Reform and Insurrection in Russian Poland, 1856–65* (Athlone Press, London 1963) is as good as his earlier work

The reform efforts of the Turkish Tanzimat are sympathetically reviewed by R. H. Davison, *Reform in the Ottoman Empire, 1856–76* (Princeton University Press 1963) and S. J. and E. K. Shaw, *History of the Ottoman Empire and Modern Turkey*, vol. 2 (Cambridge 1977), the latter unique for a Western historian in its pro-Turkish bias. The general Balkan picture can be appreciated from the social and cultural angle in C. Jelavich and B. Jelavich (eds.), *The Balkans in Transition* (California University Press 1963) and politically in D. Djordjevic, *Revolutions Nationales des Peuples Balkaniques 1804–1914* (Belgrade 1965).

English material is rather thin for Austrian politics in the 1860s; the chapters in A. J. P. Taylor's *The Habsburg Monarchy* may be consulted and any biography of Emperor Franz Joseph, notably J. Redlich, *Emperor Francis Joseph of Austria* (New York 1929) or, if more readily available, E. Crankshaw, *The Fall of the House of Habsburg* (London 1963; Sphere, London 1970), a well-written but conventional biography in all but name. G. Szabad, *Hungarian Political Trends between Revolution and Compromise* (Budapest 1977) offers a Hungarian view. Eötvös's liberalism is examined in P. Bödy, *Joseph Eötvös and the Modernisation of Hungary, 1840–70* (Transaction no. 62, American Philosophical Society 1972).

Chapter 5: Economics and society, 1850–1914

Indespensable for socio-economic development for this and later periods is the work of the Hungarian historians I. Berend and G. Ranki, *Economic Development in East-Central Europe in the Nineteenth and Twentieth centuries* (New York, 1974). They have also published *Hungary: A Century of Economic Development* (Newton Abbot 1974), and there is a convenient article by Ranki, 'Problems of the development of Hungarian industry', in the *Journal of Economic History*, vol. 24, no. 2 (1964), pp. 204–28.

Austria is less well served. German readers will have a feast from the first volume of A. Wandruszka's and P. Urbanitsch's series, *Die Habsburgermonarchie, 1848–1918*, entitled *Die Wirtschaftliche Entwicklung* (Vienna 1973) and edited by A. Brusatti, but N. Gross's chapter, 'The Habsburg Monarchy, 1750–1914' in the *Fontana Economic History of Europe*, vol. 4, part 1 (London 1973) is the only general survey for English readers. For those who know French, B. Michel, 'La révolution industrielle dans les pays tchèques au dix-neuvième siècle', *Annales*, vol. 20 (1965) is shorter and more stimulating than J. Purs, 'The industrial revolution in the Czech lands', *Historica*, (1960), vol. 2 pp. 183–272; they can be supplemented by the suggestive monograph of R. L. Rudolph, *Banking and Industrialization in Austria-Hungary: The Role of Banks in the Industrialization of the Czech Crownlands, 1873–1914* (Cambridge University Press 1976). The famous economic historian

Alexander Gershenkron raises interesting general questions about industrialization in *Economic Backwardness in Historical Perspective* (Harvard 1962) which also contains a chapter on Bulgaria. The under-development school have not concerned themselves with Eastern Europe as such. Life on the land after the emancipation of the serfs is the theme of G. Illyes's magnificent evocation of the world of the Hungarian farm-labourer, *People of the Puszta* (Budapest 1936, 1967) and D. Warriner (ed.) *Contrasts in Emerging Societies* (Athlone Press, London 1965). See also S. Kieniewicz, *The Emancipation of the Polish Peasant* (Chicago 1969).

Austro-German culture reached its apogee at this time. Ilse Barea's *Vienna, Legend and Reality* (Secker & Warburg, London 1966) is far more than a conventional guide book; C. E. Schorske, *Fin de Siècle Vienna: Politics and Culture* (London 1980) and W. J. McGrath, *Dionysian Art and Populist Politics in Austria* (Yale 1974) brilliantly point the interrelationship of culture and politics. P. G. J. Pulzer in *The Rise of political Anti-Semitism in Germany and Austria* (Wiley, Chichester 1964) takes up an ungrateful theme – summarized in part in his article 'The Austrian liberals and the Jewish question', in the *Journal of Central and East European Affairs,* vol. 23, no. 2 (1963–4), pp. 131–42 – and W. Jenks analyses the anti-liberal backlash of the conservative coalition of the 1880s in *Austria under the Iron Ring, 1879–93* (Virginia 1965).

Emerging peasant and socialist movements are best covered for Poland, by O. Narkiewicz, *The Green Flag: Polish Populist Politics* (London 1976) and L. Blit, *Origins of Polish Socialism* (Cambridge 1971). Some light is cast elsewhere in English by J. G. Polach's article, 'The beginnings of trade unionism among the Slavs of the Austrian Empire', in the *American Slavic and East European Review,* vol. 14, no. 2 (1955), pp. 239–59, Bell's and Rothschild's work on peasantism and socialism in Bulgaria (see bibliography for Chapter 7) and P. G. Edelberg's monograph *The Great Rumanian Peasant Revolt of 1907* (Leiden 1974)

Chapter 6: Politics, 1870–1918

Books on the Balkan crisis of 1875–8 are legion but M. S. Anderson's standard work *The Eastern Question 1774–1923* (London 1966) should suffice lesser fry, together with B. H. Sumner's *Russia and the Balkans, 1870–80* (Oxford 1937) which sets events in their context. Also complicated, but worth the effort, are C. E. Black's monograph *The Establishment of Constitutional Government in Bulgaria* (Princeton University Press 1943) and Petrovich on Serbia (see general section).

The theme of nationalism as the mobilization of social linkages is developed by K. W. Deutsch in *Nationalism and Social Communication*, 2nd edn (New York 1966). The general references given under Chapter 3 are still helpful, but there are fine studies by B. Garver, *The Young Czech Party 1874–1901* (Yale 1978) and S. Skendi, *The Albanian National Awakening, 1878–1912* (Princeton University Press 1967); Oszkar Jaszi, the Hungarian reform politician, explored the links between national and social repression in his famous *Dissolution of the Habsburg Monarchy* (Chicago 1929). R. Kann's *The Multi-national Empire*, 2 vols. (New York 1950) is the classic study of federal schemes; convenient, though, is A. Kogan's article on socialist federalism, 'The Social Democrats and the conflict of nationalities in the Habsburg Monarchy', *Journal of Modern History*, vol. 21, no. 3 (1949), pp. 204–17. For mounting tension in Hungary, see N. Stone, 'Constitutional crises in Hungary, 1903–6', *Slavonic Review*, vol. 45 (1967), pp. 163–82 and, in the South Slav world, V. Dedijer's vivid account of the young Bosnia assassins, *The Road to Sarajevo* (New York 1966). The memoirs of the radical Magyar count, M. Karolyi, sub-titled *Faith without Illusion* (London 1956) should not be missed either, for the light they shed on the Magyar ruling class.

For the war years A. J. May is worthily dull on internal events in *The Passing of the Habsburg Monarchy, 1914–18*, 2 vols. (Philadelphia 1966) and Z. A. B. Zeman's *Break-up of the Habsburg Monarchy, 1914–18* (Oxford University Press 1961) spiritedly revisionist in down-playing the external role of the Slav nationalist exiles. B. Kiraly (ed.), *The Habsburg Empire in World War 1* (Columbia University Press, 1977) New York summarizes recent research.

Chapter 7: Independent Eastern Europe

The inter-war period is covered in four works in English: H. Seton-Watson's *Eastern Europe between the Wars* (Cambridge 1945) offers a vividly immediate sociological analysis; C. Macartney and A. W. Palmer in *Independent Eastern Europe* (London 1962) emphasize diplomatic developments in a complex narrative, interweaving events in the region as a whole. Both J. Rothschild,

East Central Europe between the Two World Wars (Seattle 1974) and A. Polonsky *The Little Dictators: The History of Eastern Europe since 1918* (London 1975) adopt a country by country treatment, the first with great thoroughness, the second with concise readability.

No one book deals with the 1919 settlement in Eastern Europe as a whole; of many related works C. Macartney's *Hungary and her Successors, 1919–37* (Oxford 1937) is the most wide-ranging and N. Davies's *White Eagle: Red Star* (London 1972) on the Russo-Polish War of 1920 the most absorbing. Masaryk's views appear in his *The Making of a State* (London 1927). Czechoslovakia is the best covered of individual countries with W. Mamatey and R. Luza (eds.), *A History of the Czechoslovak Republic, 1918–48* (Princeton University Press 1973) the most comprehensive treatment. For Austria, the best study of Seipel is K. von Klemperer's *Ignaz Seipel: a Christian Statesman in a Time of Crisis* (Princeton University Press 1972) and of the social democrats, C. A. Gülick's voluminous *Austria from Habsburg to Hitler*, 2 vols. (Berkeley 1948). Other helpful works are H. Roberts, *Rumania: Political Problems of an Agrarian State* (New Haven 1951), A. Polonsky, *Politics in Independent Poland, 1921–39* (Oxford 1972) and C. A. Macartney's massive *October 15th, a History of Modern Hungary* (Edinburgh 1956). Bulgaria and Yugoslavia are less well covered. Unfortunately there is no really good biography of Edward Benes, a crucial figure, but T. G. Campbell, *Confrontation in Central Europe: Weimar Germany and Czechoslovakia* (Chicago 1975) offers interesting insights into his diplomacy. The slump's impact on the international economy of the region is exhaustively explored in A. Basch, *The Danube Basin and the German Sphere* (London 1944). As before, I. Berend and G. Ranki, *Economic Development* (see bibliography for Chapter 5) cover general economic issues.

On the problems of peasant society and peasantism, in addition to H. Roberts above, J. Tomashevich, *Peasants, Politics and Economic Change in Jugoslavia* (Stanford 1955) is a mine of information. D. Warriner, *The Economics of Peasant Farming*, 2nd ed. (Cass, London 1964) throws light on the economic backdrop, while the autobiography of the Croatian peasantist leader, V. Macek, *In the Struggle for Freedom* (Philadelphia 1957) and J. D. Bell's study, *Peasants in Power: Alexander Stambolisky and the Bulgarian Agrarian Union* (Princeton University Press 1977) explain much about the politics of the countries concerned. Different aspects of the communist experience are opened up by R. Tokes, *Bela Kun and the Hungarian Soviet Republic* (New York 1967), G. D. Jackson, *Comintern and Peasant in Eastern Europe, 1919–30* (Columbia University Press, New York 1966) and M. Djilas, *Memoir of a Revolutionary* (New York 1973), J. Rothschild's *The Communist Party of Bulgaria: Origins and Development, 1883–1936* (Columbia University Press, New York 1959) is the best of a number of national monographs. East European fascism can be studied from P. Sugar (ed.) *Native Fascism in the Successor States, 1918–45* (ABC–Clio Press, Oxford 1971) and the relevant chapters of H. Rogger and E. Weber (eds.), *The European Right* (London 1965).

Chapter 8: From Hitler to Stalin

The most comprehensive introduction to the Second World War in the region remains H. Seton-Watson, *The East European Revolution* (London 1950), strongly marked by the Cold War. More recently, an extensive literature has developed on patterns of occupation, resistance and collaboration; examples are V. Mastny, *The Czechs under Nazi Rule: The Failure of National Resistance, 1939–42* (Columbia University Press, New York 1971), M.Fenyö, *Hitler, Horthy and Hungary: German–Hungarian Relations, 1941–4* (New Haven 1972) and J. T. Gross, *Polish Society under German Occupation* (Princeton University Press 1979). For the dramatic events in Yugoslavia, P. Auty's solid biography *Tito* (London 1974), together with Milovan Djilas's brilliant recollections of partisan life in *War-Time* (London 1977), makes a balanced introduction. The diplomatic angle can be studied in E. Barker, *British Policy in South-East Europe in the Second World War* (London 1976), A. Polonsky (ed.) *The Great Powers and the Polish Question, 1941–5* (London 1976) and E. Benes's posthumous memoirs, *From Munich to New War and New Victory* (London 1954). Benes also wrote extensively in the American journal, *Foreign Affairs*, at this time, and this and the British *International Affairs* may be consulted profitably for the period up to 1948.

A great many anti-communist memoirs were published in English shortly after the events of 1945–8; examples are the Hungarian Smallholder prime minister, F. Nagy's *The Struggle behind the Iron Curtain* (New York 1948) and the Czech, H. Ripka's *Czechoslovakia enslaved* (London 1950). It is interesting to compare them with later works like P. E. Zinner's *Communist Strategy and Tactics in*

Czechoslovakia, 1918–48 (London 1963) and F. Fejto's sophisticated *Le coup de Prague, 1948* (Paris 1976). An official communist interpretation may be sampled from *History of the Revolutionary Workers' Movement in Hungary, 1944–62* (Corvina Press, Budapest 1972) edited by D. Nemes. For a provocative and succinct introduction to the American debate on the origins of the Cold War, see R. J. Maddox's onslaught on 'revisionist' historiography in *The New Left and the origins of the Cold War* (Princeton University Press 1975). The views of Joyce and Gabriel Kolko are to be found in their *Limits of Power: The World and United States Foreign Policy, 1945–54* (New York 1972), and G. F. Kennan's in his *Memoirs, 1925–50* (Boston 1967).

On the final Stalin years R. L. Wolff, *The Balkans in our Time* (Harvard University Press 1956) is admirably circumstantial. N. Bethell's *Gomulka* (London 1969) and the Czech purge victim E. Loebl's *Stalinism in Prague* (Bratislava 1968; English translation, London 1969) help extend the picture northwards. Not to be missed is the stimulating analysis of Stalinist mentalities by the Polish writer C. Milosz, *The Captive Mind* (Paris 1953; translation, London 1953).

Chapter 9: Communist Eastern Europe

There are many general surveys of communist Eastern Europe, of which by far the best is F. Fejtö's *History of the People's Demoracies* (Pelican, London 1973). In addition the specialist journals *Problems of Communism* (Washington), *Survey* (London) and *Soviet Studies* (Glasgow) contain much of value, the first offering the most readable format and style.

In the absence of a general, non-technical survey of the East European command economy, Oto Sik's broadcast lectures of the Prague Spring, published as *The Bureaucratic Economy* (White Plains, New York 1972), will offer the simplest critique to the general reader. Harder, but worth perservering with, are J. M. Montias, *Economic Development in Communist Rumania* (Cambridge, Mass, 1967) and A. Zaubermann, *Industrial Progress in Poland, Czechoslovakia and East Germany, 1937–62* (Oxford University Press 1964). For more recent trends see Zaubermann's article, 'The East European economies', in *Problems of Communism*, no. 2 (1978).

There is an abundance of good books on communist Yugoslavia:

D. Rusinow's *The Yugoslav Experiment, 1948–74* (London 1977) and T. B. Singleton's *Twentieth Century Yugoslavia* (Macmillan, London 1976) make complexities comprehensible, while D. Doder in *The Yugoslavs* (New York 1978) achieves a brilliant socio-psychological study of the day to day operation of 'self-management' from the complex standpoint of a Yugoslav-born American. J. J. Horton has provided a valuable bibliography in *Yugoslavia* (Oxford 1977). The Kadar regime in Hungary is equally well-served by W. F. Robinson, *The Pattern of Reform in Hungary* (New York 1973). S. Fischer-Galati's *Twentieth-Century Rumania* (Columbia University Press, New York 1970) is a succinct and convincing introduction. The writings of A. Bromke, particularly in *Problems of Communism* ('Poland under Gierek: a new political style', vol. 21, no. 5 (1972); 'A new juncture in Poland', vol. 25, no. 5 (1976); 'Opposition in Poland', vol. 27, no. 5 (1978) provide a convenient coverage of the Polish scene.

There remain the revolutionary events of 1956 and 1968, for the first of which I. L. Halasz de Beky's *Bibliography of the Hungarian Revolution of 1956* (Toronto 1963) is helpful. Recommendations must be subjective in the face of the mass of material. Mine would be, for Hungary, T. Aczel and T. Meray's *Revolt of the Mind* (London 1960), F. Fejto's *Behind the Rape of Hungary* (New York 1957) and the unusual Trotskyist interpretations of Bill Lomax, *Hungary 1956* (London 1976): for 1968, Zeman's *Prague Spring* (London 1968) a simple, vivid Penguin special, the two heavier volumes of G. Golan, *The Czechoslovak Reform Movement: Communism in Crisis, 1962–8* (Cambridge University Press 1971) and *Reform Rule in Czechoslovakia: The Dubcek Era, 1968–9* (Cambridge University Press 1973), and J. Valenta's *Soviet Intervention in Czechoslovakia in 1968* (John Hopkins University Press, Baltimore 1979. R. A. Remington's *Winter in Prague: Documents on Czechoslovak Communism in Crisis* (Cambridge, Mass. 1969) is the best source book. Two short cuts to comprehension are P. Ludz's investigation into the philosophical basis of the Prague Spring, 'Philosophy in search of reality', *Problems of Communism*, no. 4/5 (1969), and the Dubcekite Communist E. Goldstuecker's interview with the German magazine *Der Spiegel* 'The lessons of Prague', in *Encounter*, vol. 37, no. 2 (1971).

Data on current living standards in Eastern Europe are available from the annual statistical pocket books published in English by all countries in the region (along with weightier English material), from reports prepared by Western banks and other agencies, and from *The Economist* and specialist journals. Other aspects of life are harder to evaluate. Light is shed on darker corners by Canon T. Beeson's *Discretion and Valour: Religious Conditions in Russia and Eastern Europe* (Fontana, London 1974): R. R. King's *Minorities under Communism: Nationalities as a Source of Tension among Balkan Communist States* (Harvard University Press 1973): by Haraszti's intriguing account of piecework in Hungarian factories *A Worker in a Worker's State* (Pelican, London 1977) and by the *Socialism and Bureaucracy* of the dissident Hungarian sociologist, A. Hegedüs (London 1976). Perhaps the most challenging estimate of current and future trends proceeds from the dissident Hungarian Marxists, I. Szelenyi and G. Konrad, in their pseudonomously published, M. Rakovski, *Towards an East European Marxism* (London 1978).

It should be remembered, finally, that the surest way to a nation's heart is through its literature, and that most East European countries make fair efforts to translate their classics. Those who believe in mixing study with pleasure would be well advised to sample the Budapest Corvina Press's translations of Maurice Jokai's *The Man with the Golden Touch* (1963) or Kalman Mikszath's *A Strange Wedding* (1964) or G. Illyes's biography *Petöfi* (1973); alternatively the historical novels of the Yugoslav Novel prize-winner Ivo Andric, the various translations of the Polish romantic poet, Adam Mickiewicz, and novelist, Henryk Sienkiewicz, or the Rabelaisian Czech satirist, Jaroslav Hasek. Arthur Schnitzler, *Vienna 1900: Games of Love and Death* (New York 1974) and Robert Musil, *The Man without Qualities* 3 vols. (Panther, London 1968) subtly depict Viennese society in the last stages of the empire.

Index